Alfie!

Alfie!

THE GARETH THOMAS STORY

GARETH THOMAS WITH DELME PARFITT

MAINSTREAM
PUBLISHING

EDINBURGH AND LONDON

First published in Great Britain in 2007 by
MAINSTREAM PUBLISHING COMPANY (EDINBURGH) LTD
7 Albany Street
Edinburgh EH1 3UG

ISBN 9781845961916

A catalogue record for this book is available
from the British Library

Typeset in Galliard and Gill Sans

Printed in Great Britain by
Butler & Tanner Ltd, Frome, Somerset

ACKNOWLEDGEMENTS

I would love to be able to dedicate this book to specific individuals, but I have met so many people who have touched me and helped me in so many ways that there are too many to list here. So to those of you who know who you are, thank you for playing a big part in my life, which grew from a humble beginning and will keep on growing.

A very special thanks to Huw and Ben Evans of the Huw Evans Picture Agency (huwevansimages.com) for their work in providing the photographs for this book. Thanks also to Rob Cole and Westgate Sports Agency for the statistics.

CONTENTS

INTRODUCTION

The most important thing to me is that people realise I have written this book not for financial gain but hopefully to inspire people in all walks of life and to help them realise their goals. I have not written it to be derogatory about other people and in doing so to be deliberately controversial but to let you the public know how I became Alfie, captain of Wales, captain of the British Lions. I want to convey a message to people that whatever and wherever you are in life, if you haven't achieved what you've dreamed about, well, you can. If you decide to read this book, I hope you will see proof of that in my story. I went from someone who did not even want to play for Wales and didn't have a clue about what representing my country should mean, to being a captain

as proud and as passionate about leading out our national rugby side as any of my predecessors could possibly have been.

Above all, throughout this book I hope you can accept me for what I am. As soon as I was made captain of Wales, I pledged to be honest to myself and honest with everyone around me. I was never going to try to be a mix of the three or four players who had done the job before me.

I feel that most people's dream is only their dream because they see it as just that – a dream – and they will not even try to turn it into reality. In this book, I would like people to be able to relate to someone who is just a normal bloke from a normal working-class background and went on to achieve his dream.

You can be anything you want to be.

Me and my brother Dickie in our early days. (Courtesy of the author.)

I

BRIDGEND

'This kid is gonna be bloody good.' That was the word doing the rounds among the senior players who sat watching in the main stand at the Brewery Field on the August afternoon that I played what I consider to be my first proper game for my beloved home-town club Bridgend. I was still officially playing for the club that taught me the game – Pencoed – at the time but had been invited by Bridgend to play in a pre-season trial match against South Wales Police, our local rivals from just across the way at Waterton Cross, the old training headquarters for the great Wales sides of the 1970s.

OK, it was only a friendly, but for all the locals and us it was a big, big game. And apart from anything else, you have to understand that this was my big chance to make a real impression in the famous blue-and-white shirt. I remember my best mate Ian 'Compo' Greenslade saying that he had told all the people who mattered at Bridgend what a top player this 17 year old was

going to be and how they should more or less get ready to witness the next superstar in the making.

So, we kicked off with me looking like the lankiest string of piss you could ever imagine and those senior Bridgend players saying to Compo, 'OK, let's see how good this kid is. Let's see what he's made of.' Anyway, play went on for a little while with me on the wing, and before long I found myself next to the touchline in front of the main stand having to deal with a massive up-and-under kick that might as well have been coming down with snow on it. I tried to do what I had always been told to do in that situation. I kept my eye on the ball and got into the best position I could to take the catch cleanly.

It was then that it happened.

You know those odd times in life when you find yourself doing something and you have absolutely no idea why you are doing it, and for the life of you, you still can't explain it afterwards? Well, that was me at that moment. The ball was on its

way down to me, getting closer and closer to my waiting hands. And I had actually done well to get into the perfect position to receive it. To this day, I don't know why I did what I did next. Just as the ball arrived, instead of catching it, I headed it, Wayne Rooney style, back infield.

My mind had gone blank. I could have easily caught it, and I remember when it was a split second away from me thinking, 'I'm going to catch this.' But no; for reasons I don't think I will ever be able to explain, I decided to put my nut on it instead. It wasn't as if I had lost sight of the ball and it had just struck my head. No, the style of the actual header was very deliberate, as if I was trying to score the winning goal in the FA Cup final.

The reaction from the stand was a mixture of laughter and, perhaps worse still, stunned and embarrassed silence. The senior Bridgend players turned to Compo, who must have been dying with humiliation, in utter disbelief. I think 'Who the hell is this muppet?' was one of the more polite inquiries. Even the South Wales Police players stopped for a split second as if to say, 'What the hell is this guy doing?'

It did get better: I scored a try in the second half, which left me chuffed to bits. But that was my first experience playing for Bridgend – and what a classic it was! A future captain of Wales? Yeah, right.

Even now Bridgend the town and Bridgend the rugby club mean the world to me, and I guess they always will.

I recall the summer after my first season in Toulouse when I came home and found myself driving past the Brewery Field one sunny afternoon. I couldn't resist a look at the old place, which was deserted at the time. I clambered over the railings and went and sat in the middle of the pitch for a few minutes, just staring around. I looked over at the old tunnel where I used to run out and at parts of the pitch where incidents had occurred down the seasons. I even went and stood on every terrace and sat in the old stand to get a view of the ground from every angle I could.

Yet despite the place Bridgend holds in my heart, playing for the club in the amateur days of the early 1990s and for a little while after the game went professional in 1995 wasn't ever some deep and meaningful or emotional thing for me. It was simple: you thanked your lucky stars you were good enough to get in the team and then turned up every week and just, well, played. I can honestly say that half of the time I didn't even know who the opposition were before I got to the ground on any given Saturday, even when the big names like Cardiff were coming to town.

I do remember the initiations that went on during the old days: incidents of so-called team bonding that were they to take place today would probably result in the police being called. It went something like this: if one of the senior players decided you were to be initiated, then you were initiated, whether you liked

it or not. What's more, these were not necessarily one-off events only for the new boys. You couldn't simply endure them in the knowledge that once it was all over that was it. Not at all. You did exactly as you were told whenever you were given the new set of rules for whatever grisly deed they wanted to put you through. And you knew the consequences of breaking these rules would be far worse than anything they had planned for you in the first place. Any form of refusal just didn't enter into it.

One day when we had all gone up to Warrington for a lads' trip away, we were sitting in a row in some pub, which was thankfully empty apart from us. The lads had pinched all the pillowcases from the hotel we were staying in. I was among those chosen for initiation and soon found myself sitting alongside a few other unfortunate souls with a pillowcase on my head and wearing just a pair of underpants. All that could be heard was the whispering and muffled laughter of the conspirators, but if the pillowcase came off, you knew you were dead.

The next thing I was aware of was a hand coming up into the pillowcase with a lump of Deep Heat cream that was liberally rubbed into my face. It got worse. Next up, one of the players went round carrying a plastic bag of some of the most awful substances you could imagine. I won't go into the graphic details, but if you imagine a selection of the things you would least like rubbed in your face, what was visited upon us would certainly

be among them. So, when I felt the hand coming up again, I just had to close my eyes and mouth and grin and bear it.

But the guys didn't care. They might as well have been insane. And you wouldn't expect any praise for getting through it all. Oh no, it was merely seen as your duty.

I suppose some people would see this as bullying, but I don't look back on it in that way at all. It was just part and parcel of the game, and I didn't bat an eyelid. In any case, most of the time – and certainly on the occasion mentioned above – I was so steaming drunk along with all the others that I was able to get through whatever was thrown at me a little more easily.

I was man of the match for Pencoed in this District Youth Cup final, scoring three tries. (Courtesy of the author.)

There were other times when we would run shuttle races against each other in a pub and plates of cat food and raw liver, say, would have to be consumed along with pints of alcoholic concoctions containing something dreadful at the bottom of the glass. This might sound stupid to some people, but I loved it at the time. To me, this was the *craic* and one of the reasons why I loved rugby. Those days were special.

I know some players today harp on about how playing the game is not about the big money they can earn. But back then you definitely knew that was the case, because money couldn't have been further from our minds. And even when we eventually went professional, I didn't care two hoots about the cash. Without a word of a lie, I don't think I even knew how much my first professional contract was worth.

Even after we started playing rugby for a living, one of the real highlights of a Saturday afternoon for me was when the final whistle blew and I could go back into the changing-room and have a cup of tea and a fag! To me, that little moment was heaven. In later years, there would be lads there with Gatorade high-energy drinks and all kinds of concoctions that were supposed to boost this and that. But all I cared about was the sight of a great big pot of tea and the first deep drags on a well-earned cigarette after a hard 80 minutes. Every single game I went through that same little routine.

Off the pitch and on it, all that mattered was being with the boys, having a laugh and a *craic*. Nobody cared how much anyone was paid, whether anyone played for Wales or was going to move to a different club. When I played for Pencoed and Bridgend, we simply got a brown envelope after a game with a bit of pin money in it. At Pencoed, we would queue up after a match and would be given £10 if we had won but nothing if we had lost. What that meant was that if you had won, it felt like you had won the lottery. Ten pounds in those days was a lot of money – it still is, I suppose. But twelve or thirteen years ago, it meant ten pints in the club afterwards, and the boys would obviously be chuffed to bits about that. When I moved on to Bridgend, we would get £25 for a win, and I honestly can't remember whether we were paid a bean if we lost.

At the time, it was just pin money for me to add to the wages I earned working as a postman. I left school early, before my GCSEs, to work in a factory, but at that time there were opportunities to become an apprentice, on what was decent money, with the Post Office. My dad was working for them, and I was lucky that he had a quiet word with the right people and got me in there. I loved it. It was hard work, and because of the early start it meant you couldn't have much of a social life – well, most of the time anyway! But I loved getting into the great outdoors on my own. I basically felt as though I was working for myself.

I would get to work in the mornings and sort my own mail at the Bridgend depot and then go out, either around the town or to the beautiful villages in the surrounding area. Of course, like all the other lads, I had to find a way of dealing with the postman's main occupational hazard: dogs. Sometimes, I'd walk into a block of flats and inadvertently almost stand on an angry pit bull terrier. But it didn't take me long to form a cunning plan – I took to carrying dog biscuits with me on my round. I would stuff them into my coat pocket and head towards some of the rougher parts of the town, where I tended to encounter a few bad-tempered strays, with renewed confidence. But the biscuits were a double-edged sword because the dogs soon realised I had treats, and by the time I was nearing the end of my round I would be like the Pied Piper, leading a great big pack of dogs out of the estate!

As I was still an amateur rugby player, I was really lucky because I could go in and do my round in the morning, do some weights mid-morning, head back to do my second delivery, go home and sleep and then do rugby training in the evening. Sounds exhausting, doesn't it? Well, I suppose it was, but in those days I had even more bags of energy than I do now.

My dad and I used to get up at 4.30 a.m. to go to work. We would drive in together when we eventually got a car, but before that we would have to get up at 4 a.m. and hope we could flag down one of the lads on their way in to stop and give us a lift. We didn't live far from the Bridgend depot, in the Sarn area of the town, but it was too far to walk in every day. My first car was a Vauxhall Nova 1.3 SR, a real boy racer's machine, and things were better when that came along.

There were problems on Saturdays, though. I would get up at 4.30 a.m., do my round, and then head to the club to do weights and wait around to play in the game. If I tried to do that nowadays, I'd be seen as crazy, especially doing weights only a couple of hours before a game. It came to the point that my dad would get up with me on a Saturday morning and help me, because the schedule was preventing me from getting through games. On one occasion, we played Newport, and as they were taking a kick at goal I leaned against a post, my eyes went heavy and I could actually feel myself getting ready to nod off to sleep – against a post in the middle of a game! I thought to myself, 'This can't go on,' and that's when my dad started to help me.

I eventually left the Post Office when Bridgend offered me a job as a development officer, but I was sad to leave. OK, the pay wasn't a king's ransom, but as long as I had £50 in my bank account on a Sunday night to see me through the week for petrol and food, I didn't care. They were great days, and I often think now what it would be like to go back to those times. I wouldn't

For Pencoed Youth at the Bridgend Sevens. (Courtesy of the author.)

change anything that I have in my life now, but those days were special, and I recall them with real fondness, even though time moves on. I still see some of the guys I worked with around and about, and that's always great. Working on the post, playing for Bridgend, out with the boys every Saturday night – what a life!

Even though I was playing for a great club with a great tradition, it wasn't as though I thought I was playing first-class rugby. To me, it was just rugby, end of story. I never once looked at the league table and worried in the course of a season. All I cared about was that I was playing rugby for Bridgend.

I'm not the type of person who looks back on the amateur days with a sense of injustice that I never got the chance to earn more out of the game. Instead, I'm far more grateful for the characters I encountered, friends I met and experiences I had. But that didn't mean that there were no choices to be made about where I played my rugby or a lack of suitors queuing up to secure my services. In fact, as soon as I came of age, I was faced with decisions about what path I should take in the game.

As I've said, I came through the Pencoed youth system. At that time, there was a rule that you had to give whichever club had brought you through youth rugby at least one year of senior service. But that didn't stop David Pickering, who was coach of Neath at the time and is now chairman of the Welsh Rugby Union, from ringing me practically every other night trying to get me to throw in my lot at The Gnoll. I almost went, as well: I spent the summer of 1992, before my first senior season with Pencoed, training with Neath almost in the hope that the rule would be relaxed and I could make my first big break. But it was not to be. Pencoed dug their heels in, as they were quite entitled to do.

Bridgend had also contacted the club about me and been told that I was staying put, and to be honest I was a bit miffed at having to stay, not because I was bitter or particularly keen to get away, but because I had already listened to so many people telling me what a great opportunity going to Neath was and how I should jump at it. Everyone had convinced me that I was more or less being tucked up by Pencoed, and I guess I wasn't mature enough at the time to shut all that out. I was only human and saw the chance to play for a big club as one that might never come my way again.

But I had no choice – rules were rules. The pity was, though, that my final season for Pencoed was a bit of a dead loss, because I simply wasn't interested. The situation in the close season had left me on poor terms with the coach, so I ended up playing a large chunk of the first half of the season in the seconds. However, I was to blame more than anyone else, because when I played I

didn't give two hoots. I just didn't care. As far as I was concerned, I should have been somewhere else.

Thankfully, I got my head together as the campaign wore on and ended up playing some really good stuff in the firsts and enjoying it. Even now, the fact that I toughed it out at Pencoed for a year and learnt to play rugby the hard way is one of the proudest things for me to look back on. These days, I think youngsters have it too easy in many respects. Their talent is spotted at an early age, and they go straight into the academies. Everything is on a plate for them to be nurtured through. Perhaps it is better for them that way in the long run, but all I know is that when I was 17 years old I was playing senior rugby with neutral touch judges in matches against teams up in the valleys where sometimes you were relieved to hear the final whistle and still be in one piece. I vividly recall running around the pitch in some games and not knowing where the next haymaker was coming from.

Despite having to go through all that – let's face it, I'm not the only rugby player to have had to! – I now look back on it with so much pride. For all that I was annoyed at having to stay at Pencoed, in hindsight I am really glad that I did, because it gave me what I consider to be an invaluable grounding in the realities of the game. Not just that, I am proud to have given them a year of senior rugby, because they were the club that produced me, and I'm also proud of the fact that, for want of a better way of putting it, I had to fight my way to the top. I wasn't given anything on a plate.

Even now, I recall people I encountered in those early days and know that I owe them a debt of gratitude for making me the player I am today. There were two people who were really important to me when I look back on my time at Pencoed: my old youth coaches Gareth Jones and Viv Thomas. I don't doubt for a minute that rugby clubs the length and breadth of Wales have people like these two, who, for the love of the game, do so much to attract and bring on youngsters who could be the stars of Wales teams of the future. The role that they have to play in terms of guidance cannot be underestimated. That's what I and so many others received at Pencoed, which has a reputation for producing Welsh internationals and British Lions, players such as Scott Gibbs, Gavin Henson and Gareth Cooper all having passed through in their earlier days.

I was fortunate that during the one season I spent as a senior at Pencoed a lot of the youth players whom I had come through the ranks with were also making the same breakthrough as well, so we were all able to stay together. And I was by no means the only one who went on to play first-class rugby. Lyndon Griffiths went on to play fly-half for Swansea and Bridgend, Matthew Harry played for Bridgend, Neil Watkins went on to be a second row for Caerphilly and my mate Gareth Jones was good enough

to play in the centre for Bridgend and Wales.

After I completed my one season with Pencoed, I had David Pickering back on the phone to me asking me to go to Neath. 'Your year's over now,' he said. 'It's time you came to Neath.' But it never happened because by then Bridgend had already approached me. I can't remember who made the first call or exactly where the first interest came from, but as soon as I had heard from them my mind was made up.

'I'm sorry, Dai,' I said to Pickering, 'but Bridgend have been on to me, and that's where I'm going.' Fair play to Dai, who accepted my decision and wished me well.

From that time on, I concentrated on being a Bridgend player. And I have to say that the next couple of seasons were among my happiest for the simple reason that I was playing with my mates. As well as all my pals at Pencoed, I made a new bunch of mates, and we were all part of one big social circle.

At that time, it wasn't as if I knuckled down with the rest of the team to an intense period of pre-season training. No, we used to roll into the club two or three times a week at the Brewery Field or Newbridge Fields in the town, where there was a running track marked out. In my favour, I was very fit in those days – like everyone should be when they are 17 or 18 – and there was nothing of me.

It was a good job, too, because at times there would be a fair bit of running involved in the sessions, but everyone knew that come the end of Thursday night's training we would have our reward – a night on the piss together. And that would be the case every Thursday come hell or high water. Unfortunately for me, I would be up before the crack of dawn the Friday morning to do my post round, which meant I couldn't go too over the top on the beer.

I even played one or two matches for the Post Office side in Bridgend. The main reason I made myself available was that I would be given the day of the game off, which meant I wouldn't have to get up early. We may only have been playing Pontyclun Post Office, or some team like that, but it was worth it just to get a day off.

When it came to playing my first game for Bridgend – no, not the South Wales Police match, which was just a friendly – it was against Cardiff, of all sides. And it was at the Arms Park at that.

I remember the Thursday night at training when they read the team out for Saturday's match and I heard those two words: 'Gareth Thomas'. I was in the centre with my pal Gareth Jones. I was in a state of shock for a good few minutes, completely unable to believe that I had won selection to play not just for Bridgend for the first time but in a game of such magnitude. But the feeling lasted only a couple of minutes, because, as I have already said, the meaning of big

matches was lost on me in those days. All that mattered to me was playing for Bridgend, and I certainly didn't go home and think for two days about playing against one of the biggest clubs in the game at a ground that had witnessed so much history and hosted so many great players. With respect, we could have been playing some nondescript club up in the valleys as far as I was concerned, right up to the point when the team bus snaked its way into the ground in the middle of the city.

From then on, I gradually became a more senior player and started to make a name for myself in the game. We never won anything, certainly not a league title, and I think the furthest we ever got in the cup was a quarter-final. But I can't say that affected me badly at the time, nor do I look back upon what was a period of little team success with any particular regret. The only consideration for me was that I was lucky to be doing something I enjoyed at such a high level – and how I enjoyed it.

For instance, I loved sevens rugby, something I've rarely had the opportunity to play since. On one occasion when I was still a youngster at Bridgend, I was invited to play for The Welshmen team in what was a posh annual sevens event at Henley. Our team was run by the former Wales and Bridgend winger Glen Webbe. Back then, the team was quite famous and more than a bit useful, capable of winning any event we went in for. In fact, we could be awesome at

times. But one particular year sticks in my mind, because it was yet another episode in which I thoroughly embarrassed myself, even if we did go on to win the tournament.

As was the routine in those days, we all went out the night before our opening game, against Cardiff, and got legless in the local pubs. And again in keeping with the routine, I, at just 19 years of age, was as drunk as anyone else in the party, if not the worst. Anyway, the game had not been going five minutes when I was tackled heavily just as I offloaded the ball. Immediately, I knew I was in trouble, for not only had the challenge knocked the wind out of me it had also loosened my fragile bowels enough to force me to follow through good and proper. Thankfully, I was wearing cycling shorts underneath my rugby shorts, which saved me from total humiliation. But I knew I couldn't carry on in that state, not least because the hundreds watching would probably start to smell something before very long.

I sidled up alongside Compo Greenslade, who was also running himself into the ground despite having had a bellyful of beer the night before, and under my breath told him of my plight as the game more or less went on around us. 'Compo, I've shit myself,' I said in a desperate tone. 'Please don't say anything. Just discreetly ask Glen to substitute me and tell him I've tweaked a hamstring or something.'

'No worries, Alf, leave it to me,' Compo replied, and I began to see an escape route from public ridicule. I should have known better. The next thing I heard was Compo bellowing across the pitch like a town crier: 'Webby, Alfie's just shit himself!'

That was it. While the game was in full flight, I ran like a greyhound off the field to a portable toilet just a few yards back from the touchline. I sprinted through the door amid howls of laughter from the crowd and into the private haven of the cubicle, where I removed the poor cycling shorts and cleaned myself up as best I could. Two minutes later, I stepped out with my soiled cycling shorts in my hand and ran back onto the pitch through a guard of honour of around 50 people cheering and shouting, 'Well done, Alfie!'

Perhaps at this point I should explain why I am called Alfie by everyone who knows me. In fact, it has become such a well-used nickname that I'm now even referred to as Alfie by large sections of the press. But although the name is commonly used, I still hear people ask why, and that's fair enough, because there is no obvious reason to people who don't know me. Well, it comes from an old American kids' television show which used to be shown over here when I was young. The main character was a puppet creation called Alf, which stood for Alien Life Form. One day, I was watching the programme with one of my mates Oscar,

and he said, 'You look exactly like him!' For whatever reason, the name stuck and has done ever since, changing from Alf to Alfie over the years.

It's strange how certain pet names stick. It all started when I was about 14 years old, yet it's still going and probably always will. Even my grandparents called me Alf, my wife Jemma very rarely calls me anything else and there are all sorts of off-shoots to the name that get thrown my way, such as Alfonso or Alfredo. My mother is the only one who refuses to call me Alfie when she is speaking directly to me, insisting that I was christened Gareth so that's what she will call me, but even she refers to me as Alf if she's talking about me to other people. She says that she must be the only mother in the world with three sons who are all called by their nicknames, because my two brothers are known as 'Dickie' and 'Twm' rather than their proper names. It has got to the stage that if someone shouts Gareth at me in public, I quite often don't realise that it's me they are talking to.

The incident at the Henley sevens tournament summed up Compo Greenslade and Webby at that time: the two of them were *the* characters at Bridgend and would invariably be up to something. And the Henley embarrassment was by no means the only time I came off worst at a sevens competition – one incident, which coincidentally occurred in Toulouse

where I would end up going to play my rugby almost a decade later, could have ended in tragedy on another day, even though I now look back on it and laugh.

I was playing for a team called the Water Buffalos, run by the former Ebbw Vale and Wales flanker Kingsley Jones, not long after I had won my first Wales cap in 1995. Among others, the team was made up of me, Compo Greenslade, Jamie Ringer, who now plays flanker for the Newport Gwent Dragons but is a Cardiff boy through and through and used to play for his home-town club, and Nick Jones, a second row who used to go by the nickname 'Nick Violence' because he was a real hard knock.

As it was my and Jamie Ringer's first time playing for the team, we knew we could expect some form of forfeit to come our way at some stage. It began with us being locked in the dark in a toilet in the hotel we were staying at on the main square in Toulouse. The original plan had been that Compo and Nick Violence, the two guys nobody would dare mess with, would burst in on us and basically run amok. But Kingsley and a few of the others got wind of what they were planning and managed to bargain their way out of it – Jamie Ringer and I, on the other hand, were not so lucky.

Anyway, the bursting-in-on-us-in-the-dark caper was abandoned for something altogether more unpleasant, and Jamie and I, being the two young

pups, were lined up to amuse the others. Earlier in the day, Compo and Violence had been to one of those classic street markets and bought all manner of things that the French love to eat but many of us Welsh, more used to a weekly shop in Tesco, would find totally revolting, including frogs' legs. Jamie was force-fed most of them and had to get them down or the consequences would have been even more dire.

Just as I thought I had escaped, they gave me the Tabasco-sauce treatment. Quantities of the red-hot condiment were rubbed in my eyes, on my privates and up my backside. I was then made to stand at an open window that fronted onto the main square, where there was not so much a balcony as a sort of ledge and a rather short barrier, which was never going to prevent anyone from falling to the ground, some 25 feet or so below. I then had to sing the national anthem while standing to face the world in just my underpants. The task may sound simple, but by that stage I had so much Tabasco in my eyes I couldn't see a thing, and the pain of having so much of that stuff in other places was making my knees tremble as I desperately tried to get through the words of '*Mae hen wlad fy nhadau*' or 'Land of my Fathers'.

Having had my eyes shut for so long, I had also completely lost my bearings and it was then that I toppled forward towards the barrier. I was just about to flop over it and plummet to the ground when Compo quickly stuck out his hand

and grabbed my underpants to yank me back. Had he not done so I could well have met my maker, because it was one hell of a drop, and I was in no fit state to do anything to help myself.

Later on, I was in absolute agony, and I spent ages trying to get the Tabasco off with water, all the while thinking that it was bad enough doing this kind of stuff with Bridgend, let alone having to do it with a sevens team as well! What made it worse was that Compo and Nick Violence tried to convince us that they had done forfeits when they were younger, but we knew that they hadn't because nobody would have dared go near them.

At that precise moment on the balcony in Toulouse, the only thing that would have prompted further derision would have been if someone had suggested that this buffoon would one day become captain of Bridgend . . . But that's what happened shortly after I returned home from the 1995 World Cup as a fully fledged Welsh international.

The selection process for the club captaincy back then was a little like it used to be in school. Because I was more or less the only member of the Bridgend side that was playing for Wales and therefore considered to be the best player, that made me the natural choice for the captaincy. That was what the thinking used to be. To hell with whether I was a presence off the field or whether I could boast any inspirational qualities, which I certainly couldn't at that time. That was why I was lucky to have Compo by my side. The way I was then, I hardly ever talked, certainly not in a rugby context. Nowadays, it comes more naturally. I more or less know when I need to speak and also when I need to shut up. But then I was only 20 or 21, and I didn't have a clue what being a captain meant.

And while being captain of Wales became an ambition later in my career, I can assure you it never entered my head back then. If someone had put it to me at that stage of my life, I would have smiled and said, 'No hope.' I looked a bit different, too – far more like a kid with my long flowing blond locks that used to prompt people to call me the new Dai Duckham after the great England and Lions wing three-quarter.

I admit, I do look back now and think, 'How on earth did I ever do the job?' But, then again, I don't think there were any great expectations on me, because the role was seen in a different light. It went to the best player regardless, and Bridgend wasn't Cardiff, who obviously had six or seven Wales internationals. In fact, it was a bit like the old schoolyard scenario of 'you're the best player, so obviously you'll be the captain'. Because of that, there were never any qualms whatsoever from any of the other players about me being handed the armband.

I think the captaincy was also a way of Bridgend saying, 'Stay with us now that you've made a name for yourself.' They

Reawakening my career during my second spell with Bridgend.

In action for Bridgend during my successful
second spell at the club.

knew how much I loved the club, and they knew that had I wanted to leave I could have gone somewhere like Cardiff. I wasn't aware of any specific deals being put on the table, but I knew there were offers in the pipeline if I really wanted to pursue them. I did eventually make the switch, but it was somehow appropriate that the last club rugby I played in Wales before the game went regional was for Bridgend, when I left Cardiff in 2001 to go back to the Brewery Field for a second spell.

The Bridgend I went back to was a very different animal, largely because of the speed at which the game was changing as it adjusted to the professional era. Understandably, the game was no longer about just enjoying yourself and having a beer with the lads after training – although we did still find time on occasions!

No, it was far more results orientated and open to fierce press scrutiny. If you went five or six games without a win, the newspapers would invariably conclude that you weren't fit or the coach was on borrowed time or so-and-so was on his way to another club come the end of the season.

Bridgend were owned by a chap called Leighton Samuel, a local millionaire

businessman who was prepared to pump considerable funds into the club but expected quick returns on his investment in terms of results. To be brutally honest, I did not want to leave Cardiff, but there was also a part of me that did want to go back to Bridgend, and I would be lying if I said part of it was not down to the financial incentive. The deal Samuel put on the table for me back in 2001 was quite simply mind-blowing for a Welsh club at the time. In fact, it was ridiculous, and it may not comfort Samuel to know now that I would actually have gone back for much less money.

I was lucky that I had a good agent, and he'd phone me and say, 'It's just gone up five grand. I'm going to go for more.' He would then ring me back ten minutes later and say the offer had gone up even more!

Anyway, I had a call one day to tell me that the contract on offer was six figures a year, and immediately I told him to accept it. Not only that, it was on a rising scale, which meant that it would go up by £15,000 in the second year and then £10,000 in the third and final year of the contract. Quite frankly, if there was a better deal on offer in the whole of the Welsh club game at the time I would be very surprised. Put all this up against the fact that I was earning way less in my final year at Cardiff and you can see why the Bridgend move was so attractive.

Now, I am not motivated by money any more than the next man – it is not the be all and end all for me and never has been. I believe being happy in your environment, being made to feel valued, and finding your work stimulating and rewarding are far more important principles. But I would defy any human being not to feel swayed by a huge increase in their salary – a difference of more than double before you took into account the rising scale. I don't believe for a minute that I can be accused of being greedy, especially when the offer was made by Samuel before any real hard bargaining had even begun. It wasn't as if I had gone in from the start and said, 'Right, I'm not coming unless I get this much.' Instead, it was practically being given away to me. And the beauty of it was that I was being offered money to go back and play for a club that I loved from the bottom of my heart anyway.

Obviously, such a willingness to pay top salaries attracted other big names to the club, and the Bridgend team of my second spell was a totally different proposition to the earlier days. We actually had an outfit that could compete with anyone, and Samuel was perfectly entitled to expect us to put some silverware in what had become a rather dusty Brewery Field cabinet. Dafydd James, who at the time was close to the peak of his powers having just returned from the British Lions' tour to Australia, where he got his Test cap, also joined. Other players included Nathan Budgett, who was doing great things in the Wales team at the time, the Welsh international second row Andy Moore, who arrived from Swansea, the Tongan full-back Josh Taumalolo, who was hot property back then and had come on board from Ebbw Vale, and even Chris Horsman, the prop who became eligible for Wales in 2005 and has become one of the best on the international circuit.

Yet because of the money that was circulating around the club and because of the fact that Bridgend was now being seen as somewhere you could go and play for top dollar, there was something distinctly unhealthy about the team environment for a long time. We became known as a club whose players were more influenced by money – the Chelsea of Welsh rugby, if you like. Don't get me wrong. I'm in no way pointing the finger here, because I myself took the money that such a fantastic contract brought with it, although I maintain I always played for the jersey as well.

On top of that, Samuel was in the newspapers a hell of a lot, spouting on about this issue and that, and it began to feel at times as if we weren't a rugby club at all, just a business that had lost sight of the soul of the game. We were under increasing pressure because of the salaries we were earning and the fact that for a long time we were not getting the results that the strength of our team should have been producing.

Every now and again, Samuel would come into the changing-room after a bad result or a dodgy performance, and

Proud skipper of Bridgend.

you could feel the vibe coming from him that he was far from happy. What's more, all the power was with him. As players, we knew that if he withdrew his support of the club the following morning, our wages were gone and the whole place would go belly-up. Taking the money was one thing, but part of the package was taking Samuel with it, knowing that he was a sort of emperor figure in charge of everything from salaries to what make of tea bags we used for a post-match brew.

Despite this, I have to say that I never really had any particular problem with

Leighton Samuel claimed that the Welsh Premiership trophy was the most expensive vase he'd ever bought!

him, because I had very little to do with him on a day-to-day basis. I just knew he was the bloke who was paying me all that money. If you turned to any member of the public and said, 'Here's the fellow who pays your hefty wages,' then it's unlikely they would look to pick an argument with him. For that reason, I never went looking for things to dislike about him, and if anything did raise its head, I always looked to give him the benefit of the doubt rather than criticise.

And besides, Samuel, although perhaps not a fan of mine as such, was someone who saw the good in me rather than the bad. In fairness to him, he always looked to support me, and I sometimes felt as

though I could do little wrong in his eyes. He saw the club and everything that came with it as his personal possession, even down to its individual employees, of whom I, of course, was one. In a way, he was entitled to take that stance, because he was paying us all out of his own pocket. Although he was rewarding me well, his financial input perhaps made him feel that I had come to play not just for Bridgend but very much for him as well.

The early days of my second spell at Bridgend were tough, because – and there's no way of hiding it – we were an expensively assembled team that was not delivering. It was only halfway through my second season (2001–02) that things started to change. With respect to all the individuals involved, the signing of Andy Moore, the second row, and Chris Horsman made a real difference to the balance of the team, and the change of coach – Allan Lewis, the hugely experienced former Newport and Wales assistant coach, took over the reins from the ex-Pontypridd supremo Dennis John – also seemed to spark us into life. I'm not sure exactly why, but all of a sudden we turned into a proper team, not just some band of individuals all brought together by the lure of the coin, and we finally started to cheer up Samuel by delivering some results.

It all culminated in us winning the Welsh Premiership title at the end of the 2002–03 season, which up until 2005 was the only piece of silverware I

My old Wales pal Shane Howarth tries to grab me during a Welsh Cup semi-final.

had ever won in the game and the first honour Bridgend had secured since the Schweppes Cup win of 1980. Not that it appeared to mean as much to our long-suffering chairman as it did to us. After we had been presented with the cut-glass trophy on the Brewery Field pitch after beating Neath 22–13 on a sunny May evening, Samuel told waiting journalists, 'That's the most expensive vase I've ever bought!' It was the sort of quote that was always going to get a good airing, and, as expected, it was given plenty of prominence the following day. I know that it must have raised plenty of laughs around Wales,

but I can assure you that it did not go down at all well with the players at the time. And it still doesn't sit well with me when I look back on it now. The general feeling was, 'What a thing to say.' We had just proved ourselves to be the best side in the division over the course of a season, the ultimate test for any team, and even though Samuel's comment may have been tongue-in-cheek the timing of it was poor.

But we were also not helped by the fact that everybody knew that it was the last-ever Welsh Premiership in its current guise, because Welsh rugby was going regional at the start of the next season.

Celebrating our title win.

For that reason, some people seemed to regard winning the league as some sort of Mickey Mouse accomplishment that most teams didn't really care about. Well, let me give you an idea of what it meant, and still means, to me. Even now, I regard that final season with Bridgend as definitely up there with the best seasons of rugby in my life. That team, that year, that achievement: it will always mean the world to me.

I had taken over as captain in mid-season the year before when Allan Lewis became our coach, and the strides we made under him and Richard Webster were amazing. The turnaround showed what is possible if the will is there, and it gave me a huge sense of pride. We had everything a championship-winning side needs: ability, good direction and a massive spirit of togetherness – and so for Samuel to come out with a statement like that really hurt. It might have been a quip, but it was as if he was saying that the title was the least he deserved and that such success should never have been so long in coming, because of all the money he had put into the club.

But never mind an expensive vase, we would not have cared if we had been

given a plastic bag as a trophy. It was the achievement of winning the last-ever Welsh Premiership before regional rugby and making history that counted. I remember saying to the boys at the time that for all the years I had put in at Bridgend, I had never won anything. And even though I had been to Cardiff, I still counted Bridgend as 'my club', so being able to say that I had won a league title there was something that was going to stay with me for ever. It wasn't just for the players, though – what a present for the supporters of the club who had gone through so many success-starved years.

It wasn't just the end of the road for us as players before the regional upheaval, it was the end for the supporters following Bridgend Rugby Club as a top-flight entity. These days, while the club still very much exists, I think everyone will tell you that following the fortunes of a semi-professional team that plays in the revamped Welsh Premiership just isn't the same. That's not meant to sound disrespectful in the slightest, but that division, while I'm sure it is competitive in its own way, is very much supposed to be a feeder competition for the regional game and to provide a decent level for youngsters to develop in and more senior players to help them through.

So, whatever people thought at the time or still think today about Bridgend becoming the Welsh Premiership champions of 2002–03, I retain the memories of a great team, a great season and a great achievement. And nobody will ever take those memories away from me.

2

....

CARDIFF CALLING – THE KEY'S UNDER THE STONE!

Right up until just before the game in Wales went regional, many people still saw Cardiff Rugby Club as the Manchester United of Welsh rugby, even though followers of Llanelli, Newport, etc., would probably have something to say about that. But whatever they say, I don't think there is any doubt that wearing the blue-and-black jersey brought with it its own unique set of demands and standards that all tallied with the tradition of it being the self-styled 'greatest club in the world'.

If I'm honest, tags like that mean little to me these days. I'm not one who goes in for misty-eyed recollections of the game's history, even though I do have a healthy respect for those who have gone before me. But saying that, nobody could fail to be aware that playing for Cardiff brings with it something unique. It's difficult to put into words exactly what it entails. But it is there – and you do feel its presence.

For all manner of reasons, but probably mostly because of their rich 'city slickers' image, Cardiff were always resented by followers of the other top-flight Welsh clubs. Just as Sir Alex Ferguson always claims that everyone hates Manchester United, the same claim could be made about Cardiff in the very much smaller world of Welsh rugby. It's different now that the game has gone regional and Cardiff have become the Cardiff Blues. Yet even now I'm told that there are still some catcalls at grounds when the Welsh regions face one another in the Celtic League, harking back to the old order of things.

Nowhere was this resentment fiercer than at Bridgend in the mid-to-late 1990s and particularly in the 1997–98 season when I bit the bullet and decided to take up an offer to head east to the Arms Park. To be blunt about it, going to Cardiff was nothing short of a monumental decision for me, because I knew full well that our supporters not so much disliked their big-city neighbours

People say I don't act my age.
I say, 'What is age?'

as completely hated them. And I was unsure as to whether I would ever be forgiven for going.

The root of such ill feeling? Well, as in most such situations, it probably means different things to different people, but a common source of annoyance was the number of top Bridgend players who seemed to migrate to Cardiff as soon as they became hot property in the game. Mike Hall, the Wales and Lions centre, Mike Griffiths, the British Lions prop, the second row Mike Budd and number 8 Owain Williams were just a few who had made the switch to the disquiet of the Bridgend faithful. Rob Howley actually went through the whole business twice after returning briefly to the Brewery Field when his first stint as a Cardiff player didn't work out. And rightly or wrongly, the consensus was that these players always failed to make

I found my second home at Cardiff Arms Park.

the progress at Cardiff that they would have done had they stayed put with the club that made them. In a nutshell, everyone connected with Bridgend hated the idea that they were perceived as Cardiff's feeder club.

This naturally ensured that whenever Cardiff came to play a match at Bridgend you were guaranteed it would not just be a packed house, but a noisy and angry packed house. In fact, the atmosphere would be horrible. You could feel the hatred dripping down from the stands and terraces as soon as you took to the field. You even felt it in the warm-up.

So you can understand why I took a while to decide to follow in the footsteps of some of the guys I've mentioned above. That said, in the end the decision was made a little easier for me and for one main reason: the Bridgend coach, a New Zealander by the name of John Phillips, who had already been the cause of a few other senior players deciding to leave before me. I have to be honest about this: as much as I loved the club, I just couldn't come to terms with the way Phillips went about things.

Now, back then I would say that I probably didn't know the true difference between a good coach and a bad coach. I just loved playing. I had such enthusiasm to get my boots on and get out on the field that I felt as though I had never been coached and didn't need to be. As I mentioned earlier, the game was far simpler back then, certainly the way I looked at it. Even now, I can't help but

feel that if you are charged with the task of coaching someone as enthusiastic as I was back then, you can only dim some of that enthusiasm by telling him to do it this way or that. I think there's a danger of turning a real flair player into a robot.

As for Phillips, his bizarre methods and unusual personality had a negative impact on me. And in my opinion, he proves wrong the notion that a southern-hemisphere accent automatically makes you a rugby genius.

Leaving Bridgend was the first time in my entire career that I put myself first. I had reached a stage when I had to start thinking about myself rather than the team. The rugby world was changing: professionalism had been introduced, and, whether people liked it or not, the game was now a means of making a living for the likes of me and hundreds of other former amateurs in Wales. Therefore, I had to think like anyone in any other profession would in terms of financial incentives and job security.

I also had ambitions and wanted to climb the ladder. For example, the Heineken Cup had been created, and I really wanted to play in that competition. Unfortunately, Bridgend didn't look like a team that was capable of playing in the best tournament in Europe at that time. I felt selfish, even though plenty of people were saying to me, 'Go on, put yourself first for once.'

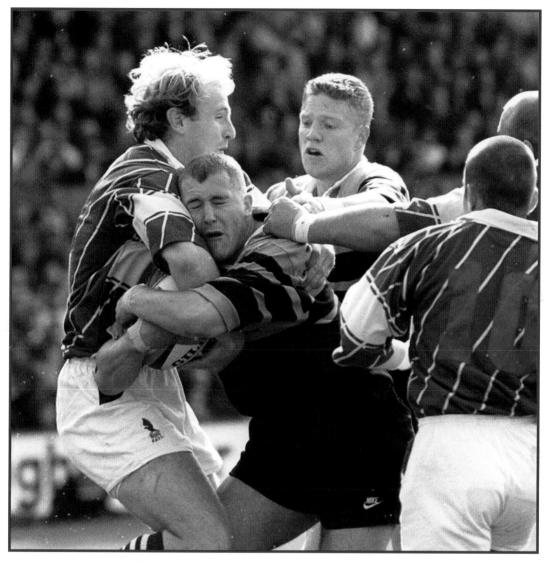

Leigh Davies hits me hard in a Cardiff v. Bridgend match
before I joined him at the Arms Park.

I told the chairman Derek King, a really top bloke who in fairness had both the club's and my best interests at heart, that I wanted to leave. Derek was always great with me – he was one of the game's true gentlemen – but for a long time I got nowhere, as the club committee didn't seem to want to accept my decision. It all came to a head one evening when I went before the committee for what seemed like the umpteenth time to ask for a move. I entered the room above the main stand at the Brewery Field with the attitude that I had already had a complete gutful of the whole business, because

negotiations had been going on for so long.

Cardiff were nagging me all the time, and I just wanted to leave Bridgend. I told the committee as much, but the problem was that I had to keep saying it. They wanted me to stay for the good of the club, which was fair enough, but it reached the stage that I felt I was banging my head against a brick wall. They kept saying, 'Why do you want to leave? This is your club, and we need better reasons than the ones you have given.'

It all became too much at this one particular meeting, and I ended up bursting into tears and running out of the room. That might sound a bit melodramatic, but it was an indication of the depth of feeling I had for the club. And I think that moment was the straw that broke the camel's back.

Derek, who had been a father figure to me ever since I had joined the club, finally realised that I wanted out for genuine reasons and would not be for turning under any circumstances. He realised that I had to try and go for it – go and do more in the game. It never came to Bridgend offering me any financial incentive to stay – I am not sure whether they were in a position to do so anyway – but it would have made no difference because none of this was about money.

Do you know, the first year the game went professional I honestly don't think I was even on a contract. If I was, I didn't know about it! I certainly cannot recall ever signing on any dotted line. I was getting paid what I thought was a decent wage, and that was enough for me. I was not the highest-paid player at Bridgend by any means, but I was happy with what I had, and I didn't have any issues or grievances. And I am honestly unclear to this day as to whether I was on a contract when it came to me leaving for Cardiff. There were definitely no contractual matters talked about at any length between me and the board, and in any case contracts were never an issue to me back then.

John Phillips wanted me to stay, and even though he had only been there a year he was trying to insist I did just that. But Derek had obviously told him that enough was enough. I remember Tonga were touring in the autumn of the 1997–98 season and came to play us at Bridgend. Phillips came up to me before kick-off and said, 'After this game, you are free to go.' And that is what I did, leaving the club I loved halfway through the season and playing my first game for Cardiff against Newport at Rodney Parade a few weeks later.

Despite the hatred some Bridgend supporters felt towards Cardiff, it was not as if anyone burned an effigy of me in the streets of my home town when I crossed the great divide to the Blue and Blacks. But I do recall the first time I returned to play against Bridgend for Cardiff when I almost ended up jumping from the pitch and starting a fight on the terrace. Remember the infamous

Eric Cantona kung-fu kicking incident when the volatile Frenchman jumped into the stand at Crystal Palace and practically tried to decapitate a fan who was barracking him? Well, it didn't quite get to that stage, but it wasn't far away. When I think about it now, the reason I lost my cool was simply because even though I had left Bridgend I still loved the club deeply.

Anyway, as the match went on there was this fellow at the front of one of the terraces who was hurling non-stop abuse at me. It doesn't take a genius to imagine the gist of it, but, needless to say, it was foul-mouthed nonsense about how I was a Judas for leaving Bridgend, as well as everything else under the sun! What was probably inflaming the situation was that we were stuffing them. I took it for a period, trying to tell myself that he was just a moron who didn't even deserve my recognition. I didn't want him to know that he was getting to me. But he was getting to me.

I was playing on the wing and was very close to him. Also, I had seen little of the ball, which might have taken my attention away from his vitriol. Suddenly, after another mouthful, I snapped and ran over to the barrier that separated the pitch from the terracing. I was just about to jump over and got as far as having one leg on top of the rail when the Bridgend water man stopped me from scaling it. Luckily – for me and him, I suppose – I saw the guy move away into the crowd and disappear out of sight. I'm not

altogether surprised that he did, because he would have seen that not only was I coming to get him but that I really meant business as well.

So, I didn't quite get to follow in the footsteps of Mr Cantona, which in hindsight was best for all concerned, but I would be lying if I said that the incident didn't hurt me in a big way. I still loved Bridgend, and I so wanted people to appreciate the reasons why I had left. Fortunately, because of the way the game was going at the time and because it happened on the far side of the Brewery Field away from the grandstand, it wasn't really noticed by the press and little was made of it. I suppose from a distance it wouldn't have been clear what I was doing anyway, and I was grateful not to see it splashed across the newspapers the following day. I certainly said nothing, not because I was embarrassed by my actions, but because I was embarrassed for the poor idiot whose tirade, had it been made public, might have given all Bridgend fans a bad name. After all, he was probably one of the many fans who had been as nice as pie to me over the previous few years. That was what was hard to accept – that someone's opinion of me could change so much when I was still so passionate about Bridgend the club and that someone's discontent could be so venomous.

Little did I know that the following few years of my career as a Cardiff player would be some of the best I would ever

experience. But if you spoke to many followers of the game who recall that period, I am sure many would say that it was one of underachievement for Cardiff, and they would have a point. Back then, we used to make winning the Heineken Cup our prime goal every season, and we believed, along with many of Welsh rugby's most respected pundits, that we had a squad that was capable of doing so. But we never managed it because we seemed to save our worst performances for the biggest matches in the competition.

Painful defeats that stick in the mind are two Heineken Cup quarter-final exits – to Llanelli in 2000 and Gloucester the following year. The match against our Welsh rivals at Stradey Park was just one of those horrible days when we allowed the Scarlets to make a good start and could not get back into it, going down by the horrible margin of 22–3. The Gloucester disappointment at their Kingsholm fortress was more damning than the final 21–15 score line suggested, with a couple of late scores painting a misleading picture of an afternoon when we again failed to turn up when it mattered most. I wouldn't say that those defeats were because we couldn't handle the pressure as a group; it was just that for reasons I cannot explain we didn't seem able to turn it on when the really big games came along.

But it is all too easy to forget some of the things we did achieve. I loved it there. We had an awesome team, and I would love to see the complete record of the time I spent there between 1998 and 2001. We had proven performers like Dai Young, Jonathan Humphreys, Rob Howley, Leigh Davies, Neil Jenkins, Nick Walne, Craig Quinnell, Dan Baugh and John Tait. They are all still great mates of mine.

From memory, I would say you could count on one hand the number of matches we lost at home, because we turned the Arms Park into a fortress. Two defeats to Swansea at home do stick in my memory, but we saw off teams like Toulouse, Saracens, Ulster and Montferrand in the Heineken Cup, big European scalps of which we could justifiably be proud. Those results gave us the right to be regarded as contenders every time the tournament came around, and to my mind that's exactly what we were.

That said, we did take a couple of hidings away to Montferrand when we were drawn in their pool twice during my time at Cardiff. In December 1999, we took a battering at the Parc de Sports Marcel Michelin, going down 46–13 in a match that we were never in from start to finish. But then we beat them in the return game after Christmas, which was played on an absolute quagmire of a pitch at the Arms Park. It's not just the brilliant 30–5 victory that I recall that day, but something altogether less pleasant as well.

During the 1999 World Cup, the pitch at Cardiff had been used for

the housing of hospitality marquees because of its position next door to the Millennium Stadium. Anyway, if a surface resembling Barry Island beach with the tide out worried us players, the fact that the soil smelled of sewage was arguably of greater concern. I kid you not; if you picked up a clump of the earth and put it to your nose, you were hit by the stink of the one thing we all hate to smell. How that came to be, I cannot be totally certain, but our suspicions were that the contents of Portaloos that had been put up for the hospitality guests had somehow leaked onto the pitch. No wonder the French were knocked out of their stride that day!

But it wasn't just that: the field was also extremely wet – we were in the middle of a typical Welsh winter – with vast pools of water lying on top of the soil. I remember as we lined up in the tunnel that day I had a huge pair of swimming goggles that I was going to wear as I ran out, the added bonus being that the encounter was live on television. I wanted to take the mickey and make a point in the process. All our boys were pleading with me to wear them saying, 'You've got to, you've got to.' But I'm afraid I chickened out at the last minute, and to this day I'm gutted I never went through with it.

So despite what some sections of the press were saying at the time, we did have plenty of team spirit when I was at Cardiff. And while there, a big thing in

my life happened – I met Leigh Davies, who came to the club from Neath and burst onto the international scene at centre to quite devastating effect in the mid-1990s.

Davies, as I have always called him, became one of my best mates – we were together all the time. And we used to indulge in the most savage drinking sessions. For example, every Saturday night without fail we would go out in Cardiff and drink ourselves stupid. We would go to a variety of watering holes – Jumpin Jaks in the city's Mill Lane was a favourite, then there was Kiwi's in the Wyndham Arcade and The Square bar at the bottom of St Mary's Street.

We had a nice little routine going on a Saturday. After the game, we would both get steaming in the Cardiff clubhouse before going anywhere. Stella lager was my tipple – still is. Even now, on the odd occasion that I have a drink I prefer to drink Stella. But back then whatever was wet, we drank, the only guarantee being that by the end of the night the two of us would be absolutely leathered. By then, we would both easily be in double figures in terms of pints; in fact, there were occasions when we were in double figures before we even left the clubhouse! But there would be shorts thrown in a lot of the time as well. We used to smash the drink down our necks like there was no tomorrow.

At the time, Leigh had a place in the Llandaff area of Cardiff, and I lost count of the number of times I kipped over at

his house. There were times when there would be what seemed like around 50 people staying there on a Saturday night, half of whom I had never met in my life and wouldn't see again. The classic saying if ever we parted company at any stage during the night was, 'The key's under the stone.' You see, Leigh had a massive stone just outside his front door, under which he always left the key. I swear at one time hundreds of people across Cardiff must have known that the key to Leigh Davies's house was 'under the stone'. Whole groups of people used to go up to him to say that they were heading off, and if Leigh was still going full pelt on a bender in some nightclub, he would say, 'Key's under the stone.'

I loved that time. Leigh became such an outstanding mate, and we had some brilliant evenings. But our drinking antics were by no means confined to evenings. No chance! Not only had we developed a routine for Saturdays, we'd also developed one for the entire weekend. I would park my car outside his house on a Saturday morning, and we would go to the match together. That meant that on a Sunday morning after the boozed-up exertions of the night before, I could go and do something that my teammates suspected me of doing for years, but I never really admitted to anyone other than Davies: 'secret training'. Secret training? I suppose you can define it as work put in alone, totally separate to the work

you do with your club, which is meant to be enough to ensure you are fighting fit every match day.

I still do it now, but back in my Cardiff days the most intense sessions were on Sunday mornings. I would drag myself out of whatever bed I had managed to find at Davies's house, having been utterly wrecked the night before, and would go and run the alcohol out of my system. It was the only way I could justify in my own mind going back on the booze on the Sunday, which me and Davies did on a regular basis. I would go on a treadmill at a gym back in Bridgend and keep going until I was physically sick if I had to. And nobody knew. I told none of the boys at the time, although most of them now know what I was up to. As I say, Davies was the only one who knew, because he was my closest pal.

After running myself ragged in the gym, I would head into Bridgend, followed by Davies. Like most normal people, Davies preferred to sleep off the effects of his hangover, but come lunchtime, or early afternoon at the very latest, we would go for it again in the pubs around my home town. Years ago, Sunday was the day to drink in Bridgend. It sometimes seemed like everyone who mattered was out on the piss on a Sunday. And we're not talking about a few sociable beers either side of a roast dinner. Far from it. We would be out by 1 p.m. and would still be knocking them back at 2.30 a.m. the following morning.

Me and Davies – best of pals. (Courtesy of the author.)

There was a place called The Roof in the middle of the town that wouldn't shut until midnight, and then we might go for an Indian or a Chinese meal before heading on to a nightclub. There was always one open somewhere. Most of the time our girlfriends would be with us as well, so there was a big crowd of us and very much a 'more the merrier' type of feel to it all.

Sunday is still a big day for drinking in Bridgend, though not as big as Saturday. And, even now, if you give me a choice of when in the week I would most like to have a good drink, Sunday wins hands down. I love it. It's quieter,

and I just feel you can sit down and chill out without a place being chock-full of rowdy people.

But there was a potential downside to the 'Super Sundays' that Davies and I used to enjoy so much. Every Monday morning at Cardiff we had to deal with the dreaded 'F' word – 'F' standing for 'Fitness'. Someone in their wisdom had decided that the weekly schedule would not begin with a gentle warm-up followed by skills practice, but fitness. As you can imagine, after two days of drinking like fish the two of us were not overly enthusiastic about pushing our bodies to the limit. No matter though,

Me and Davies doing what we once did best! (Courtesy of the author.)

because Davies and I had a potentially awkward situation sussed. Would you believe that at the time the pair of us were learning to play tennis? Not only that but we managed to convince the Cardiff management that our lessons were actually harder than the club's fitness session! To this day, I don't know how we convinced them to fall for such nonsense – or maybe they knew all along and just couldn't be bothered to argue.

It meant the two of us would have an hour and a half of tennis tuition at the David Lloyd Centre on the outskirts of the city – which was in fact an absolute doddle – while the rest of the team sweated buckets by running themselves into the ground. Yet despite the fact that we were clearly deceiving people, I justified it in my own mind because I felt that, as a centre partnership, Davies and I were doing nothing at all wrong on the park. More than that, we were a bloody good pairing who bowed to nobody on match day and produced the goods week in, week out. With Davies at inside-centre, me outside him and Neil Jenkins at number 10, we used to call ourselves 'the wall', because we considered our defensive unit to be unbreakable.

Even these days there are some top-flight professionals who do not train

adequately and definitely do not do enough weights. But my attitude is that if you are doing the business on the park on a Saturday, it doesn't really matter. We were doing the job, and nobody ever had any qualms about the way we were playing. The typical response to that is to claim a player may be good but could be so much better if he mended his ways, but that's not a mantra that should necessarily be seen as gospel in my view. Some players have a formula for leading their lives that works for them and that's that. If you tried to change them, you would probably only end up getting less out of them.

What Davies and I were producing in the 1999–2000 season in Cardiff colours was obviously impressing the rugby-league fraternity, because we were both approached by Warrington to switch codes as the end of the season neared. They were a club who had a bit of a connection with Wales through the players they had taken from the union game down the years, including Jonathan Davies, Allan Bateman and Kevin Ellis.

At the time, Darryl van der Veldt was their coach, and the club had expressed an interest in both of us. Neither of us seriously saw our futures in the 13-man code, but we were made up because we had a free weekend up in Warrington if nothing else. The plan was to go up there to watch their game and then meet the coach and the players the day after our Heineken Cup quarter-final against Llanelli at Stradey Park.

As mentioned earlier, we were thrashed 22–3 at Stradey, and while Davies played really well in defeat, I had an absolute shocker. But we quickly got over the disappointment, and we set off up north the following morning with Kevin Ellis, a very good friend of mine and a legend up in Warrington, making all the arrangements and Compo Greenslade also joining the travelling party. When we arrived, we booked into a posh hotel – all on Warrington, of course – and almost straight away Compo and Kevin, or Champ as he's called, suggested a quick beer in the hotel bar. 'No way,' I said, speaking for me and Davies. 'We're meeting the coach after the game, and we can't go drinking before that. We'll have a couple tonight.'

So, we all set off for the match, getting to Warrington's ground in good time, where Champ received a hero's welcome. We had tickets for a box, but the Warrington equivalent of the Kop was behind the posts at one end, and Champ suggested we go and stand on the terracing just to savour the experience. That was fine with us. If we were going to come here to play – though I was only up there, if truth be told, because I had said I would come to the Warrington people – it would be nice to mingle with the true fans and get a real feel for the place. So, off we headed to take our places.

Unfortunately, we found a spot that was right next to one of the bars, which was dispensing the usual selection in

I always loved playing for Cardiff.

plastic cups, and Champ decided to get a round in. 'Get us blackcurrant squash,' I told him. Two minutes later, he returned with four pints of cider and black! There was no way we could refuse to drink them, and once the taste was in our mouths that was it: the end of me and Davies.

By half-time, we had sunk about six pints and were steaming drunk. This carried on, until about ten minutes before the end when the pair of us were, not for the first time, totally legless. 'Right boys,' I slurred. 'No more now. We're meeting the coach and the players in ten minutes.' By this time, Compo and Champ had begun laughing at us, but we weren't entirely sure why and thought that it was just because we were pissed.

Anyway, we managed to get to where we were meeting Darryl van der Veldt. We were paranoid about the state we were in and desperately trying to act as if we were sober. A Warrington official introduced us, and I could immediately see van der Veldt looking at us funny. He shook our hands and continued to look at us as if we were from outer space, before making conversation by asking us about the game at Llanelli the day before. God knows what we came up with, but whatever it was it was slurred.

After a couple of minutes, van der Veldt suddenly said to us, 'Boys, do me a favour. Bugger off and come back when you're serious!' Then he looked at us and began to laugh. Compo and Champ had also come along, and they began to laugh as well. We couldn't think what was tickling them other than the fact that we were steaming drunk, then Compo said, 'Go and look in the mirror.'

When the pair of us looked in the mirror, we discovered that, because we had been drinking from plastic glasses and were so drunk, we both had the biggest blackcurrant smiles you could ever have wished to see. Mine stretched from the corner of my mouth halfway towards my ear lobe, and Davies's wasn't much better. We looked like a couple of drunken fools, and Compo and Champ had known all along that the moment van der Veldt saw us he was in for a shock. To make it worse, Davies and I were so far gone that we hadn't spotted our 'smiles' on one another, as enormous as they were.

So, that was that. We never even got to meet the players or any of the sponsors. Instead we went into Warrington and continued on our bender. If nothing else, we had a good weekend away.

When I first went to Cardiff, the Australian Alec Evans was coach. He was someone who had a reputation for a no-nonsense and straight-talking style. He had tried to persuade me to join Cardiff's ranks at the 1995 World Cup when he was in charge of the Wales national team on a caretaker basis after the sacking of Alan Davies following the Five Nations whitewash that year. Mike

Hall, the national captain who was at Cardiff at the time, also had a good go at enticing me.

I was keen, sure, but hardly bursting to make the move – and for the right reasons. I had only just started to make a name for myself at Bridgend, and it did not seem like the right thing to do at the time. I was really happy at Bridgend, and the offer was something that I found flattering rather than genuinely tempting. It was certainly nice to have a player of Hall's stature on at me to join his club. But although I refused, the interest never went away.

In the early days at Cardiff, I used to travel back and forth to training with my pal Gareth Jones, who had also made the switch. I never felt awkward at the time about joining a new team and introducing myself to new faces, because I knew so many of them from the time I had already spent in the game and at the 1995 World Cup, of course. On top of that, I knew that moving to Cardiff was something I had to do for my own good, and so I just knuckled down and got on with whatever confronted me.

Things were much more professionally run at Cardiff, and you could not help but realise that everything was on a much bigger scale compared with Bridgend. For instance, at Bridgend we had one secretary at the club who ran everything, whereas at Cardiff there were offices with different departments full of dozens of people looking after the running of the place. It was a new feeling to sense that it was not just a rugby club but a business.

One of the real plus points at Cardiff was the relationship I had with Terry Holmes, the former Wales scrum-half who took over when Alec Evans departed. With Charlie Faulkner and Mark Ring on board to help him, I thought it was a great coaching team, all of them offering something different. I had loads of respect for Terry, not just for what he had achieved in the game, but for the way he went about his role. He was great at dealing with the players and handling them in an adult manner. Terry was never one to put players down in front of other players. If he had a problem, he would pull you aside and let you know in the correct way – a private way. Before anything else, he was a good coach, but I found he had the sort of personality to which I could relate and trust, and for me that is one of the most important elements of any player–coach relationship. Whether a coach is the best or worst in the world tactically, he will more than likely extract enough from a player if there is a healthy level of mutual trust.

As mentioned earlier, my time at Cardiff heralded the height of my so-called drinking years, and Terry helped me to sort out a lot of things – not just with rugby, but in other spheres of my life as well. Most of the time, Terry knew full well that I had been out on the piss, but to him the most important thing was first that I had respect for him

Davies and I were in our element at the Arms Park.

and second that I was doing my job, which was to perform out on the field on a Saturday. He realised that I was doing that to the best of my ability and doing it well. Terry could have come down hard on me and imposed all sorts of rules and restrictions, but he never once gave me any ultimatums or dire warnings of the consequences of me not conforming.

Terry parted company with the club after we were hammered by Llanelli in a Welsh Cup semi-final at the Brewery Field of all places. It was during our rebel season when Cardiff and Swansea had fallen out with the Welsh Rugby Union, which wanted to tie the Premiership clubs up on a ten-year loyalty agreement

that would in turn guarantee each club a sum of money every year. The two clubs refused, saying that the game would have changed beyond recognition by then, and decided to play a series of friendlies against English clubs rather than bow to WRU demands. It led to all manner of claims and counterclaims about whether Cardiff and Swansea or the Welsh clubs that had stayed loyal to their domestic league were playing the better standard of rugby. And so when we lost that match at Bridgend 39–10 – after taking a 10–0 lead early on – there was an outcry and an extended inquest into what was supposedly going wrong at Cardiff. Terry paid the price a few days later when he more or less

47

had to fall on his sword after a series of damning press stories, and I and plenty of other players were extremely sorry to see him go.

His replacement at the start of the following season was Lynn Howells, whose greatest attribute as a coach was his sheer passion. Lynn will talk passionately about the game all day if you will listen – and he'll mean every word he says. I've since worked with Lynn with Wales and the Celtic Warriors, and he has always had the perfect balance in terms of his henchmen. At Cardiff, he brought in Geraint John, and at the Warriors he had Allan Lewis by his side, both of whom were the perfect complement to what he brought to the party, being more methodical, more tactical, calmer and more relaxed in general.

People listened to Lynn because he was honest, but if you wanted more specifics about the game, you would go to Geraint or Allan. As it happened, Lynn left the Arms Park at the same time as me, right after we had won the Welsh Premiership title. While I had no real inside track on his departure, to this day the feeling is that he was treated badly after a season in which he had delivered success, being made as he was to reapply for his own job. Ultimately, it was probably the failure in Europe that accounted for Lynn, and in particular those two Heineken Cup quarter-final failures against Llanelli and Gloucester. But whatever people at Cardiff thought

of him at the time, I held him in high regard – and still do.

What made me even happier at Cardiff, though, was the marvellous rapport I had with the supporters, who always seemed to respect me for what I was and never expected me to change. They appreciated that I didn't think I was someone special just because I played for Cardiff. I had so much positive feedback from them for being like that, and I think that is one of the reasons why I am the way I am now.

I cannot stress what a massive thing it was to play for Cardiff back then, although I never felt that I was on the same wavelength as the chief executive Bob Norster. I do not bear a grudge against Bob, and he may think differently about this, but I just felt that I did not fit into the version of what he believed a Cardiff player should be at that time. And when it boiled down to it, I had a choice: I could either change; or I could just carry on being myself. I was always going to choose the latter option. But in the end I think the relationship I had with Bob, or the lack of one, was instrumental in me leaving. I think the same could be said of Davies as well.

Let me stress, I didn't want to leave Cardiff in the summer of 2001. I was actually trying to organise a deal to stay, and it was not as though I was asking for money that they were not prepared to give me – there were certainly no outlandish demands on my behalf. But

Secret training at Cardiff left me out of breath on very few occasions.

I always had a great rapport with the terrace faithful at Cardiff.

despite negotiations, Bob never even came back to me with an offer, and so in the end I left because time was running out, and, as a professional player, I needed to secure a new contract.

At the club dinner at the end of my final season, I was introduced to a South African by the name of Rudi Joubert, who was to become the next Cardiff coach. He asked me about the club, and I told him that although I was leaving it was not what I really wanted at that time. Joubert asked me if I wanted to stay and was there any way this could happen. But I told him no. By that stage I had already signed my new contract

with Bridgend, and there was no turning back. Anyway, I was set on going back to the Brewery Field.

Funnily enough, the wrangling over the contract which never actually came at Cardiff proved to be a sign of things to come, as I later found myself embroiled in a mix-up that ended with me pulling out of a deal to join Pontypridd at the 11th hour. I was vilified in the press with certain newspapers claiming I had done the dirty on the Sardis Road club by messing them around and leaving them in the lurch having given my word to go there. I didn't bother trying to defend myself at the time, but it was

certainly not a case of doing the dirty on anyone.

I was actually ready to sign for Pontypridd, one of the real forces in the Welsh game at that time, and would have done so had they not forgotten to bring the contract to a 'signing on' ceremony at the headquarters of the sponsors Buy As You View. For the cameras, I held a pen over a fake piece of paper, but that evening I received a telephone call that convinced me I was making the wrong decision. I won't say who precisely it was from, but suffice to say that it was a prominent Ponty figure who reminded me that I would not necessarily be seen as a centre at Sardis Road and would more than likely have to play a lot of games on the wing. This was news to me – I had expected to be seen primarily as a centre who would fill in on the wing if the team was really stretched. So I pulled out of the move, because I felt I had been misled. Whatever people think, it was for a very valid reason and not just some late whim.

Despite the circumstances in which I left Cardiff, I am extremely chuffed to be going back there to finish my career with the Blues. I love the place and still have a deep affinity for the Arms Park. I regretted that I finished there under a little bit of a cloud and never had the chance to say a decent goodbye to the supporters, but I can put that right now. Bridgend will always be 'my club', but Cardiff, in whatever form they come, will always occupy a special place in my heart.

3

. . . .

1995 AND ALL THAT . . .

Can you imagine a young rugby player being picked to play for his country on the eve of a World Cup and then deliberately getting himself lost on the way to the first training session in order to get out of going? It's difficult, isn't it? In fact, it's almost too bizarre to believe that it could be reality. But, yes, you've guessed it, that is exactly the situation I chose to put myself in when I got the call from Wales just a few months before the 1995 World Cup in South Africa, a tournament that was to launch Jonah Lomu as the game's first real global superstar.

At the time, I had barely ever been out of Bridgend in terms of rugby, and although I hadn't actually been chosen to go to the World Cup itself at that stage, it was clear that the selectors were very much thinking along those lines and that I had a golden chance to make the cut – if I wanted to. The letter had landed on the doormat requesting me to turn up to the first proper gathering

of players who had a shout of going, and I knew full well where I had to be, what time and how to get to the place in Cardiff, which was the Welsh Institute of Sport in Sophia Gardens.

Most guys in my position – I hadn't then played for Wales – would have seen it as their big chance and been planning their trip to the get-together with military precision weeks in advance. But, instead, when the big day arrived I chose to get myself lost on purpose, because deep down – and I know so many people will find this hard to understand – I did not want to go to the World Cup.

To this day, I remember exactly what I did. Quite deliberately, I came off the M4 at the wrong junction at Llantrisant, which is about two stops further west than the actual route I should have taken. After getting off the motorway, I picked a country road that I knew reasonably well, which took me to the western outskirts of Cardiff. A few more left and right turns later, I found myself

in the middle of a housing estate. At that point, I pulled the car over and just sat at the side of the road for about 15 minutes. Then I popped into a nearby shop, bought myself a bar of chocolate and went back to the car to sit in silence for a bit longer, the clock ticking all the while.

Time seemed to pass really quickly, and I was in a kind of haze. After about two hours, I just drove home without ever turning up at the session or even telephoning anybody to say why or to offer some lame lie as an excuse. I think I even told my parents that I had gone to the session, but it was all a big porky just to save myself from having to explain why not.

Oddly enough, there was never any comeback that affected my progress in any way. We had a schedule of training, and there was a session planned two or three days later, which I was able to bring myself to attend. Nothing was said by the coach Alec Evans about my no-show a few days earlier – don't ask me why.

I'm sure that some people will shake their heads in amazement at this, but have you ever had to go to something you don't want to and deliberately gone the long way round in order to be late for it? The idea being that if being late means you miss a section of it, then it is all worth it. Well, I guess that is a watered-down version of what I did, although I admit that not arriving at all is taking it a bit to the extreme!

But whatever anyone else thinks, I had my reasons. I was very unsure as to whether I deserved to be there, and that made me feel really uncomfortable. The bottom line was that I just didn't want to go. I was happy playing for Bridgend, I was happy working as a postman, and I was happy going out on the piss with the boys. The World Cup was something that was going to take me away from the lovely little comfort zone that I had created for myself.

I was only being asked to go twenty minutes down the road to Cardiff, but I was more used to going five minutes down the road to Bridgend, and Cardiff might as well have been on the other side of the world. I was secure and didn't want anything that would require me to prove myself invading my settled little world. I was not scared, but in a weird kind of way I wished that I didn't have to meet the people who I knew would be there, because I felt as though I didn't belong. I was worried what the reaction of the other players would be to me – it's just the way I am. Even now, when I walk into a room of Welsh supporters, I feel embarrassed, because I do not expect people to know me – I never expect that. I'm naturally stand-offish and wonder what people think of me and what they are saying about me. In 1995, it was even worse, and I had this vision of the more established players taking one look at me as I turned up for the first time and saying to themselves, 'Who's this lanky string of piss?' Yet deep

down I knew they would all know me. They had to, because I had been playing for Bridgend for two or three years. It is a feeling I have never forgotten, and it is why whenever a young player makes a breakthrough into the Wales squad these days and turns up for the first time, I go out of my way, as the captain, to make them feel part of it all – to make them feel that they are there on merit and do indeed belong in our company.

While I did eventually get through a number of training sessions with the Wales squad, these feelings refused to go away, and I was devastated when I was selected to go to the World Cup! I can remember the day I found out. I was working on the post with my dad, who brought the letter around and stood next to me with a smile to end all smiles, pleading, 'Open it, open it.' So, I opened it – and was absolutely gutted to read the 'good' news. I did my best to smile while my dad was hopping around in delight, but it was a false expression, and there was one thing in particular that horrified me.

Driving to Cardiff for an afternoon training session with Wales had been hard enough; now I was going to have to spend five or six weeks with these people thousands of miles away. What made it worse was that I had been pinning my hopes on going on holiday with the boys to somewhere on the Mediterranean, where I could just relax, have a few beers and fade away into anonymity. To

me, missing out on a summer of fun on some boiling-hot beach and countless nights on the beer with the lads was just unimaginable misery.

The one thing I can say that might shed a little bit of light on this is that back then the Welsh rugby scene was slightly different. Today the media circus surrounding the national team is far more intense than it has ever been, with stories seemingly every other week about who is going to be the next best thing. There were plenty of people talking about me as a fine prospect, and I remember the ex-Wales and Bridgend centre Steve Fenwick doing a piece in one of the Welsh papers, saying, 'Bring him on. This guy is good enough to go right to the top.' (He obviously hadn't been at Waterton Cross a few years earlier to see my infamous header!) But it wasn't as though I was making the back page every day. In fact, the only paper I was ever interested in reading was the *Glamorgan Gazette*, the local rag which wouldn't break rugby stories but told you all about what people in the area were getting up to, who had been in court and who hadn't paid his television licence. I barely knew that any other papers existed.

When I got the call for the World Cup, everybody I knew – friends, family, even just acquaintances – was going nuts and falling over themselves to congratulate me. All I could manage to say in reply was a fairly half-hearted, 'Yeah, it's great,'

before flashing that big false smile and going along with it all. Throughout the build-up to our departure, I never had the guts to tell people how I really felt, not even my mum and dad. So many times I was bursting to say, 'Actually, everyone, I don't even want to bloody go.' And there were occasions when I thought to myself, 'Go on, just say it now and get it over with.' But the words just wouldn't come out. It got to the point that I started wishing people could read my mind so that they would know without me having to say it. I don't think anyone ever even suspected – why would they? Why would someone not want to go to the World Cup?

Sometimes, I wonder why I felt that way when at the age of ten or eleven I used to watch the national team on television and hope that one day I would play for Wales. It always comes down to the removal of my comfort zone, something I just found difficult to handle. I was happy with my summers off, although when we eventually met up for the training camp in Cardiff the week before we were due to fly out we might as well have been on holiday in many respects. For starters, we were on the beer most nights of the week. We stayed in the Marriot Hotel, which, as anyone who knows Cardiff will tell you, is right in the middle of the city surrounded by bar after bar. Most nights, we would go across to Kiwi's and get steaming drunk. And I'm not just talking about one or two of us, as was the case with me and

Davies at Cardiff – I'm talking about virtually the whole squad, although one or two abstained.

From what I remember, it wasn't as if we did that much training anyway, and most of the time you didn't have much of a clue about what was in store the next day. In any case, I never really asked questions in those days. I was told to turn up that week and didn't know in advance whether it would be an intense training camp or just an extended bonding exercise. All I did know was that we went out on the piss and half the time got back to our rooms in the early hours of the morning.

The key thing, though, was that back then it was still an amateur game, so it was difficult for coaches and management to dictate to grown men what they could and couldn't do off the field. They had nothing on us, so they couldn't really stop us. Nobody had signed a contract, and while we did get paid something, it was next to nothing, really.

However, something happened that week that changed everything. While I struggled to come to terms with what I was going to have to go through for the next five or six weeks and to rid my mind of all the things I thought I would be missing out on at home, I met someone who became a huge influence on me and who made that World Cup a truly worthwhile and unforgettable experience: Robert Jones. The man who by 1995 had been there, done it and got

the T-shirt as far as top-flight rugby was concerned became a friend for life and a huge influence on my career. It was a huge relief that I found him. Not only had he helped Wales to third place in the inaugural World Cup in 1987, but he had also been on two British Lions tours, including one to Australia in 1989, in which he had played a starring role in a monumental 2–1 series win against the Wallabies.

Rob was nearing the end of his time at the top, while I suppose I was just starting out on mine, but the difference in our standing in the game didn't come into play at all. We just hit it off from day one. I roomed with him in Cardiff and throughout our time in South Africa, and there was none of this 'let's change around who we share rooms with'. It meant that in an environment in which I was certainly uncomfortable I had found someone whom I was completely comfortable being with.

The squad at the time was a little intimidating to me, with big-name players such as Mike Hall, Scott Gibbs and Neil Jenkins. Rob was easily as big a name as any of them, but he might as well have been my next-door neighbour for the way he behaved towards me. We had such a great laugh – every day. I wouldn't describe our relationship as childish, but it was certainly based around us doing plenty of silly things. We would be lying in our beds at night, and out of the darkness Rob would suddenly pipe up with, 'Right. Alphabet. Sing a

song beginning with "A".' We would then go through the whole alphabet singing a song beginning with each letter along the way, and we would invariably dissolve into fits of laughter every couple of letters. If I had been rooming with someone whom I had known really well, they probably would have told me to shut up if I had suggested something like that when they were trying to get to sleep. But the degree of familiarity between me and Rob was perfect for things like that.

The next night, having sung songs beginning with every letter of the alphabet the night before, I would switch off the light and climb under the duvet. Five minutes of hush in the darkness would elapse before Rob's voice would break the silence with, 'Right. Name a film beginning with "A"!'

I saw so much of myself in Rob at the time, even though he was already a legend and I was a relative unknown. He was the joker in our pack, if you like, always ready with a one-liner or cracking a joke that would break the ice at a training session. Nothing was ever too serious for him, and I just connected with his personality. Rob was awesome. He helped me through the World Cup every step of the way, taking me out on the piss countless times, bringing me out of myself and just generally making me feel at ease.

Of course, the one downside to the trip was the way we performed on the field. Some would argue that we barely

stood a chance from day one, given the upheaval of a late change of coach and all the accusations thrown at Alec Evans that he had shown bias in selection towards Cardiff players. But we could still have done better than we did, going out at the pool stage by losing to New Zealand and Ireland, the latter being a decider fought out by two poor sides.

The game against the All Blacks, of course, offered me the chance to play against the great man Lomu, who amazingly returned to Wales, a nation he has always described as his second home, for a spell with Cardiff Blues last season. I didn't mark him – which was probably for the best – as I played in the centre that day and he was on the wing, but I can definitely recall the aura that surrounded him. It did have an effect on a Bridgend lad playing only his second-ever Test match, which just happened to be against New Zealand. I remember looking at him as we were walking out onto the pitch and thinking to myself, 'Oh my God!' He truly was a monstrous specimen back then. That said, he didn't actually worry me in the real sense of the word. All I was concerned about in those days was myself and that I was enjoying playing rugby.

Nowadays, we do so much video analysis that sometimes I think it can actually have an adverse effect on you and put doubts in your mind. If an opposition player is in your face on a television screen having a great game, there can be a tendency to focus too much on what he may do to you. Watching someone throw an outrageous dummy and go scorching through a gap to score is only going to start you worrying about him getting the better of you in the upcoming game.

Back then, though, there was no such attention to detail, so the nerves were never allowed to get to you. All you knew was the team you were coming up against and a few names of the individual players. You just went out and got on with it. Not that any of that appeared to work for us, because the whole tournament turned into the worst kind of damp squib after I made a dream debut by scoring three tries in the opening match against Japan, a game that we were expected to win by a big margin – and did.

That hat-trick inevitably sent the Welsh press into a bit of a frenzy, with all sorts of proclamations that I was the new hero of the hour. The best thing for me, though, was that the match was not in Wales, so I was able to get away with doing one or two short interviews after the match and then slope off back to the hotel, even though all of the other players were congratulating me like there was no tomorrow. I think if it had been in Wales there would have been a hell of a lot more hype around me; instead, I could ignore whatever was being written back home from a distance of thousands of miles.

But it was all downhill from there on as we finally went out after that

In action on the 1996 summer tour of Australia.

dreadful affair against an Ireland team that was only marginally better than us. We were awful in that match, which had we won would have clinched a respectable quarter-final berth against France, a game I would have loved to have played in. But it all went over my head. I still believed that the World Cup was something for me to get through and then forget about when I got home. I fully expected to be discarded by the Wales set-up after the tournament – to be told, 'Thanks, youngster, but you only came because we were short of numbers, and you'll have to wait your turn a while now.'

An example of my naivety was that one of the boys had said to me that I would get a World Cup cap for representing Wales in the tournament. 'How gutting,' I thought. 'All I want is a Welsh one.' I honestly believed that I was getting a World Cup cap alone, which would have meant nothing because to me it was just another tournament.

After it was over, the most important thing to me was that I could go back to my Bridgend comfort zone and be one

of the boys again – get back to normality and be able to say to myself, 'Yeah, great few weeks away, but it's good to be back.' Even though I had gone to South Africa, I didn't even expect to get a cap, and it wasn't as if any of my family came out to watch or anything like that. I just assumed I had gone there because someone else was injured, and if I had ended up carrying the tackle bags and water bottles, I wouldn't have been unduly put out. It certainly never occurred to me to see an international career past the World Cup.

That's why when newly capped players say that a taste of international rugby has left them craving for more, it's not a sentiment I can ever really relate to. I didn't want more; instead, my attitude was that I'd done it all: I'd played at a World Cup, I'd scored three tries on my debut, I'd played against New Zealand and I'd found a great new pal in Robert Jones – but now just take me home to my mam's in Bridgend.

On top of all that, it wasn't as if I felt being around the international camp was making me a better player in any way. I never felt as though I was learning much worthwhile, getting an inside track on how to handle coming up against the world's best or picking up any tactical tips I could take back with me to Bridgend and use in club rugby. In fact, I don't think that I learned a single thing off any international coach I played under until Steve Hansen came along in 2002. Up until that point, the whole attitude when

you were with Wales was always win at all costs and to hell with improving individuals or creating an environment in which we could develop as a team.

That's not to say that I don't have respect for people like Alec Evans, Kevin Bowring and Graham Henry. But in none of these regimes did I feel that there was much of a desire to nurture a player who was new on the international scene. It was more a case of, 'You're playing for Wales on Saturday. There's your jersey. Get on with it.' It was very much a case of sink or swim: 'Let's see how you get on.'

When I went to the 1995 World Cup, I didn't go with any detailed thoughts about the coach, because, and I say this in complete honesty, I wasn't even aware of who the coach was. I knew that Alan Davies had been dismissed, but I only gained a clear idea that Alec Evans was in charge on the day I first joined up with the squad. Because I had not expected to be involved, I simply hadn't been interested in who was leading the team, and, as I have said, I was never one to read the newspapers.

I do remember the infighting in Wales at that time about Evans's team selection and the perceived bias he had shown towards his own players at Cardiff. The impression among more cynical observers was that all you had to do to get into this Wales squad was play for Cardiff. There was Adrian Davies, Andy Moore, Derwyn Jones, Mike Hall and others, and there were howls of protest

from different corners of Wales that the whole selection process was rigged.

I now realise that Evans was probably only doing what scores of coaches in all sports have done for donkey's years – putting faith in what he knew. But that did nothing to quell the political storm. I accepted the gripe about bias as more or less fact, but it didn't bother me in the slightest. It was way too deep a subject for me to get my head around, and I didn't want to get embroiled in any of it.

The great pity was that the moans and groans of the general public had clearly seeped into the psyche of many of the squad. Whether it was a safety mechanism for those who were not chosen for the team, I don't know, but all I heard from those left out were unhealthy remarks like, 'Oh well. We don't play for Cardiff, so we should expect to be left out.'

None of this sullies my memories of Evans, mind you. I found him a fair enough kind of guy, and I will always be grateful to him for giving me my first Welsh cap. I've always tried to speak as I find in rugby and in life in general. I've always been wary of people prejudging me, so I make a point of not doing it to others, and I hope I have stayed true to that belief down the years.

As it turned out, as much as I was expecting – even hoping – that the World Cup would be a one-off and that I would not have to worry about any future Five Nations, it didn't quite

work out like that. I had three Welsh caps; little did I know that there would be in excess of ninety more to follow. And I must have done something right at the tournament, because it was after the 1995 World Cup that I received my first approach from rugby league.

When I got home, I had a letter waiting for me from Bradford Northern, now known as Bradford Bulls, and I also received telephone calls from either Widnes or Salford, I honestly cannot remember which. Back then, I used to say yes to everything, and when one of them rang me up to arrange a meeting at one of the service stations halfway between Bridgend and the north of England, I gave assurances that I would be there, even though deep down I had no intention of going. 'Yes, yes, I'll definitely be there,' I said.

At about midday on the day I was supposed to meet them, I had a call. 'Are you on your way?' they asked.

'Yes,' I said, sitting in Bridgend Rugby Club with no intention whatsoever of moving. They must have arrived at the service station, sat down and waited, and then after a while just given up and gone home, realising that they were dealing with a total muppet. I never heard a thing after that – hardly surprising, I suppose. I'm not particularly proud of having given people the runaround like that, but that was just the way I used to operate at that time. My head was in the clouds about things like that.

1995 AND ALL THAT . . .

In the autumn of 1995, after Alec Evans decided he did not want to take the Wales job on full time, Kevin Bowring, then the Wales A coach and a teacher who had played flanker for London Welsh years before, took over. It was not a reign, with respect to Bowring, that was covered in glory.

4

THE BOWRING YEARS

When a Sunday league football team turns up every week to some churned-up field in the rain, they invariably do so hoping to win and enjoy themselves, the twin aims of most people who play sport at any level. But on the parks pitches there is, for 99.9 per cent of teams, no overall strategy for the next couple of seasons, no grand plan, no template to work to that will ensure the sound development of the side and a solid foundation for future campaigns. No, quite rightly it's a case of, 'Let's just turn up and enjoy it. If we play well and win, then great; if not, well it's just been a bad day at the office.' As amateurs who play for the love of the sport, they are quite entitled to approach it like that. But the responsibility is of course different for those who are being paid to perform.

Unfortunately, as I look back on it now, the amateur attitude was far too dominant in the Wales side of the Kevin Bowring era between the autumn of 1995 and the spring of 1998, and that

is in no way entirely down to Bowring, who was respected and highly thought of by most of the players during his time in charge. And I'm not trying to make out that I was leading any kind of campaign for attitudes to change, either.

Bowring's was the first Wales side since the game had gone professional, and subsequently we were open to scrutiny like never before. If we turned in a bad display, you can bet that one of the main planks of criticism would be that we were not adapting to the demands of the professional era and that we really needed to look at ourselves on that score. It was claimed, and quite rightly, too, that the southern-hemisphere nations in particular had stolen a huge march on us in terms of approaching the game in a professional manner. And the dominance of their big three in terms of results at the time admittedly spoke volumes. We were certainly a considerable way behind being able to beat New Zealand, Australia or South

My first try for Wales against Japan at the 1995 World Cup.

Africa, and conditioning was probably one of the major reasons why.

Yet physical limitations were in many ways not the primary reasons for our failures. No, it was our mental outlook that needed an overhaul, in my opinion. When I compare the attitude then with the all-for-one team ethic that we have now fostered in the Wales camp of today, well, it simply doesn't bear any comparison.

During Bowring's time, if we turned up, performed well and beat, say, one of the other home nations, then we were going places and were a good team. The opposite and, well, things just hadn't come together for us because of reasons beyond our control. We would try to do better next time with no real need for any soul-searching or rigorous self-examination other than a token shrug of the shoulders. There was nobody driving us, nobody navigating us towards some ultimate goal, nobody ensuring that our overall standards hit a level that would allow us to progress up the international ladder.

I stress again, Bowring was certainly not to blame for all our failings, but, at the same time, I did not find him much of an inspiration either. His school-teacher background seemed to fit in with some sort of vogue in Wales at the time – every coach seemed to be

an ex-school teacher, and, yes, I found Bowring to be like a school teacher in the way he behaved towards us players. I didn't consider him to be a bad bloke for one minute, and I definitely did not dislike him, it's just that he was unable to have any significant effect on me as a person or as a player.

But I am ready to admit the part I myself played in that situation. At that time, I was totally going through the motions as far as Wales was concerned, just turning up as if it were some habit and counting caps. A game would arrive on the calendar and one of the first things I would say to myself was, 'What number cap is this?' I was counting tries, as well, and I recall one that I scored in a 28–19 defeat to Australia in autumn 1996 as a real cracker. I intercepted a pass in midfield deep in our 22 and raced the length of the field to touch down in front of the Arms Park's old East Terrace. But if you think it meant the world to me, you'd be wrong – it didn't. All it meant was that it was a feather in my own cap in terms of being picked for the team again. That's what it was all about as far as I could see. It was look after number one before you worried about the team, and when I think about the values that are dear to me these days, I can barely believe that it was me who thought like that. I simply don't recognise those types of feelings any more.

Yet if my teammates at that time are really truthful with themselves, I reckon most of them would admit that they felt exactly the same way. Back then, we had nothing approaching the squad spirit that we have now. Don't get me wrong, there were great guys involved, but, strangely, I seemed to become good mates with some of them completely outside of rugby. My friendships with people such as Leigh Davies and Andy Moore were not really based on anything that we were doing in the game. Our companionship did not develop from within the team environment, but outside of it.

And the way we prepared for Test matches was, to put it mildly, suspect and born out of an ignorance on so many levels as to what was really needed to compete. One of the problems with the professional game, particularly with coaches, is that some of them feel they have to justify their wages by having the team train for more hours of the day than is really necessary. Such an outlook can be very counterproductive, because players soon start to ask questions and become demotivated. Ask any player and they will tell you that if you train for just fifteen minutes and it's a great session that sinks into the brain and makes you feel like you are learning and improving, then it beats hands down a two-hour slog of mind-numbing drills that have no real relevance to what you might be able to do on a Saturday.

If only that lesson had been heeded by the Wales set-up of the time, but, again, I wouldn't be too vitriolic in attaching blame because, in my opinion,

it is only now, 12 years or so after the advent of professionalism, that coaches are truly beginning to view rest as being as important as training for modern-day players. Unfortunately, much of the thinking around the Wales camp in the mid-to-late 1990s was, 'Right, we're paying you, and you will do as much or as little as we want, whenever we want.' With hindsight, it was a very silly way indeed of greeting professionalism. When a game was on the horizon, it was as if those in charge said to themselves, 'Get the boys in now. This is such an important game, and we have to put in loads of training.' Even in quieter spells, you were never allowed to forget that you could be called in for fitness testing at the drop of a hat. It felt massively demanding and was very hard to deal with, especially as nothing had been done to prepare the players for this new life. Professionalism had, quite literally, come in overnight.

The players were adapting, coaches were adapting, fitness coaches were adapting, but the sorry fact of the matter was that most of it was, understandably, being done wrongly. It all translated into a frustrating time results wise. As I say, we were never in the same ballpark as the southern-hemisphere nations, but our record in what was then the Five Nations tournament hardly pulled up any trees either. Instead, we just ambled along in a kind of neutral state of mind, losing slightly more than we won and every now and again producing something

that offered real hope, only for it to be punctured a week or two later just as everyone thought that the corner was being turned. The really frustrating thing was that we had the players to be doing so much better – Rob Howley, Scott Quinnell, Scott Gibbs, David Young, Colin Charvis, Allan Bateman, Neil Jenkins – and every so often I would get a strong feeling that if only one or two of the players – although not necessarily those guys – had turned up the gas a little we could have won matches that we went on to lose.

The 1997 campaign was a perfect example of the hot-and-cold nature of the times. We travelled to Scotland for our first match and got a 34–19 win, scoring four tries in the process, including Arwel Thomas's famous 'Forrest Gump' touchdown when it looked as though he was going to run out of the stadium, like Tom Hanks did in the film, before he eventually touched the ball down inches from the end of Murrayfield's renowned deep in-goal area. The fact that a display like that had come in our first game gave the nation a real sense of hope that we could achieve something, even if England and France were still supremely strong at that time. But it all came crashing down just two weeks later when we lost a dismal game at home to Ireland, and it got no better as we lost our remaining two games, away to France and at home to England, only managing to avoid finishing bottom of the table on points difference.

Whether it was because of my own state of mind, I don't know, but I never once detected that it was a really big deal to the squad. As I have said, a neutral state of mind was evident all the time – or at least that is what it felt like to me. To my mind, the most important consideration among most of the Wales players, me included, was how we were perceived by the general public. Newspaper write-ups started to take on a greater significance for individuals than they ever should have done. It had reached the point that even if the team had lost a match but a newspaper report had said that you had played well and given you a good mark in its ratings section, then all was well with the world. It was dog eat dog, if you like – look after number one because nobody else was going to.

There was no better example of this than our defeat by England at Twickenham in 1998. Well, I say defeat; it was more of an annihilation as we went down 60–26 to our great rivals, despite getting off to an amazing start by crafting two superb scores through Allan Bateman. If I was involved in such a defeat now, I would be close to inconsolable. Sure, I'd do my press duties afterwards and mix with the other side like I always do, but when my head hit the pillow that night the feeling of dejection on behalf of the team and the nation would be absolute, and boy would it take some getting over. But I can distinctly remember walking off the field at Twickenham that day and not

feeling dejected, but, incredibly, not that bad at all. You see, I had managed to put in a decent performance, even if the team had been thrashed. Again, I can barely believe that this was true of me, but it was important that I was happy with my own game. It wasn't me personally who was going to get the flak for what had happened, and there was even every chance that I would retain my place for the next game which I did!

There have since been stories of how Lawrence Dallaglio supposedly came banging on the door of our changing-room afterwards shouting, 'You've been dicked, you've been dicked.' Well, if he did, I didn't notice it, and even if I had I wouldn't have cared less as long as I had done OK. Dallaglio, who I have since come to regard very highly as a player and a bloke, could have said what the hell he liked, and it would have gone straight over my head.

The truth was that nobody in the Wales camp expected to beat a team like England at that time, so the thinking was, 'OK, let's pull together and see how far we can take them, but when the shit hits the fan everyone's on their own.' And, sure enough, once the game had slipped away from us that day – and it happened on numerous other occasions, too – it was every man for himself. Only one question needed to be answered: who could defend their own little corner well enough to escape a caning in the press and the ignominy of the axe for the next game?

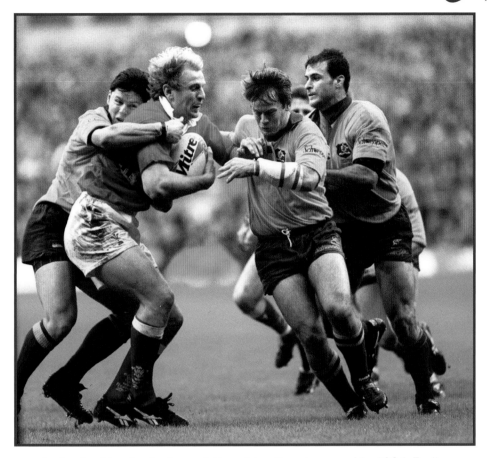

Ambushed by Australians at the old national ground in 1996. Earlier,
I went the length of the field for a memorable interception try.

The same went for one of the blackest days for Wales in modern times and the match that eventually proved to be Bowring's last: the ugly 51–0 battering dished out to us by France at Wembley in March 1998. I played on the wing that day up against Xavier Garbajosa, who would later become a teammate of mine at Toulouse, and I felt I did a good job of nullifying one of the real danger men of the French team. I did what I had to do and never let him get away. Later in the game, I got switched to centre and made a couple of decent breaks, so, all in all, it had been a pretty decent afternoon. I'm embarrassed to say this now, ashamed even, but I spent the game watching cock-ups go on all around me and thinking to myself that none of it was my responsibility.

Even the fact that thousands of Welsh fans had made the trip to London that day to support us wasn't enough to change my outlook. Oh sure, I walked around that evening with a long face, but only because that was what was expected of us all. The expression was certainly not representative of how I was

feeling deep down – disappointed, yes, but my disappointment was outweighed by huge relief that someone else had played worse than me and was going to cop all the stick. I now ask myself how I could have thought like that, but I want to be honest in this book about the way I felt.

As rugby has evolved so professionalism has evolved and so players have evolved. And I have had to go through that process to become what I am today and change the way that I think about the game. Yes, it's taken a while. But though I may think of myself as a selfish bastard for thinking like I did back then, I do feel that I was very much one member of a group who felt the same, and I am by no means the only one to have gone through the process mentioned above.

Thankfully, I have gone full circle, and nowadays I am uncomfortable with any emphasis on the individual in the game – there is far too much of that in the media for my liking. I suppose we just have to accept that is the way of the world. The press loves a hero – and a villain – and so do the public. But I detest the build-up to a Test match when a disproportionate amount of column inches is devoted to a duel between just two players or there is a big discussion about what just one player might be capable of doing to the opposition. And I also have to admit that I am not a fan of individual player ratings, which so many newspapers are inclined to print these days. The reason

for that is primarily because I have read so many times the little blurb that accompanies a journalist's verdict on the way that my teammates and I have played and wondered what the hell he or she was talking about.

Honestly, I feel I have a good rapport with the press. I always try to be myself when speaking to them and am as forthright as I possibly can be. I also accept that there are a lot of very talented writers and broadcasters out there who do a terrific job, not just in imparting information to the public, but also in analysing the game and promoting it. But I'm sorry, ladies and gents, you've got to up your game on the ratings!

When I heard about one exchange between a journalist and one of our younger more inexperienced players regarding ratings, it left me staggered. As I understand it, the journalist told the player that he had given him four out of ten for his display in an 11–10 win against Fiji during the 2005 autumn series, which was admittedly not Wales's finest hour in recent times. But he went on to confess to the player that he had not even seen the whole game! I couldn't believe it when I heard that; in fact, we all ended up having a good laugh about it – if we hadn't laughed, we'd have cried.

The players, me included, look for the individual marks and ratings before anything else, and I think that is only human nature, even in these days of vastly improved team spirit. I chuckle to

Alfie!

Me with (from left to right) Leigh Davies, Arwel Thomas and Nathan Thomas.
We decided to dye our hair blonde on the 1997 tour of the USA.

myself when I hear coaches and players claiming to journalists that they manage to stay above all criticism because they don't read the papers. Believe me, in 99 per cent of cases that's complete bull. I know because I'm one of the ones who has said it! The truth in my case is that I hardly ever go out and buy a newspaper. But I don't care who you are or what you have done in the game, if a colleague was sitting at a coffee table in some hotel foyer, or anywhere else for that matter, and there was a newspaper lying there, I would defy any one of them not to pick it up and scan for comments about himself, in particular the dreaded

ratings. And if you see a four out of ten or some other poor mark accompanied by a damning paragraph or two next to your name, again, I don't care what your standing is in the game, it has an effect on you. It's a negative that nags in your head, and for a good few hours, sometimes days, it doesn't matter how many times you tell yourself that the journalist is talking rubbish and you know best.

Conversely, there are times when I have felt I have had an absolute nightmare then gone and picked up a paper in trepidation and seen a nine out of ten next to my name. Of course, it's

Celebrating a try with Arwel
on the 1997 USA tour.

I think there was a particularly poisonous period not long after we turned professional when a lot of ex-players came into the media, watched us lose matches and then concluded in rather spiteful language that they would have done so much better had the game been professional in their day. It's tough not to surmise that some of them might have been motivated by pure envy. I think it's different now, because people, ex-players included, have much more of an idea of the demands on players and subsequently what is and isn't a wage that is fair and par for the course. In the early days, nobody had a clue, and I'm sure some people didn't really believe that rugby union was a sport that warranted being professional at all. If a player was earning £25,000 a year and not performing heroics every week, some people threw their hands in the air and said, 'These guys don't know they're born.' And I suppose you can understand an ex-player who earned two pounds a match for twenty years feeling like that to some extent.

The advice I pass on to the guys is to not just read the press when they have had a great game. It's something that Compo Greenslade and Glen Webbe used to say to me in the early days at Bridgend. They always insisted that if you read newspapers in the good times, you should be man enough to read them when you've had a shocker as well, otherwise you will be fooled into thinking that what you read about yourself in the press is always good.

different then. In those instances you want to believe that the writer has it spot on and that you've been too hard on yourself all along. But you still know the truth deep inside of you.

The ratings do rile me. Even if you are involved in fifty incidents in a match and only mess up three of them, each mistake seems sometimes to go against you, as if you start a game with ten out of ten and can only lose marks from then on, rather than the other way round. It strikes me as an exercise in spotting negatives, and the frustrating thing is that this is what becomes ingrained in people's minds.

Neil Jenkins in support of me in our 1997 Five Nations defeat to Ireland.

I don't suppose Bowring ever felt like that. If he had stopped reading the newspapers long before he left the job at the end of the Five Nations in 1998, nobody would have blamed him. Like his predecessors, his failings were not for the want of trying. As a coach, he had our respect, and he was a decent innovator who had some fresh ideas about how the game should be played. But I don't think he dealt that well with the pressure, especially when it came on strong towards the end of his reign. While it never got to me particularly because of the way I was, there were

suggestions that Bowring was passing on the heat to the players. But he is obviously still highly thought of in the game.

Little did we know that with his departure an era of New Zealanders leading Wales was about to begin. It lasted for six years and included some of the most tumultuous times the Welsh game had ever seen. It began with the big-money appointment of, you've guessed it, yet another former school teacher. He arrived in Wales with a reputation the size of the new Millennium Stadium, which was being constructed for the

Going over for a try against Romania in August 1997.

Another try, this time against Tonga, in the wet at Swansea.

1999 World Cup at that time. Just a few months into a tenure that would last for four years, he was christened the 'Great Redeemer' by an adoring public. Welsh rugby had never seen his like before and probably never will again, and to describe our relationship as interesting would be an understatement. His name was Graham Henry.

5

REGARDING HENRY AND THE CLASS OF '99

'I could be on a beach somewhere soaking up the sun rather than being here.' That was more or less the first sentiment conveyed to the Wales team by Graham Henry when he took charge in a blaze of publicity in the late summer of 1998. I think it's safe to say that as far as I was concerned it was not a good start. It was almost as if he was saying to us, 'Hey, I don't have to be here. I could be somewhere else putting my feet up, and you lot are lucky to have me.'

Now, I know he had given up his life in New Zealand to come over to coach Wales, but it was not as if he was doing it for nothing. In fact, if you believe the figures being bandied about in the newspapers at the time, he was on in excess of £200,000 a year, which was an extraordinary amount in those days – and still would be now.

His appointment was a real departure for the Welsh Rugby Union, and you sensed it was done in complete desperation, though I am not suggesting that it was the wrong move for the time. After a string of Welsh coaches had failed to live up to expectations, there was all manner of hype about how Glanmor Griffiths, the then chairman of the WRU, had trawled the world looking to find the very best coach, no matter what the cost or the new man's nationality.

Henry came to us with a track record of success in the Super 12 with Auckland Blues and was the bloke who everyone said should have been in charge of the All Blacks but had been denied his chance by internal politics in New Zealand. But right from the off to the day he walked away four years later, we never got on. The main reason for that was that it was the biggest teacher–pupil relationship I have ever experienced in my life when it comes to interaction with a coach.

Another core problem as far as I was concerned was that the whole ethos of the side revolved around a band of senior

The second-ever try at the Millennium Stadium in our historic win against South Africa in June 1999. At least I pleased the cameraman!

players who seemed to be the only ones who mattered to Henry. I'm talking about the likes of Rob Howley, who was kept on as captain even though he had been Kevin Bowring's appointment, Scott Quinnell and Scott Gibbs. It was a difficult place to be unless you were a senior player. Graham put people like those three almost on the same level as him, with the rest, including me, on a level below. Effectively, there was a 'them and us' sort of situation within the team environment, and I never felt comfortable enough to speak up about matters I might have thought were important. And if that was the way I felt at a time when I was nearing 50 caps, I dread to think how youngsters who had just been called into the set-up must

have seen it. My personal feeling, and I know others will see it differently, was that when matches came around it was as though we had a squad of twenty-two players that revolved around six senior names with the rest of us just there to ensure that the moves worked out.

Now, before I go further, let me stress that although I had by then been around for some time, I was probably not the easiest person in the world to coach. Put it this way, I wouldn't have wanted to have coached me! I wasn't very stable at the time in terms of how a professional rugby player should act; in fact, in some respects I was as far away from what a professional rugby player should be as I possibly could have been. What I mean by that is that I was

still in a frame of mind whereby I just enjoyed playing rugby for my club and was getting paid big money to play for Wales.

And that was one thing that Henry did achieve as far as the players were concerned – he managed to ensure that we got more money for playing Test matches than we ever had before. There were all sorts of criteria that entitled you to rake in the cash. For instance, the more caps you had the more you earned for every appearance. And another key financial incentive was a £5,000 individual win bonus for each and every game. I don't know if people can remember this, but in Henry's early years whenever we won a match there would be Welsh players going up to the television cameras to celebrate by holding up the palms of their hands with all five fingers spread wide. At the time, there must have been plenty of people who wondered what it was all about – well, it was us lot saying, 'We've just landed £5,000!' To be honest, it was probably a good thing that the vast majority of people were in the dark about what it meant, because I am sure many would have been appalled that we were each getting such an amount for delivering a result in our country's shirt. Yet if that was what was on offer, who were we to turn up our noses?

The money up for grabs was bordering on the obscene. On top of the win bonus, if you had more than ten caps you would get £50 for every cap you had won, each time you played. In other words, if you had won 20 caps, your fee on your 21st appearance would be £1,000. If you had gained 50 caps, you would rake in £2,500 just for turning up, and if you won the match, you'd be going home with an extra £7,500 in the bank. This wasn't just for Six Nations matches either – it was for each and every Test match. And don't forget that we went on a ten-match unbeaten run under Henry in 1999, so you can just imagine the amount of money that was sloshing around the place.

Yes, I know, they are astonishing figures that are next to impossible to justify – and people wonder why the WRU was struggling for cash at that time. But for an idea of how such attitudes changed, let me take you behind the scenes after Wales's win against Australia in the autumn of 2005. I can vividly remember standing in the shower of the home changing-room at the Millennium Stadium about two hours after the game thinking to myself how brilliant it was to have beaten one of the southern-hemisphere big three for the first time since defeating South Africa in 1999. Sure, we would have a nice win bonus, but then it dawned on me that not a single player in the team in those two hours had spoken about the extra money we would be due and how great it was that their pockets would be lined.

I turned to Martyn 'Nugget' Williams and told him that I believed that because

of this, the day had been something of a turning point. 'You know what, Nugget?' I said. 'Nobody in this team has even mentioned the word money since the final whistle went.' I was suddenly hugely chuffed that we had at last managed to create that kind of environment, and when I broached the subject to some of the other boys later that evening a good few of them replied that they weren't even aware how much they were due.

What a difference. In Henry's time, even before the final whistle had blown in some matches you would hear some of our players shouting nonsense like, 'Come on, boys. We've got five grand on this.' Henry had chosen to make money our main incentive – and we had accepted it, which is why I am not blaming Henry for such a lamentable situation. We were all culpable – me as much as anybody.

After that Australia game in 2005, even the day after when we were all having a good Sunday drink together at the end of the autumn series, players were still telling me that they had no idea what the victory meant in cash terms. This was real evidence that the money issue had faded into the background thanks to Steve Hansen tackling it when he took charge in the spring of 2002. At that time, there were a fair few frank discussions between the management and the players about match fees, with the gist of the management's argument being that

there was no way such generosity could continue. Understandably, the players were not exactly over the moon at first, and we went through a stage when we were playing international rugby for £1,000 a game.

I know some people will find it objectionable that players are paid at all to represent their country, with the usual line being, 'I'd give my right arm just to wear my country's shirt.' That's understandable. But being paid for international appearances is a fact of life in professional sport, and when you go from earning £7,500 in some matches to just £1,000, you are bound to at least stop and think about it. But Steve put his cards firmly on the table by telling us that because we had all earned such good money for so long, there would have to come a time in the future when people would have to pay the price for that by accepting vastly lower fees. He said that the WRU could not only ill afford to maintain the level of payments we had become accustomed to in the Henry era, but that they were now no longer in a position even to pay a decent match fee. The pot, he explained, was empty, and it was about time that we realised that all we could do from then on was start performing, start winning and accept that we would be playing for Wales for the foreseeable future for next to bugger all.

It was difficult not to feel a little guilty at hearing all of this, as if we had been greedy in accepting Henry's loot in the

There were low times under Graham Henry when I doubted my Wales future.

first place and were now to blame for the WRU's mountain of debt. But the truth was that back then I couldn't have cared less if the union went bankrupt in five years' time if it meant that I could carry on raking in a fat match fee for the time being. Nobody cared about the union then. It was totally separate to the players, and our attitude was that, above anything else, we had to look after number one. A coach had come in who was willing to give us an astronomical amount of money, so, bloody great, let's take every penny we can while we can.

In Henry's day, I barely knew any committee member, and I certainly had nothing whatsoever to do with Glanmor Griffiths. It seemed to me that most of the grey-suited guys who ran the WRU were only interested in hanging around with one or two of the influential senior players. They weren't interested in speaking to the likes of me, and the feeling was very definitely mutual. It's different now. You turn up at dinners, and the boys know all the committee members as well as fellows from the smaller clubs who come along.

As much as I didn't see eye to eye with Henry, I would never try to suggest that he is not good at what he does. His track record proves that he is an

outstanding coach. Although as far as I was concerned, and I must stress that this is only a personal opinion, I did not regard him as being superior to anyone else I have played under. Why? Well, he just didn't motivate me.

One of the things that used to annoy me was that he was always comparing me with other players. For example, he would tell me that I needed to play like the former All Black winger John Kirwan and advise me to go and dig out some videos of the great man and watch them. I would think to myself, 'I'm not bloody John Kirwan, and I never will be. If you are going to pick me in your team, pick me because I am Gareth Thomas, not because I may remind you of someone else.' Don't get me wrong, I admire John Kirwan hugely and wouldn't mind being half the player he was. But rubbish like that did nothing for me whatsoever. I just didn't see it as relevant in any way.

Furthermore, whenever Henry spoke to me, I felt he always spoke down to me. I was always in the wrong, and it had a really negative effect on my outlook, even though I have always accepted that I am no angel. For example, when we would meet up for team briefings after matches he would pick up on things that I had done and bark, 'Gareth, you should run low and run hard in that situation,' but it was his tone of voice and the hand signals he made as he strutted around the room that made me feel small.

There was one incident involving the two of us that was a real low for me. We were playing Scotland away in the 2001 Six Nations, and I was picked on the bench. On the Friday morning before the match, I walked past Henry in the corridor of our hotel on the outskirts of Edinburgh and exchanged a nod and a simple 'good morning' with him, not for a moment envisaging that there was any kind of issue bubbling away.

I went into the breakfast room and was tucking into a bowl of cereal when Trevor James, whose official title was National Squads Manager but who in essence was Henry's 'Mr Fixit', sat down next to me. 'There's a bit of a change of plan,' said Trevor, at which my ears immediately pricked up. He told me that Stephen Jones, who was on the bench as a replacement outside-half for Neil Jenkins, was 50–50 to be fit because of back trouble and that subsequently they had to call up Lee Jarvis, the former Cardiff and Pontypridd pivot who at the time was with Neath, as kicking cover from the Wales A squad.

'What's all this got to do with me?' I asked Trevor.

'You're out of the squad, and you're to join the A team for their match in Glasgow this evening,' replied Trevor. 'Get your things. We've got a taxi waiting for you.'

I could barely believe what I was hearing. 'Hang on a minute, Trev,' I said. 'I've just this minute passed Graham in

the corridor, and he didn't say a word about this to me.'

'I know,' said Trevor. 'He asked me to have a word with you!' I thought the whole business was incredible.

So, I had to hastily stuff what I could into a bag and travel all the way to Glasgow in a taxi. I played for Wales A against Scotland that evening and was then forced to stay in Edinburgh for the rest of the weekend to watch the senior international. It was torture. Worse still, throughout the entire time I was up there not a single word was spoken to me by Henry, never mind any hint of an apology for giving me the runaround and not telling me himself.

I was devastated by the whole episode, and I remember ringing home to my parents in absolute pieces about the situation. I had rung them in despair plenty of times before during Henry's reign, usually after having been axed and not been given a word of explanation. But this time, I recall, I was particularly desperate, and I told Mam and Dad that I was determined to pack in playing for Wales altogether. It was the fact that there had simply been no dialogue between me and the coach that was the toughest element of it all to swallow. I had woken up on the Friday morning thinking that I was going to sit on the bench for Wales at Murrayfield. I had ended up in the evening at some anonymous little ground in the middle of Glasgow on the bench for Wales A without a single word from the coach!

The only things I had been able to take to Glasgow with me were my Wales tracksuit and my tuxedo, which we were all expected to wear after matches. I got on and played the last 20 minutes of the match. Mike Ruddock was coach of the A side, but he didn't say anything to me to try to make me feel better, and, to be honest, I don't blame him – he could probably see by my face that words would have been pointless. Don't ask me the score. I didn't give a toss at the time, and there was no way I was ever going to remember a thing about that match.

Looking back, what other conclusion can anyone expect me to reach than that Henry just couldn't be bothered telling me to my face that I would have to switch squads, a part of the job that all coaches have a duty to confront head-on. If you are faced with having to make an awkward decision, you should make it and tell those affected, not use someone like Trevor James as a messenger – although I must stress that I had a lot of time for Trevor and will always think well of him. He did his best to help me on that occasion. I was in one hell of a huff and knew that the longer I stuck around the hotel the more of a fool I would look. But he saw that I was OK for money, because I didn't have a bean on me at the time, and tried, bless him, to offer me some words of consolation.

• • •

Upended during my 50th cap – a win against Italy in Rome in 2001.

By the time of that incident in Scotland, Henry had long since ceased to be the Great Redeemer in the eyes of the Welsh public and was more than a little embattled, having come through the furore of the 'Grannygate' scandal the previous year. His honeymoon period had been the well-documented ten-game winning run we'd put together in 1999 leading up to and into the World Cup for which Wales was the host nation.

The Welsh public were going bonkers at the time, because it had been so long since we had done anything like that, and it wasn't just the run of victories but the fact that we had beaten England, France (twice) and South Africa that excited people so much. Wins like that were even prompting some observers to claim that we were capable of lifting the Webb Ellis Trophy, especially as we were on home soil, but in the final analysis that was to prove wildly optimistic. We were still not equipped to beat the southern-hemisphere big three when it really mattered, and so it turned out as we were eliminated at the quarter-final stage by the eventual winners Australia, who beat us 24–9.

I do not look back on that ten-game purple patch with any real satisfaction or affection because at the time it just didn't feel that great to be a part of

that regime, even though it comprised a great bunch of lads. In fact, if we had not won the Grand Slam in 2005 and someone had asked me what the best spell of my Wales career had been up to then, I would never in a million years have gone back to that period, despite the success.

It should have been Welsh rugby's finest hour, but for me the 1999 World Cup was a total washout, a real let-down and a tournament I have few fond memories of. To this day, the only thing about the whole sorry episode that I recall with any fondness was when I scored a try against Japan in the pool game after Colin Charvis had been banned for a punch on the Argentine forward Roberto Grau in the opener. I had got a T-shirt made saying 'Free Colin Charvis' and pulled up my Wales jersey to reveal it as I celebrated my score. It says it all that it was a moment like that when I was just larking around that sticks in my mind.

I have since asked myself how something that should have been so big could have ended up meaning so little to me later in life. Yet that is what has happened. And I have to be honest, I find it impossible not to compare what being in the Wales set-up was like then with what it is like now – a group of players who care passionately about each other and what they are trying to achieve as a collective unit. Not only that but my attitude to playing for Wales became so

different. It meant the world to me to lead out a group of guys who would all but die for one another. It never felt like that to me back in 1999, yet I so wish it had done because I am never going to get those years back, and I'm certainly never going to get the chance to play in a World Cup hosted by my own country again.

It says it all that to me the 1999 quarter-final that we lost to Australia pales in comparison with the 2003 last-eight clash with England, even though the 1999 game was played at our home ground and the 2003 encounter was in Brisbane. We had a buzz about us in Brisbane that was light years ahead of the feeling we had four years earlier – it felt like we were a proper team fighting a proper cause. Other players may see it differently, but the Australia game was just another Test match to me, and I don't think in hindsight that it meant all that much to the public either. You certainly rarely hear people talking about that game, whereas the opposite is true about the 2003 match.

But *c'est la vie*. Life is not a rehearsal, and when it comes to some experiences there are simply no second chances. Some sections of the press, and subsequently the public, were beginning to believe that we could lift the famous gold pot as the 1999 summer turned to autumn and the big kick-off approached. Yes, we were on a roll. And, yes, we would be playing on home soil in front of

Free Colin Charvis! After Charv's ban for punching in the opening game against Argentina in the 1999 World Cup, I had this T-shirt made in his support and showed it off after scoring.

our own fans at our new fortress, the Millennium Stadium. But we were never going to win that tournament in a million years.

It wasn't just because we were emphatically inferior to the southern-hemisphere big three, but also because so much of what we were doing in and around the team was not preparing us as it should have done for the biggest moment in our professional lives. For a

start, we were staying in the Copthorne Hotel at Culverhouse Cross on the western outskirts of Cardiff. There was nothing wrong with the hotel – it was very comfortable and the staff couldn't do enough for us. But that was part of the problem. We were basically allowed to eat and drink what we liked, when we liked, and such leeway was like a ticking time bomb, because, like it or not, some players took advantage and piled on

the pounds. They were clearly way too comfortable in their surroundings.

An example of this was that if we had played on a Friday or a Saturday we were allowed to go home for the weekend and did not need to return to the hotel until Monday night. However, the rooms were kept open for us should we want them for any reason, and because of the luxury of being able to order room service and basically have whatever they wanted, some of the boys didn't even bother to go home. They would stay put in the hotel for the weekend without the rest of the squad.

You could never do that now at the Vale of Glamorgan Hotel, which we use as our base, because the arrangement is quite rightly different, and there just wouldn't be food especially laid on for you. But at the Copthorne in 1999, you could just waltz into the restaurant and order off the menu. And by the way, they had the biggest dessert selection you could have wished for! You could take whatever you wanted – you didn't even have to ask. As well as desserts, there were toasted sandwiches and hot chocolates. If you wanted it, you could have it.

I was lucky, because I always trained hard, but I was also one of the ones who would think nothing of going down to the restaurant and tucking into a generous slice of gateau. In lots of ways, I took advantage as much as anybody. I wouldn't dream of doing that now, because we are in a different regime in which a lot of the responsibility is put on your own shoulders if you tip the scales and it turns out you are carrying a couple of pounds too many. That's a situation that forces people to become better trainers. OK, you can have someone there all the time telling you what you can and cannot do, but in my experience players will do the opposite nine times out of ten.

The gateau is still there these days, but the players are strong enough to walk past it. Back then, though, all I would have said if someone had questioned me stuffing my face was that our fitness coach Steve Black, who I thought the world of, despite the fact that I didn't think his methods really worked for me, had said I was allowed it. I can understand Blackie's thinking in a way, because he just wanted people to be happy. And in a different environment, his methods would probably have worked well. But I think that what we lacked was that there were no individual fitness programmes for each of us, so someone like Dai Young, a prop, was on the same diet and fitness programme as Rob Howley, a whippet of a scrum-half.

The time bomb I referred to above exploded with the resignation in 2000 of Blackie, a wonderfully warm and unique man who had been with us all through 1999 and won the hearts of almost everyone involved in the Wales set-up. Let me make it clear before going any further: it is almost impossible to criticise

84

Blackie, as he is affectionately known to everybody in the game, because he is such a top, top guy. I cannot speak about the methods he uses nowadays, but during his time with us they were unorthodox to say the least.

Blackie was far more concerned with trying to make us all believe that we were the best players in the world, rather than ensuring that we were unarguably the fittest and using statistics to prove as much. His superb personal qualities also made him the perfect antidote to Henry – players felt Blackie had their best interests at heart, and he was always a sympathetic shoulder to cry on. But I'm afraid to say that for too many players in our squad at that time, Blackie was the ideal fitness coach – one who wasn't too concerned with fitness! He had a different outlook from anyone in his position I have ever known. There were hardly any times when he ran us into the ground. And with respect to Blackie, the routines he used were never, on their own, going to ensure the fitness of an international rugby team.

One classic example of how Blackie operated was when we all took off up to Brecon for a day's training before the World Cup. We were told to split up into groups of about four and pretend that we were playing rugby. There was a bit of running involved, because some of the guys were pretending to score length-of-the-field tries, but we didn't even have proper rugby balls. Most groups had to use tennis balls, and the group I was part of actually had to make do with an orange! Picture the scene: our group was throwing an orange around pretending that it was a ball in a real game of rugby. Half the time, I felt a bit like a madman.

Later on, we would be made to lie on the floor, close our eyes and imagine a series of events that might take place in the course of a game. For instance, the forwards would be told to imagine hitting a scrum, and the backs would be asked to think about breaking through a tackle and charging through a gap. To Blackie, this kind of concentration on the brain was more important than anything else, and loads of the boys liked it because it was something they had never done before – and because they didn't have to run shuttles!

I have bags of time for Blackie. It's impossible not to, and I must stress again that I would not say his methods were wrong, just different. But I can definitely say that those methods didn't work for me. At the time, I was doing a lot of my secret training anyway, so I was cool with the idea that what I needed to do fitness-wise I was doing myself. I am someone who has always ensured his fitness on his own accord. But the difference compared with when the New Zealander Andrew Hore was in charge of our physical preparation was that if ever I did fancy doing a bit of secret training I was more often than not too exhausted to go through

with it. If Horey and Blackie sat down together, I'm sure there would be fireworks when the discussion turned to whose methods were best. Horey dealt in statistics, Blackie the mind. There was a good example of this that still embarrasses me to this day. In fact, I'd go as far as to say that at the time I was dying with embarrassment.

While training up in Brecon, we went to a little cricket pitch, around which about five or six people were walking their dogs. At certain points, they came over to us and asked what the hell we were doing – they were so bemused watching us. The crux of it was that Blackie wanted us to play imaginary games. We had to imagine that we had just scored a last-minute try in the World Cup final, which had won us the tournament. That was bad enough, but it wasn't the end of it, because we then had to climb a flight of steps onto the balcony of the cricket pavilion. The local club had kindly allowed us to borrow one of their old trophies, which must have been about the size of a chess piece. Rob Howley then lifted it up with us all cheering in pretend euphoria, shouting, 'Yes, we've won the World Cup.' We then had to take the cup and run around the pitch, showing it to the onlookers and their dogs on a make-believe lap of honour.

Throughout the whole business, I was standing there thinking to myself, 'Oh my God!' I had done some things in my time, but I had certainly never won the World Cup in Brecon, having scored the winning try in the last minute in front of five people – with an orange! It was an absolute classic. And some of the boys were so deeply into the whole thing that I could only stare in amazement. A few of them were going around saying, in all seriousness, 'I really believe it. We've won the World Cup. This is really it. This is the moment!'

'No it's not,' I thought. 'Just look around you.' Not wanting to spoil things, I humoured those who appeared to have been converted by replying to their claims of winning the cup with a half-smile and a 'Yeah, we have haven't we.' They were getting so carried away, and I think most of it was for Blackie's benefit. They so wanted to be utterly behind his methods.

But whatever you thought of episodes like that, by God we missed him when he decided to leave us the following year. Blackie was always a happy person who never spoke ill of anyone. Even if deep down he hated someone – which I can't imagine could be the case – instead of slagging them off he would say, 'Well, he does have his good side.' I wouldn't say that he was soft, but maybe it was easier for people to get around him at times, because he would never see that they were trying to pull a fast one. Blackie truly was one in a million.

I've said in the past that I am not and never will be a politician. And so in

talking about Grannygate, I can only convey my personal feelings, rather than pretend to be in possession of every single fact related to the whole sorry episode.

Undoubtedly, the guys I felt for most were the two players who were caught up in it all – Brett Sinkinson and Shane Howarth. I remember writing a letter to Shane when he was dropped from the squad after the story had just broken. I had always got on very well with him, and he had always seemed genuine to me. I said in my letter that it had been an honour to play alongside him, that he had stood shoulder to shoulder with us all in a Welsh jersey and not let any of us down, and that consequently he was as much of a Welshman to me as anyone else in the team.

Howy, as we called him, always supported me, always backed me up and never got on my case, and to play with someone like that was a privilege. It was such a pity that when the storm erupted, Howy and Brett were, in my view, more or less hung out to dry and left to face the consequences with minimal support.

I've since thought about a conversation I had with a guy called Paul Arnold, who I roomed with as part of the Wales A squad. It was March 1999, a year before the scandal had surfaced, and Arnold was a Kiwi who played his rugby for Newcastle. He said that although he played for Wales, he was no more Welsh than Nelson Mandela.

'I haven't got an ounce of Welsh blood in me and no other connections to Wales whatsoever,' Paul told me. But he was still progressing through the ranks and had already made it as far as the Wales A team. After Grannygate, Paul disappeared off the Welsh-rugby map altogether, never to play for any of our representative sides again, and for me that spoke volumes. And I am sure that had the smelly stuff not hit the fan, there may well have been a steady influx of 'Welshmen' with dubious heritage coming through the ranks.

The effect on the team of Howy and Brett being caught out was not as detrimental as some people might have thought; in fact, it says a lot that we won the two remaining games of that year's championship, beating Scotland at home and then Ireland at Lansdowne Road. But it also shows, in my view, how lacking the team spirit was that we just shrugged our shoulders and got on with it. If that sort of situation happened in today's climate when there is such a ferocious team ethic, I have no doubt that all hell would break loose, and the team would most definitely be adversely affected by the loss of one of its valued lieutenants in such shabby circumstances.

Back then, Henry remained very much the man in charge, so it was very difficult for any player to air any controversial opinions in public. If anything, the players tried to laugh about it; after all, it was about as farcical a situation as you

could imagine, and there simply wasn't any point in getting worked up about it.

I certainly don't regard Howy or Brett with any less respect than I did at the height of their playing success with Wales. Remember, when they were producing the goods out on the field in a red jersey – and didn't they both produce the goods at times – people loved them. They were legends at one point, and then all of a sudden people were lining up and shouting, 'Get rid of the pair of them.'

I think the aftermath of the affair was more difficult for Howy because he genuinely believed that he did have Welsh heritage and for personal reasons couldn't expand on the details. Howy was a passionate bloke who wore his heart on his sleeve on and off the park. I'm not surprised that he went on the record after it all to say that he would still love to play for Wales again some day and that the whole business had left him terribly down.

In Brett's case, I think he always knew deep down that he simply had no real Welsh claims, despite some rumours of a granddad who hailed from Carmarthen. But because he proved his character in our team, I still cannot bring myself to think any the less of him.

For all that Henry so often made me feel miserable, there were precious moments when I did feel I had got one up on him. It's been documented that after our fabulous 33–32 win against France in Paris in 1999, our first there

All smiles as I run in a try against Italy at Treviso in 1999.

since 1975, Henry turned to me as I celebrated with the boys on the team bus afterwards and said, 'Remember, Gareth, you were only sub.' And, yes, it did happen, although the actual words might have been slightly different. A comment like that, together with the timing, would have destroyed some players. But after what I had got away with a couple of nights before, I was able to take it on the chin and then privately stick two fingers up at him after he had turned around.

I was actually originally picked for the Wales A team that weekend, and we were stationed out in Dax in the south of the country for our match on the Friday

night. Compared with Paris, it might as well have been the middle of nowhere. I hadn't played for a while, because I had been injured, and I went into the A game having played just one comeback match for Cardiff against Aberavon in the cup. There was speculation about whether I would be called up for the senior match, but Henry blocked my path, insisting that I play for the A team, and I had no problem with that, because I hadn't even expected that much. In any case, I loved playing for Wales A, because the understanding among the players was that when you went away on the Thursday for a game like this you would get on the piss that night.

Anyway, Arwel Thomas and I went out and got completely and utterly leathered. It must have been 5 a.m. before we got to our beds, and we had to be up reasonably early for a light training session the next morning! When the alarm sounded a few hours later, we got up, still pissed as farts, and somehow got through the session, but the only thing on my mind was getting back to the hotel room and sleeping for the rest of the day so that I would be in a half-decent state to play the game.

As soon as my head hit the pillow, I was out for the count, but only around half an hour had elapsed when I was rudely awoken by Alan Phillips, who was the A team manager at that time, hammering on the hotel room door. 'Alfie, get up, get up. I want to see you downstairs in five minutes,' he bellowed.

When I got down to reception, bleary-eyed, he told me that Allan Bateman had pulled out of the senior squad with injury and that my plane for Paris left in about an hour. I was horrified. I couldn't tell Alan, or Thumper as we call him, that I didn't feel up to it because I had been so pissed the night before. So, I blathered on about how I didn't feel ready, because I hadn't played a full-on game for so long and how one match against Aberavon was hardly adequate preparation to face France in Paris. 'I can't do it, Thumper. See if someone else will go,' I said.

'I can't, I can't,' he said. 'Graham wants you.'

'Well, have you told him that I haven't played much?' I countered.

'Yes,' he replied bluntly.

After trying every excuse in the book and failing to get anywhere, I headed for the airport.

Now, you have to realise that Arwel and I were not just tipsy the night before after one Kronenbourg too many – we were insanely sloshed out of our minds! We'd been on the lager and then graduated to Pernod, which, as anyone who has ever suffered after drinking the famous pastis will testify, is supremely hard to shift out of your system. The main problem I found was that I was dehydrated and wanted to drink water.

Not surprisingly, then, I still felt more than a little fragile and soon discovered that my body violently objected to being placed on an aeroplane. In other words, as we made our way north to the French capital at 30,000 feet, I began spewing into a sick bag for all I was worth.

I got to the hotel in Paris, and the boys and Graham greeted me, although I made sure I kept my distance from the coach in case he got downwind of me and whiffed the booze. In the end, I got on for the last 20 minutes of the match the following day, with my guts still turning over, so I played a small part in a famous victory that was almost snatched away from us when Thomas Castaignède missed a last-minute penalty. We were all celebrating, and although I had not played a major part I just joined in with it all – as you do.

We got changed as normal and got on the bus, at which point the beers were offered around. Because I was still steaming from the day before, it only took three or four to get me rocking again, and there was every chance I was being a bit louder than usual. Then came Henry's comment, which, as I remember, was said more in passing than with a fixed stare and was slightly different to what was later alluded to in a book by Rob Howley, who was captain that day. Giving me no chance to reply, Henry said, 'I don't know why you're celebrating. You did bugger all.' And then I recalled my antics before the

match and thought to myself, 'If only you knew what I have got away with, you old git!' I then started to grin and stifled a snigger or two. He didn't have a clue, and that pleased me no end. It was one of the very few times that I felt I had got one over on him.

These days, I sometimes get younger players to ask me if I have ever been pissed, say, on the Monday before a Test match the following weekend. You'll understand why I struggle to keep a straight face.

But that time in France was not the only instance of me falling foul of Henry. It happened again when we played Italy in Rome in 2001. And once again, the demon drink was involved.

I had won my 50th cap against the Italians, and when that happens you always get toasted by the boys. Toasted? Well, put it this way, whatever they drink, you've got to drink (this is after the game, by the way!) and more often than not they all take the chance to absolutely kill you. It began when one of the boys came up to me at the post-match function with a glass of red wine and said cheers, which meant I had to drink it. Unfortunately, that was only the start of it, because more or less all of them then started coming up to me at intervals doing the same thing with various different drinks. It meant that even before the presentation of my cap, I was rolling drunk. To make matters worse, the room we were in was

small, which only highlighted my bad behaviour – which was about to get even worse.

As the speeches started, I began to sing Cardiff City football songs, more or less at the top of my voice. I couldn't tell you which songs they were. I think I was making half of them up as I slurred and struggled to string a sentence together. Official speeches from the top table were broken up every now and then with my cries of 'Bluebirds! Bluebirds!'

The toilets were just off this small room, which was convenient in one way but not in another, because when I stumbled out to relieve myself I sang my songs for all I was worth and could be clearly heard by everyone in the function room, much to the amusement of the lads. Not only that, but when I tried to make my way back to our table from the toilet I got lost, bumping into chairs along the way.

Anyway, there was obviously going to come a time when I would be pulled to one side, and, sure enough, Trevor James was sent over by Henry. Rather than bother to try talking to me, he whispered in the ear of the relatively sober Martyn Williams. 'Sort him out, will you. He's an embarrassment,' said Trevor, before informing Martyn that Henry was threatening to cut our win bonus if I didn't stop running amok.

Fair play to the lads, they told Trevor to leave me alone and that I should be allowed to enjoy myself on the occasion

of my 50th cap. I'm not sure whether tiredness then took over, but I must have improved a little because our bonus was never cut by Henry, although I had clearly done nothing to alter his opinion of me as a nuisance. However, the next time I stepped out of line, Henry brought down the axe.

One night, I had been out having a few pints in Jumpin Jaks in the café quarter in Cardiff's Mill Lane. As I left, I realised that I was bursting for a pee, and rather than head back inside and climb the big staircase to the toilet, I decided to quickly relieve myself next to a tree in the street. Yes, I am fully aware that you shouldn't do that sort of thing, but, hey, I must be one of thousands of blokes who have been caught short like that at one time or another.

Anyway, I remember that a guy whom I had never seen in my life saw me in full flow. He didn't say anything and neither did I, but, lo and behold, within a day or two the news that I had taken a pee in the street had filtered back to Henry. I won't name names, but I know exactly who relayed it to him, and let's just say that it was typical that nobody who had been involved in the chain of whispers had seen fit to confront me directly about it. Instead, when I turned up for the next Wales training session, Henry walked over to me and said, 'Due to your actions, you will not be required for these autumn internationals.' He didn't mention the Mill Lane incident

specifically – he didn't have to. We both knew why I was being asked to leave, and I had gone to the session knowing full well that Henry knew about what had happened. I just took it on the chin. 'Fine, no problem,' I said. I finished off the session and left.

A week or so later, I took a telephone call informing me that Henry wanted me to play for a Wales development side against the USA in a midweek match at Neath. My immediate thought was that Henry was trying it on. I'm not saying I was some legend of the world game at the point, but what the hell was the purpose of someone like me, who had 50-plus caps, playing for a development side? I know some players in my position would have told the management to stick it where the sun doesn't shine, but there was no way I was going to hand anyone the moral high ground. 'Sure, no problem,' I said. 'When do you need me?'

In about half an hour, I was told.

I got on my motorbike and drove all the way from Bridgend down to the team hotel – the Marriott at Swansea Marina – and reported fit and ready for the game. I checked into my room for the overnight stay – the game was the following evening – only for events to take another twist. I'd only been in the room for an hour when I received another message from the development-squad management. 'We don't need you now. Graham says you've got to join up with the senior squad. You're on the

bench for the match against the USA on Saturday.'

So there you have it. It had obviously been a test to see if I was willing, after all that had happened, to make myself available for the development side – and I guess I passed the test.

After benching for the USA match, I was picked to start the next game against Australia, and the Mill Lane peeing incident appeared to be behind me at last, though not before Compo Greenslade had intervened. He rang me up after he heard about my trouble and told me that a mate of his who worked for South Wales Police at their headquarters in Bridgend had revealed to him that the police had CCTV footage of my indiscretion and were intending to prosecute. It turned out to be a wind-up, of course . . . thanks for all your support, Compo!

Now, as I've already conceded, I don't think anyone could ever say that Henry is not a great coach. His track record speaks for itself, and the year he enjoyed with New Zealand in 2005 when they clinched the Tri-Nations, a 3–0 series win against the Lions and a British and Irish Grand Slam was remarkable. But undoubtedly one of things that hastened his demise as coach of Wales was his infamous pod system, which as I understand it was also a contributory factor in his failure to beat Australia as coach of the Lions in 2001.

I remember the first day he presented

it to us. My immediate reaction was, 'Oh my God. What the hell is this?' We were at the University of Wales Institute, Cardiff, commonly known as UWIC, sitting in a room looking at this pod system thing which he had made Trevor James draw on a board. I'll try to keep it as simple as I can – it was basically a detailed map of where each and every individual had to be and what they had to do over ten, yes ten, phases of play.

I looked around at the other guys in the room and straight away picked up on what they were thinking: it looked good on paper, but rugby is not played on paper, and you couldn't possibly expect any game to fall obligingly into place so that we could take up the positions that we were supposed to memorise over ten phases. What was going to happen if someone lost the ball or someone else came in from the wrong side of a ruck and conceded a penalty? What if a gap suddenly opened up after the third phase? Were you meant to go for it or keep to what the pod system had taught you?

But although everyone thought that the system was doomed, not one of us had the guts to tell Henry as much. We all went along with it, and this was just three weeks before we were due to play England at the Millennium Stadium in the first game of the 2001 Six Nations. We trained and trained and trained in an attempt to hone this bloody pod system, but I knew, and so did the other lads,

because we said it to each other often enough, that it just wasn't feasible and was never going to work.

It didn't. Sure enough, England pulverised us on their first visit to the Millennium Stadium, and to make matters worse they did it playing some glorious off-the-cuff rugby that enabled them to run in a string of lovely tries. So, what we all feared would happen, did happen. But still nobody had the balls to tell Henry that we felt he was barking up the wrong tree, and he stuck with it. He stuck with it and stuck with it, even though in the opinion of so many of us it would not work, and the rumours are that he tried to implement it with the Lions as well.

Because of the pod system, you may as well have picked 22 robots in the squad. The bottom line was that you could not expect rugby players to envisage what was going to happen next before the last phase had finished.

I find myself asking from time to time whether I should have spoken up. I don't think so, because as I have explained there were five or six senior players who had clout in that set-up, and in that respect it was incumbent on them to register the team's concerns. Even if I had piped up, the chances are I would have been dismissed.

Rugby moves on, but I cannot imagine that in 50 years' time we will have reached a point at which that blasted pod system could be implemented. The essence of rugby is its unpredictability,

and planning further ahead than three, at the very most four, phases is futile. On paper, you would have thought you could mount an attack from behind your own posts and there would be no way you would fail to score a try with the pod system. On the pitch, though, you never felt like you would get out of your own 22.

To Henry, it was revolutionary, and you have to have some respect for the guy for wanting to try it out and for wanting to do something different. He was obviously looking to win the 2001 Six Nations and was thinking, 'How can we beat these teams?' His answer was, 'I've come up with this game plan. Let's give it a whirl.' And that took some guts.

I just wish we could have had the team environment then that we have now, in which the emphasis is on every member of the squad down to the newest arrival speaking their mind should they feel the need. If there are doubts about some part of a game plan, even if they are not aired straight away in a team meeting early in Test match week, you can guarantee that at some stage someone will pipe up with, 'Look, fellas, this ain't gonna work.'

Worse than the 44–15 caning that we took at the hands of England was the fact that Henry refused to drop his pod system, and we went through the rest of the Six Nations trying to play something we knew was doomed. We could only beat Italy and France and

draw with Scotland that year, while we lost to Ireland in the October after our clash with them in Cardiff was postponed because of the foot-and-mouth outbreak.

Henry capitalised on his Great Redeemer tag with a series of speaking engagements at smaller clubs. During the high point of his tenure, they had been hanging on his every word. But the irony is that within a few months those very same people didn't have a good word to say about him as our results dipped. In fact, by the time of his last game in charge, a horrible 50-point thrashing against Ireland at Lansdowne Road in February 2002 in which I didn't play, the team touched down at Cardiff Airport to be greeted by a crowd of fans singing, 'We've got the worst team in the world.' Enough said – or should I say sung?

I had played for Wales A against our Ireland counterparts that weekend on the Saturday, and after flying back to Birmingham Airport on the Sunday morning of the full international, my brother picked me up in the car. We were in a rush because we both wanted to get home, get down the pub and get on the piss to watch the game.

What I'm about to tell you shows you how much I have changed in the last four years or so, but I'm not going to lie about it because it was the way I felt at the time. As we drove back in the car, the game was on the radio. Ireland scored after a couple of minutes, and

before long their scores started to come thick and fast. After almost every one of them, I shouted in delight – I'm embarrassed to say that I was pleased Wales were losing. The main reason was that I could sense the Henry era was coming to an end, and I wanted whatever was going to hasten that process – nothing would be better than a heavy defeat – to come about. The truth was that by then I had reached the end of my tether with him and all that he stood for.

Also, whenever you are not playing in a side, and I defy any player to honestly say this isn't the case, there is always a small part of you that does not want the team to do well, purely for your own selfish reasons. There will be do-gooders queuing up to condemn me, I'm sure, but I can guarantee that those who have played the game at any level will all have experienced the feelings I have just mentioned at some stage. But before anyone calls for me to be publicly beheaded, perhaps I could share with you an example of just how much I have changed since then. In our 2005 Grand Slam year, after I had broken my thumb against France in the third match and been ruled out for the rest of the tournament, I went to find Kevin Morgan, the guy who would be playing in my jersey, before our fourth match against Scotland at Murrayfield. I said to Kevin, 'Look, butt, you're playing and you're playing in my position, but I'm saying this to your face because I

hope you realise that I would never lie to your face. I genuinely hope you do well. I really mean it.' That was how strongly I felt about the team by then and how strongly I wanted them to do well, in spite of my own absence.

But back in those darker days in 2002, it was so different. I remember by the time we got home from Birmingham to The Swan in Aberkenfig, we were losing by 40-odd points. I ordered a pint of lager with glee. The pub was packed, and Kevin Ellis, Allan Bateman and his missus, and a host of other ex-internationals were also in there enjoying themselves. To a man, none of them could care less. Oh, they wanted Wales to win all right, but to them the state of the team was awful, and most of them were just remarking with rueful smiles on their faces on how bad it had all become.

Another episode that in my view did not paint the Henry regime in a flattering light, although I wouldn't hold him solely responsible by any means, was the handling of Iestyn Harris's conversion to union from rugby league. Henry had previous in terms of helicoptering players in from outside the Welsh game, the Jason Jones-Hughes affair being the most high-profile example. Jones-Hughes was a centre who did have legitimate family claims to wear the Welsh jersey through his grandfather. He had grown up playing in Australia, and the fact

that he had experience of playing in the Super 12 sent everyone in the Welsh game into an excited lather, with the general consensus being that he must be an absolute world beater.

There was enormous fuss when he came, but as it turned out he barely played a handful of matches for Newport or Wales because of an appalling run of injuries, and throughout it all he made a shed-load of money. Before Jones-Hughes even arrived, he was disliked by the players. Perhaps that was a bit unfair on him, because nobody had anything personal against him. Instead, what grated was Henry's apparent view that because this guy was coming up from the southern hemisphere we should all bow to his expertise in much the same way as we had done with the coach. It seemed like all anyone needed was a southern-hemisphere accent. For us, Jones-Hughes was given the Welsh jersey all too easily and was far from better than what we already had within our own boundaries. In fact, I think the whole episode was a total disaster.

Iestyn was a different story. For starters, Iestyn was a great bloke who instantly endeared himself to the boys. The worst thing that happened to him was the fact that he scored three tries in his first full appearance for Cardiff in a Heineken Cup match at the Arms Park. It meant that he set the bar at a level that was never really going to go any higher. But the trouble was people expected him to improve and expected his three-try match to be his minimum standard from then on.

Because of that, I did feel sorry for him, and poor Iestyn had something of a rude awakening on his debut for Wales against Argentina in the 2001 autumn series just a few weeks later. He played at outside-half that day, and it was soon obvious that the guy had been thrown into something that he simply wasn't ready for. I think Iestyn has since admitted as much himself. One incident not long into the game proved he was far too green to be playing. He received the ball from a set-piece or a ruck – I can't remember which – in our 22, and several of us immediately shouted at him to 'kick it'. Of course, we meant to touch, but Iestyn, not familiar enough with the game, just booted it downfield, and Argentina ran it back at us and scored in the corner. We told Iestyn that we had meant him to put it into touch, but how could we blast him considering the position he had been placed in? He had come from a different sport and had been told to play at the highest level of a new one almost straight away.

The Welsh Rugby Union was run by different people back then, but I think it's fair to say that their handling of him was not one of the governing body's finest hours. Iestyn should have been nurtured into the game, sent to every training camp under the sun and then brought through at A level. Instead, he was slung in, probably to boost gate

receipts for the WRU, which was in financial desperation at that time, with nobody prepared to put his best interests as a player first. Jason Robinson wasn't treated like that by the England set-up, and the WRU's thinking on Iestyn was so short term. It was as though their attitude was, 'Right, we've paid a fortune to get you here, so now it's sink or swim. And if you sink, you're on your own. And, what's more, you'll take the grief if you fail, not us.'

There is no doubt that Iestyn is a quality player, and by the time he decided to go back to league he was really developing into a top-class union performer at Test level. But nobody ever backed him. The union built up his profile but didn't allow him to come down here, settle with his family and ease his way into the game. He was under the spotlight from the day he arrived. The management of him was scandalous, and I think his decision to go back north was the best one he could have made.

Henry quit less than a week after the loss in Ireland that I was so pleased about, but I wasn't exactly cracking open the champagne, because his successor was his right-hand man – Steve Hansen. If Henry had been bad, I thought that Hansen might as well have been the devil himself. He was a nightmare as far as I was concerned. I have nothing but the utmost respect and admiration for the guy now, but at the time he took charge I and plenty of others in the squad just couldn't stand him, and we've since told him as much to his face.

In his time as deputy to Henry, Steve really made us sit up and take notice of him. For a start, he was the first person who seemed to have the audacity to stand up to Henry. As I have said, nobody would ever dare question him, but Steve would think nothing of piping up in team meetings with, 'Actually, I think you're wrong about that, Graham. We should be doing it like this.' The players couldn't believe what we were hearing at first. 'This fellow's got some cheek for a deputy,' was the gist of what we were thinking. He also felt perfectly entitled to give players a rollicking, and he would always try and have the last say on any issue that was spoken about in team meetings, even though he was more than prepared to throw open the floor for viewpoints.

But while Henry and Steve went on to work together in the All Blacks set-up and clearly have a very good relationship, there were moments when they did not see eye to eye in Wales. On one occasion, they had a heated row in one of the computer rooms set aside for players at the Vale of Glamorgan Hotel. One of the players was sitting at the back of the room on his own on this particular day and had just gone down to fiddle with one of the wires that was connecting his machine to the mains when Henry and Hansen burst in, clearly in a state of disagreement.

The player thought about revealing himself, because the two of them obviously hadn't realised he was there, but he decided to stay put. He said that the two of them were going berserk at one another for fully ten minutes with Henry accusing Steve of being after his job and Steve strenuously denying it. Whatever was actually said, within two weeks Henry was gone and Steve was indeed the boss.

6

STEVE HANSEN AND THE NEW ALFIE

It's true what they say about first impressions – they can be so misleading. If you had told me in the early days of Steve Hansen's reign in charge of the Wales team that by the time he left I would see him as one of the most important and valued figures in my career, I would have laughed out loud, but that is what happened. And to think that his tenure in charge could so easily have resulted in the end of my international days.

After succeeding Henry, Steve was a coach who made us clean up after ourselves for the first time ever. If you dropped a bottle on the floor of the changing-room and left it there, he would go mad and make you pick it up; if you wore the wrong kit in training, he would go mental. In short, he was just like a tyrant. By the time he left us, we knew there had been method in his actions all along – he had been doing it for a reason – but when he first came along, well, if he had suddenly announced that he was quitting, it would have been hard to stifle a grin.

But I almost never played under him at all. When he took charge in early 2002, I was going through a period of serious disillusionment with all that playing for Wales entailed. Quite frankly, the Henry era had left me indifferent to the whole business of putting everything into something that always seemed to leave you feeling gutted one way or the other. I had been dropped so many times without ever really knowing why. Playing for Wales didn't seem to be special any more, just something that was guaranteed to cause me grief. I was doing something that I thought I loved doing, but when I sat back and dissected what I was getting out of it, the story was different. I wasn't enjoying the training, I was getting dropped more often than not and, as I saw the situation, everyone other than me was to blame.

What's more, I was getting pissed way too often and smoking too much. I've never been a forty-a-day bloke or anything like that; in fact, during the day

Everyone in life will come to a crossroads.

I would perhaps have just one or two. But when I went out and had a pint or a bottle in my hand, I would lose count of the number of cigarettes I got through, and nobody needs to tell me it wasn't good for me.

I would never behave like that now, because I so badly want to stay at the top of the game, and I know that to do that I have physical targets that have to be reached. But back then I didn't give a monkey's. Actually, I was even thinking along the lines that it would be good to fail to reach a target because then I would be booted out of the international set-up without having to make the decision for myself. The bottom line was that I was sick and tired of being called in and

booted out – I either wanted in for good or out for good. And I had grave doubts that the first option was what I wanted. To be blunt, I was thinking of quitting Wales.

I would speak to my mother and say, 'Right, I'm going to reach X number of caps and then I'm quitting.' I would always bring that situation up when I had been dropped, and I always wanted people to sympathise with me. I wanted them to think of me as the one who had been hard done by, and I know now that I was not seeing the other side of the story. I should have been looking at myself more. But it mattered more to me to get my version of events across to them so that they would back me up and be on my side.

It was at that time that I began to change from the old Alfie, who would think nothing of pissing it up and to whom playing for Wales was an individual rather than a team affair, into the new Alfie, who began to see playing for his country for what it really was and who looked after his body like never before. I didn't quite appreciate it at the time, but I was at a crossroads: I could have retired and just faded comfortably away, playing club and regional rugby and being content with the 50-odd caps that I had; or I could push on to bigger and better things at the highest level and prove to myself, my family and the people who had always supported me that I was capable of doing so much more. I will be eternally grateful that, with the help of my family and friends whom I will always respect and admire, I chose the latter option.

Fittingly, the process began at Bridgend at the start of the 2002–03 season. Allan Lewis was in charge for his first full season, and we had signed the likes of Chris Horsman, Andy Moore and Sililo Martens. During the pre-season, I can remember looking at the people around me in one training session and thinking, 'Hang on a minute. We've got a bloody good side here.' The momentum had been building from halfway through the previous season when Allan had first taken charge, and the partnership he had with Richard Webster was really beginning to strike a chord with the whole squad. For the first time, I had a pair of coaches

whom I felt a deep commitment to. I felt responsible, because they had made me captain, and I was starting to get the sense that here was a group that was special – on and off the field. The team was beginning to mean more to me than any team had ever done.

I felt a loyalty towards Allan in particular that I had never felt towards any other coach. Allan would always speak to me and treat me like a responsible adult and a rugby professional. He put his faith in me, and I felt as though I had to give it everything I had – not just for myself, but for him as well. And these were very much new feelings for me.

Allan would enlist my help in picking the team and making decisions about the club and the players we should look to bring in. I had suddenly gone from being someone who just turned up and played to someone who made big decisions, and picking the Bridgend side at that time was definitely a big decision in my eyes, particularly when somebody had entrusted me to help him do it.

So, I was undergoing a serious change in my approach to the game, and Allan was the one triggering it. He pushed me to get back into the Wales team at a time when I really was in danger of fading out of the picture altogether. At the end of the 2001–02 season, I had a big chat with Steve Hansen after he had bombed me out, and I was sent away to train with the Wales sevens team for the 2002 Commonwealth Games in Manchester. Steve knew I was a pisshead, and he

ordered me to train with the sevens team every Monday. In earlier days, I might have stuck two fingers up at the idea and if not walked away, then treated it half-heartedly. But the responsibility I felt towards Allan helped me to take it seriously. Not once did I have a drink on the Sunday before those Monday sessions, and I promised myself I was going to dig in and do it.

That sevens team was a brilliant bunch of lads – there were no superstars, just everyone rolling up their sleeves and helping one another. And it turned out to be some of the hardest fitness training I had done in my life. I was absolutely out on my feet at the end of some sessions, but I felt superb for doing it and got a real sense of achievement out of the whole thing. I went away to the games with the team, which was outstanding, even if we never really got a sniff of a medal. Then, a few weeks later, I remember Allan calling me over and telling me that Scott Johnson, Steve Hansen's assistant, wanted to meet me and that he would be down to the club in a few days' time.

The day arrived, and it was just like when I had been called up to the Wales squad for the first time back in 1995, with me not wanting to confront something head on for fear of the outcome. I remember going for a walk around Bridgend town centre before Johnno was due to arrive, and I was cooking up a plan to arrive 15 minutes late for the appointment. That way I would hopefully miss him but still be able to offer the excuse that I was only 15 minutes late and that it wasn't really my fault – I wasn't prepared to go as far as I had done in 1995 and not turn up altogether!

My little plot failed, though, because when I returned to the Brewery Field around 15 minutes later than scheduled, Johnno was there waiting for me in all his glory. 'Let's go for a cup of tea,' he said. We went to a café that one of my mates runs in the centre of the town. We sat upstairs, and Johnno laid it on the line to me. 'We've been watching you lately, and you've been playing well,' he said. I told him why that was, and Johnno soon left me in no doubt that Steve Hansen wanted me back for the 2002 autumn internationals.

Again, I was hit by a 1995 kind of feeling. I was happy in my Bridgend comfort zone back then and fearful of that comfort zone being invaded by something as huge as an international career. The same feeling came racing to the surface once again on hearing Johnno's words. I had found a new happiness with Bridgend away from the Wales set-up and was experiencing feelings of responsibility I had never really known before in a rugby environment. Did I really want the physical and emotional demands that playing for Wales would surely bring back into my life? I had grave doubts – I hadn't been involved with Wales for some time, and if truth be told, I hadn't missed it.

We chatted for about half an hour, and Johnno didn't mince his words about what I could potentially be if I came on board lock, stock and barrel with what he and Steve were trying to do in the national set-up. I just gave him all the lines about how I had found new happiness and was as content as ever with my home life having just married Jemma. Although deep down I wanted to go back and do it, I also wanted him to know about my doubts – and for him to carry on telling me how good I could be! In the end, Johnno told me that the Cardiff wing Craig Morgan was injured and that if I wanted it there was a place in the team for a game against Romania at Wrexham on the Saturday week.

We chatted a bit more, and I finally agreed to give it another go. At that stage, though, the decision was not a cause for celebration in my eyes. There was no sense of relief that I'd finally seen the light and was now going to enjoy many more happy years at the top with Wales. Instead, I was blasé about it all, conveying the attitude to Johnno that I would give it a try and no more, and that if I didn't feel it was working out, I'd be on my bike.

I met Steve a few days later, and he also told me straight down the line what he expected of me, saying I had dozens of caps but had never really achieved anything. He added that he never heard me speak up in camp and did not see me as any kind of potential leader. The boys, he said, all thought the world of me and

were glad to have me around, but I needed to become more of an influence about the place. If someone like Graham Henry had said that to me a few years earlier, I would have simply nodded my head and tried to look serious, but it would all have gone in one ear and out the other. This time, though, Steve's words hit home big time and really shook me up. I somehow realised deep inside that I had come to my crossroads.

Yes I had been blasé after meeting Johnno, but Steve had drummed the message home good and proper. Not only that, after a couple of days training back with Wales, even though I loved it at Bridgend at that time, I realised that this was the first ever national side I'd been involved with that was not about individuals but about what should always be the most important thing – the team. That had a profound effect on my entire approach. Whereas before you only let yourself down if you cocked up, now you could never just let yourself down – you could only let the team down. That was the new responsibility that I felt on my shoulders.

I began to see things in a whole new light. If I wanted to go out on the piss on a Sunday and then stroll in half-soaked on a Monday, that was fine. But it would be the team that would pay for it, not just me. I realised that I could never again go in pissed on a Monday and say that I had a twinge in my leg in order to get out of training, because it would mean that I would hinder the

I hated Steve Hansen at first, but he helped save my career.

preparations of the team and everyone would feel my absence. There was no way I was prepared to do that.

It's funny but there were still a lot of times during the Steve Hansen era when I sat at the back of the bus with the lads on the way home from training and we all said how much we hated him – and I've since told Steve this to his face. But now I realise that Steve had a plan all along. He knew that he would never be able to change us and our attitudes overnight. But the way he forced us to learn new values without us ever even realising that that was what he was doing was a stroke of genius. And there was one day, I cannot remember exactly when it was, when all the players got together and

agreed that he had been right all along to put us through all the things that he had.

I remember on one occasion we were in camp out in Lanzarote. We were doing five training sessions a day, the first of which was at 6.30 a.m. One day, we were out in a field going through moves and balls were being dropped left, right and centre. 'What's the matter with you lot today?' Steve barked.

'Steve, butt,' we replied. 'It's still dark out here, and we literally cannot see anything.'

'Don't use the bloody light as an excuse,' he countered.

'We're not,' we replied. 'We genuinely can't see what we're doing!'

It was 6.30 a.m., and we were out training in the dark with a coach bellowing orders at us. Every player in the world would have hated that, but somehow it was bringing us closer together, and that is how Steve Hansen changed the Wales team. It was done almost by stealth. Now that he has gone, there are still times when the lads recall things we did with Steve and say that it would be good to do them again, even though at the time we hated doing those things.

Under Steve's guidance, I found myself as a rugby player. And although we were whitewashed in his first full Six Nations in charge of us in 2003, I will, without hesitation, look back on that period with fonder memories than the ten-game winning run of 1999. To somebody who doesn't have a clue about what went on behind the scenes in both those eras, that type of statement probably sounds ludicrous. But the Steve Hansen team was so special – what we had off the field was unbreakable. We had a wall of commitment around us, and in our eyes nothing could penetrate it – and nothing ever would. People outside the squad understandably refused to believe us when we spoke of the spirit within the camp during times such as the winter of 2003 when everybody and anybody was beating us. But that is what we had created – that was the environment. And personally, as strange as this may sound, I was all of a sudden actually thriving on defeat. In other words, people were

having a go at us from all angles, and I found myself wanting to be at the front of the queue to wait for the next assault. For the first time ever, I wanted to be the one standing up for the team, and in an insane type of way I was loving it. 'If people want to have a go at this team, they will have to come through me first,' I thought to myself. When I look back now, I reckon that this was the period when the seeds of a potential Wales captain were sown within me. Because I loved that team so much, I was finding that I was turning into someone I had never been before, someone who was prepared to stand up and really fight for the boys.

I remember that the *Wales on Sunday* newspaper ran a poll asking the public who was the most hated person in Wales at the time of all our defeats in 2003. Osama bin Laden was top, Colin Charvis was second and Saddam Hussein was third! I'd love to know how many people actually took part in that poll, but the players thought that the fact that Saddam Hussein was behind Colin Charvis was pathetic, even though we actually had a good laugh about it. How many people in Wales, you have to wonder, would have sensibly said that they hated Charvis more than Saddam Hussein?

Much of it, I'm sure, had to do with the fact that Charvis was caught 'smiling' by a television camera after being substituted in the Six Nations defeat to Italy in 2003, the first game of

that year's tournament. But do people think he was actually happy we had lost? Of course he wasn't. In my opinion, that whole incident was shamefully blown out of all proportion by the media before Charvis had even had a chance to defend himself. It was all complete bullshit as far as I was concerned.

In any case, one of my sayings to the lads since becoming captain has been, 'It's not illegal to smile.' After we had been trounced 41–3 by New Zealand in the autumn internationals of 2005, I told all the lads, 'It happens. Let's not dwell on it.' And I always tell them to remember to enjoy it, because they are doing something that everyone else in the stadium would love to be doing. There are always people who would love to take the place of the players, and they will always think that they would be better given the chance. But you just have to accept that and not be dragged down by people standing in judgement of you. And I believe that mode of thinking applies to the Charvis smiling incident.

If anything, that episode brought us closer together as a team – it galvanised us. We were all prepared to admit that we were doing rubbish at that time, but I had also never felt so good while doing so badly. And it was every player's opinion that while we were getting no reward in terms of results for the moment, we soon would.

Put it this way, if you had asked a Welsh supporter on the day we lost to Italy in 2003 whether we would win the Grand Slam two years later, he or she would have probably told you where to go. But if you had asked the team, they would have said, 'Well, yeah, we'll have a good chance.' And Johnno said as much to the press only to be laughed out of court by the majority of them. Now most of them don't remember him saying that because they don't want to admit that they were wrong about us.

I captained Wales for the first time under Steve Hansen in a warm-up match ahead of the World Cup, in Ireland in 2003. He gave me the honour out of the blue when Colin Charvis was rested for the day, but the awful results continued. We lost in Dublin, and, worse still, we were then annihilated 43–9 by an England second team at the Millennium Stadium. I still cannot fathom why we were so horrendously poor that day, but horrendously poor we were, and there didn't seem to be too many excuses we could offer.

At that time, Steve was under as much pressure from a disgruntled Welsh public as he had ever been, and he was told by despairing WRU chief executive David Moffett to play his best team against Scotland at home a week later or face the consequences of another defeat. But he told Moffett to keep out of it, that he had a long-term plan ahead of the World Cup and that nobody was going to make him alter course. In other words, he put the team before his own precarious

position and thankfully got his reward as we ran out 23–9 winners in a game I didn't play in. But that was a mark of the kind of bloke Steve was and showed that he had massive guts, belief and bravery. He put his job on the line for us that day and stuck to his guns. The fact that it paid off was justice in its purest form.

Of course, the most memorable period of Steve's tenure was the 2003 World Cup in Australia, a tournament in which we produced two performances against New Zealand and England that many pundits now believe signalled the rebirth of Welsh rugby. And yes, in hindsight, I think they were probably right.

In his earlier days, it seemed to us that Steve could be unbelievably petty about things that happened on the training ground, screaming at us over what seemed like the most trivial mistakes. For example, we would be going through a planned move and everything would seem to be going well. Steve would be watching us from behind one of the posts at the other end of the pitch. All of a sudden, he would yell, 'Stop, stop,' and storm down the field ranting that so-and-so had been slightly out of the correct alignment – sometimes it was a matter of inches – and that we would therefore have to start all over again from scratch. The number of times I and others cursed him under our breath in those situations, I couldn't say. But just as there had been method in his madness when he was yelling at us to pick up

litter in the changing-room, so it proved with his apparent nitpicking when we were going through drills – and our mesmerising performance against New Zealand in the final pool game of the World Cup exemplified that.

Everyone remembers that match – even though we lost it – as the one in which everything finally clicked together for a team that had been on its knees for some time in terms of results. Some people called it a fluke, but nothing could have been further from the truth. Things like that don't just happen out of thin air.

And for me personally, that evening in Sydney represented a change of path for my career, because it was the night everyone discovered, me included, that I could be a pretty decent Test full-back if I wanted. Up until that point, I had never filled that role at international level, even if I had slotted in there a few times in club matches. But, quite by accident, all that changed.

I remember being devastated when Steve told me in the week leading up to the match with the All Blacks that I would be on the bench. His reasoning was that he wanted to keep me back for the quarter-final against England a week later, as we had already secured our berth in the last eight with pool wins against Canada in Melbourne and Tonga and Italy in Canberra, the latter of which was a real winner-takes-all clash that we were under fierce pressure to win. I accepted Steve's reasoning but was still gutted to

be missing out on playing against New Zealand at the World Cup.

Then the next thing he said stunned me a little. 'You'll be covering Garan Evans at full-back,' he said.

'No problem,' I replied, trying to mask my surprise. 'After all, I'm one of the best kickers we have in this team!' That last statement was obviously said as a joke. I think my kicking has improved tenfold in recent years, but back then I was probably better known for slicing the ball at right angles into touch more often than not. But, again, I respected his decision and took comfort in the fact that I wasn't being dropped but rested.

Realistically, nobody thought we could beat New Zealand. Italy the week before had been the big game, and like all the other lads I was just pleased we had already achieved our target of qualifying for the knockout stage. I was in for a major shock, though.

The New Zealand clash was just four minutes old when poor Garan Evans took an almighty clatter and had the senses totally knocked out of him as we defended our line. He was in no fit state to continue, so there I was, after four minutes, peeling off my tracksuit and getting ready to step into battle against the mighty All Blacks in a position that was unfamiliar to me to say the least. I hadn't been through a single team run in the number-15 slot, hadn't taken part in one training-ground move from full-back and I didn't even warm up before I went on.

When Garan went down, Martyn Williams and a few of the others who were not even on the bench but were sitting close by began to take the mickey out of me. 'Whey-hey,' they shouted, as it seemed Garan wasn't going to get back up. 'You're going on as full-back, Alfie. This should be a laugh!' By that time, I was just trotting up and down the touchline in a world of my own, thinking, 'Oh my God. This can't be happening to me.'

Almost as soon as I went onto the pitch, I found myself standing behind the posts as we faced either a New Zealand penalty or conversion. But by then I was of the attitude, 'Bollocks to this. Let's just have a bloody go.' I conveyed my feelings to the rest of the lads: 'Boys, let's just enjoy this and chuck it around a bit. If it comes off, then great; if not, at least we won't leave the field never knowing.' What subsequently happened was the subject of quite a bit of debate in Wales in the following months, years even. We stormed back with a Mark Taylor try almost immediately, and when Shane Williams sidestepped out of the way of about five black-shirted defenders soon after, the whole team just exploded into it. We actually went ahead early in the second half, but our downfall in the end was that New Zealand also relished the blitzkrieg free-flowing style we played and, being more accustomed to executing it, ended up running out 53–37 winners.

Steve Hansen was the first to play me at full-back for Wales.

So, was it a case of us players ripping up everything that the coaches had told us and just playing by instinct? Or was it all part of Steve's grand plan? Did we throw caution to the wind under his instruction? Those were the questions being asked and commented upon by the media. Well, what unfolded was part by accident and part by design, but be under no illusions: it could not and would not have happened had it not been for Steve's influence. What I said behind the posts after first coming on hardly mirrored Steve's team talk, but the very fact that we were able to play like that was because of all the attention to detail and accuracy Steve had instilled in us up to that point. We found that style ourselves on the night, but Steve was the creator, there's no question about that. All of a sudden, the little things that Steve had annoyed us with were actually allowing us to produce the accuracy we needed to perform.

I recall leaving Sydney's Telstra Dome early after the game because I had picked up a minor injury, and as I drove away in the car with Scott Johnson I sat back, blew out my cheeks and reflected on what I had just been involved in. Yes, it did, as far as I was concerned, represent a new era for us. I turned to Johnno and

said, 'You know, I didn't want that game to end.'

All the lads had been like kids in a sweet shop as the encounter wore on, suddenly realising that, yes, we could actually play like this – we were capable. We had been defeated, and although defeat is something I have always been able to handle reasonably well, it wasn't as if I had to gather myself together and bite the bullet of massive disappointment. Nobody was down. We were happy because we knew we had found a way of playing. Steve had banged on for months about the importance of performance over result and taken a fair bit of criticism from the media for it. But if there was one night to sit back and be truly proud of a performance rather than a result, that was it.

Nobody needed to say anything after the match. We knew what had just happened and what the implications were. The atmosphere in the stadium had been electric, the crowd had loved every minute of the game and we knew that we had been part of something special. It must rank as one of the best-ever games of rugby in a World Cup – the rugby that was played was simply sensational on the eye.

Yet as much as the New Zealand performance had been something of a first for us, it did not significantly change our outlook, because it was a display that we had always believed we were capable of. It was just that because we had done it on such a big stage, it magnified the amount of confidence we took from it. All Steve's nitpicking had, in the end, produced the goods. What's more, we then went and won everybody over for a second time in the quarter-final against England a week later when we outscored the team who would become world champions by three tries to one and for an hour or so looked quite capable of conjuring up what would have been to outside observers the shock of the century.

Whichever angle you come at it from, we played all the rugby that evening at Brisbane's Suncorp Stadium. Stephen Jones rounded off a brilliant flowing move for our first try and another by Colin Charvis before half-time gave us a lead of 10–3 that could easily have been more. England, as they were perfectly entitled to do, resorted to pragmatism in the second half, wearing us down with their giant forwards and relying on Jonny Wilkinson to kick his goals. But even then it was us who had the last word with a try by Martyn Williams that had Clive Woodward on pins for the final few seconds of the game.

Afterwards, we were all on a high again, despite the fact that we knew our World Cup was over. We felt like winners, even though we had not won the trophy. We had patented a new style, we had got the Welsh fans back on our side and the rugby world was once again looking up to us because of the way we played. Yes, to have gone there and beaten England in a World Cup quarter-

final would have been momentous, but we had to be happy to a degree with the progress we had made.

When all is said and done, 2003 was England's time. They had a great team that was peaking – some people said that it was even a little way past its peak – and deserved their glory. We were some way off our own peak, but boy had we begun the climb.

But I will not just remember Australia 2003 for what we did on the pitch. No, the way we lived our lives off the pitch and on the training ground will also be forever memorable for me. Back in 1999, it was all about being cooped up in a hotel stuffing our faces with food and just generally doing the things you do when you are away with a professional sports team. But in 2003, we decided to go at it differently.

For the bulk of the pool stages, the squad was booked into a basic hotel on some suburban street on the outskirts of Canberra. We were stationed in the Aussie capital for most of the time before the New Zealand game, spending just a few nights in Melbourne ahead of the opening clash against Canada. Now, anyone who has been to Canberra will tell you that it is a perfectly pleasant place to be, but as cities go it is not the most inspiring or exciting. In fact, if you go into downtown Canberra looking for a night out – not that this Welsh team did that – at most you will find one or two bars worth going into.

Anyway, that was far from the issue for us. More important was our hotel, which consisted not of your run-of-the-mill rooms but of studios complete with cooking facilities. It was like having your own little flat. It was brilliant. There is nothing worse than lying on a hotel bed for six weeks, watching television or listening to your iPod for hours on end. You get so lazy doing that, but the arrangement we had was never going to allow for that.

There were two of us to a studio. We had our own bedroom, our own bathroom and our own kitchen, and we were responsible for keeping it clean, just as you would be in your own house. There were four studios to a floor, and every night one or two of the boys would have to take their turn to cook for the rest – and it wasn't as if there were any Jamie Olivers amongst us, I can assure you! I think Adam Jones, the prop whom I roomed with, and I were the only ones who got away with not preparing anything – when I'm at home, I struggle with beans on toast, so it was probably a good thing! But the effect this type of arrangement had on the bonding of the squad was immense, and whether we were inviting another floor down for food or all arranging to go and eat out as a treat, it was always really well organised.

Adam, who along with the blonde-haired Duncan Jones is one half of what the Welsh supporters call the 'hair-bear props', because both sport a

mass of long curly locks, was great to room with. I suppose in some ways it was like rooming with a woman. I used to go into the shower in the morning after he had used it, and there would be pieces of his hair everywhere: hanging from the shower head, up and down the walls, embedded in bars of soap and, of course, blocking the plughole. I don't know how he had so much left on his head after emerging every day.

It all added up to make 2003 ten times the experience 1999 had been. The team was tighter, the spirit was better and we were there for each other – and all those things were lacking four years earlier. It was silly little things that made all the difference, such as us having to do all our own shopping at the precinct across the road. Whenever someone was going over there, you could guarantee that there would be a knock on your door asking if you needed anything.

Yes, we went through a difficult time with Steve when his apparent pettiness was the predominant topic of conversation. But by then, he had won us over. We knew that everything he did was for our benefit, and, what's more, he was backed up by fitness guru Andrew Hore, whose methods and personality have made an imprint on the squad to this day, even though he left us after we beat Australia in the autumn of 2005.

Horey had joined us in the later Henry days when I had been kicked out of the squad. When he paid a visit to Bridgend around that time, he was confronted by Simon Thomas, our club kit man. 'Hey, why don't you pick Alfie any more? He's playing brilliantly,' Simon shouted over to him.

Horey replied, 'It's not just about playing any more. It's about everything you have to offer.' I thought that remark summed up what the squad had turned into. No, it wasn't enough just to play well any more; it was about what contribution you were prepared to make for the cause as a whole. Were you prepared to throw yourself into it body and soul?

What was Horey's overall contribution? Where do I start? He brought a whole new dimension to fitness coaching, but not necessarily through his methods, which were not enormously different to those of others who are similarly respected in the field. It was Horey's approach to it that marked him out as special. As a fitness coach, you have to be quite strict, because no player really likes your department. Therefore, there is a fair chance that you are going to be disliked to a certain extent, simply because of what your job entails. But Horey never needed to shout at us, because, before anything else, he worked on gaining our respect, convincing us 100 per cent that what he was going to put us through would ultimately be for our benefit. He would never just say to us, 'Right, get your trainers on. I'm going to run you into the ground.' He would always explain why we were doing something, until, in the end, if

he had told us all to jump into the sea and swim as far as we could out into the ocean, I'm sure we would have! We would have done anything he said, such was the respect we had for him.

The public and the media were probably quick to forget about him, because he was obviously not in the limelight like Steve was. But Horey's ability to bring an element of fun to our fitness work was absolutely priceless. He realised that if we didn't enjoy fitness work, we inevitably wouldn't put as much into it. We used to train with one of those tiny American footballs, and we'd run ourselves into the ground, having little games and going through drills with this ball. Time flew, and we didn't even realise just how hard we were training most of the time, but, by God, we were going at it.

Horey was also not afraid to introduce things we had never done before. For example, we would train the day after an international, and I mean proper fitness training. We would all rather have stayed in bed, but if there was one person who could get us up on a Sunday morning, it was Andrew Hore.

And although Horey was a New Zealander, he was also extremely passionate about Wales, something that really came to the fore in his final few weeks with us at the tail end of 2005. He called Wales his home, and the night before our final Test match under him we all gathered into a room at our headquarters to make a farewell

Rob Howley and I celebrate a try against Italy in 2002.

presentation. The famous Grogg Shop in Pontypridd had made a Grogg of him, and, as captain, it was my job to make the presentation. I was dreading it, because I knew the little ceremony truly marked the beginning of the end of Horey's time with us, the start of what would be an extremely sorry farewell.

After we had settled down, the atmosphere became fraught with emotion, and, sure enough, it all got a bit too much for Horey, who ended up crying like a baby. In such circumstances, there usually would have been a few sniggers from one or two of the boys, trying to lighten the mood. But not this time. I looked around at the lads, and to a man they all had lumps in their throats – and I very much include myself in that.

A few were biting desperately at their fists, trying to stop themselves from breaking down, and all around the room there were puffy eyes, full to bursting with the most heartfelt tears.

Horey tried to make a speech, but he couldn't do it. Every time he attempted to string a sentence together, his voice wobbled with emotion and he broke up. That was what working with us for all those years had meant to him. Horey's tenure had never been just a job for him; it had almost been a state of mind, as it had been for us all. It was a huge decision for him to leave, but every player now stays in touch with him and, again, me as much as anyone.

You may wonder how on earth we cope in his absence, such is the emphasis I have placed on his contribution. Well, that was another one of his masterstrokes. When Horey left, the Wales squad essentially had two people who did his job. Huw Wiltshire – who has since moved on – was in charge of what Horey used to do outside the squad, such as going around each of the regions and making sure that what they are doing fitness-wise broadly corresponds to what the national team was doing. Then there was Mark Bennett, the old Cardiff and Wales flanker who is still involved, who had a more hands-on role with the Wales players on a day-to-day basis.

But the fact that they slipped seamlessly into Horey's role was down to Horey himself, because before he left us he made sure that Mark in particular shadowed him for his last three or four weeks. So, when we did a session, Mark took it, but Horey was there on the sidelines prowling, not saying a word, but all the time endorsing Mark as his man – and that was enough for the lads. It might have been Mark talking, but it could just as well have been Horey. When Horey left, we already had respect for Mark, because we knew that Horey would have wanted it that way. Moreover, Mark is brilliant in his own right, bringing in new ideas and really making his impact felt, even though, as I've told Mark to his face, Horey could never be replaced.

Steve Hansen left us after the 2004 Six Nations, keeping a promise he had made to his family to return to New Zealand, and by that time it was also clear that he was going to become Graham Henry's right-hand man in the All Blacks set-up. I would be amazed if Steve is not one day in charge of New Zealand, a role he would thoroughly deserve. However, the days surrounding his departure left me frustrated and a little annoyed, to tell you the truth, even though Steve ended up leaving with the Welsh public's best wishes for having turned our fortunes around. But I suppose that was precisely what bothered me.

After Steve's last game, a win at home to Italy, he was given a standing ovation by the Millennium Stadium crowd, which prompted a tear or two from the big man. But I was never able to get it

out of my head that just a few months earlier most of the nation had hated him. How could so many people, all of a sudden, change their minds about him? Was a few positive performances really all that it took? Why had they been so deaf to what we had been saying when the picture was far less rosy in the dark days of 2003? As a nation, I really believe we are too quick to make up our minds about someone, and then we change our views all too easily when the prevailing wind starts blowing from another direction.

After the Italy game, when Steve's emotional farewell was in full flight with the crowd applauding and him wiping his eyes, I just walked off the pitch, as much out of principle as anything else. It wasn't as if I was in a fury or hugely pissed off about it all, because more than anything I was pleased for Steve that at last he was getting the recognition he deserved. But I could not get it out of my head that only a year before we had been booed out of Rome Airport by our own fans after losing to Italy.

OK, we didn't deserve anything else, and as far as stick from the fans goes I've definitely heard of worse. But so many of the delirious supporters in the Millennium Stadium that day were probably the very same ones who had been baying for Steve's blood at one time. Now, though, the two World Cup games against New Zealand and England had changed people's minds altogether.

Anyway, that evening, I found myself unable to deal with Steve's departure in the way that everyone expected me to. A going-away do had been arranged back at the hotel for the team, officials and management, but I told some lie about having a family commitment – my brother's wedding, I said – and got myself out of it. I ended up jumping into my car almost as soon as I had showered and changed, and I headed back to my house before going out on the piss with a few of my mates in Bridgend that evening.

Steve had been such a big part of my career that I didn't want to have to say goodbye. It almost felt as though I might not have to accept that he was leaving if I didn't go to the party. I so didn't want him to leave. Not only that, but because the boys knew how well I got on with Steve, I realised that they would have had me up there presenting him with all sorts of stuff had I gone to his do, and then they'd have ripped me to shreds with mickey taking. I suppose everyone has someone who they see as having had a profound effect on their career, and it's tough sometimes with the boys around, because there's always banter and there's always teasing. And it was difficult for me to say anything about Steve in print or on television, because you can guarantee that the boys would have been straight on my case about it afterwards.

It was a pity that I never actually caught up with Steve before he left, although I am in regular contact with him now, sometimes by telephone,

sometimes by email. I also made sure I caught up with him for a coffee when New Zealand came over to play us in the 2004 autumn series. Steve left a message on my telephone after I had my funny turn during the furore of Mike Ruddock leaving. He said, 'I'm not ringing to see if you're OK, Alf. I know you're all right, because you are strong. I'm just ringing to check everything is OK in your life.' I think it was Steve's way of saying that if I wanted to talk about things during a difficult time, I knew his number, and I very much valued his concern.

I sometimes think to myself, 'If only more of my career had been spent under the guidance of someone like Steve.' But life is never that simple, as I discovered when Welsh rugby underwent its regional revolution of 2003. I returned home from the World Cup to embark on a whole new era – the Celtic Warriors era. Given the upheaval it had taken to set up this new side, I expected it to be a long and hopefully successful time in my life. I was wrong on the first count, but not necessarily the second.

7

I'M A WARRIOR...AND THEN I'M NOT

When it became clear that Welsh rugby was going to go from eleven top-flight clubs to five regions, I was devastated with the whole business and totally convinced that the new structure wasn't going to work. Anyone outside of the game in Wales needs to realise that this was a tumultuous time for our game, representing as it did the wiping away of more than a century of club tradition.

Despite the fact that Cardiff and Llanelli had decent track records in the Heineken Cup, in the first weeks of 2003 it emerged that the much talked about move from clubs to provincial rugby was now gathering pace and was going to happen whether people liked it or not. The inability of our clubs to punch their weight in the company of their English and French counterparts and the Irish provinces, as well as the notion that our domestic league was not providing a tough enough environment to hone players for Test rugby, were the main factors driving it all, factors which

you couldn't really argue with when all was said and done. But that didn't mean anyone had to believe the new system could work in Wales.

David Moffett had taken over the running of the debt-ridden Welsh Rugby Union, and having been in the job just a few days, the Australian, who had previously headed up the New Zealand Rugby Union and Sport England, infamously announced that he had not come to Wales to 'rearrange the deck chairs on the Titanic'. The difference in the WRU under this new, professional and some would say ruthless management was that people such as Moffett knew how to get their way. 'You're either with us, or you can bugger off,' was Moffett's rather original approach to the haggling that had traditionally gone on in the Welsh game's corridors of power.

Moffett wanted regional rugby. And he was going to get it, even if he had to rip up every page of the WRU

117

I help launch Welsh rugby's regional revolution with a few beers with my teammates.

constitution. Glanmor Griffiths, the old WRU chairman who had seemingly been in power since the year dot, was still hovering around in the background when the new man first arrived, but it was clear that Glanmor's days as Welsh rugby's godfather were numbered and that the new executive would not be prepared to pussyfoot around the sensibilities of the clubs any more.

The whole process began with the seemingly never-ending haggling over how the regions should be carved up and subsequent threats of court action and dire predictions of the impending demise of rugby in Wales. Eventually,

though, a formula was agreed. It was decided that Newport and Ebbw Vale would form the Gwent Dragons, whose name was later changed to Newport Gwent Dragons because Newport fans just could not accept their name being left out of the title. Then Bridgend and Pontypridd would form the Celtic Warriors, Neath and Swansea would come together to make the Neath–Swansea Ospreys, while Cardiff and Llanelli each fought tooth and nail to preserve their stand-alone status. They got their way, much to the annoyance of the others, and became the Cardiff Blues and Llanelli Scarlets.

But the situation all but provoked a revolt among the supporters, and the disaffection was worst among the Bridgend and Pontypridd fans, now expected to follow the Warriors. They quite understandably complained that the identity of the clubs they had formerly followed had been completely wiped out. Fans of the old Newport club who could not accept the death of the Black and Ambers as a top-flight entity were also thumbing their noses at the idea of getting behind an all-Gwent team.

Critics had warned from the beginning that you couldn't expect 100 years of rugby culture to change overnight, and these complaints seemed to suggest that they had a point. But things carried on regardless, with fans and players forced to get on with the new arrangement as best they could. To those who were miffed about the fact that Newport, Neath, Swansea and others were effectively being consigned to history, the WRU pointed to the fact that those clubs would still exist in the new semi-professional Welsh Premiership. But it was a silly point to make, because, with all due respect to those playing in it, that league is a pale shadow of its predecessor, lacking in intensity and significance, even if it is potentially a decent breeding ground for future regional players.

Yes, something had to be done in Welsh rugby. We had eleven clubs and, again, without being disrespectful, beneath the top five there was very little

true competition, apart from perhaps the odd tricky away encounter. It was not an attractive league, and it was not a good grounding for Test rugby. But I still think that what happened was wholly unsatisfactory in terms of the process and the outcome. The competing vested interests in the game ended up sullying what could have been an exciting and bright new dawn for rugby in Wales.

For me, the worst thing about the whole business was that we were effectively going to lose the Bridgend side that went on to win the final Welsh Premiership prior to regionalism, the team in which I had finally found a new responsibility for myself, my teammates and the coaches. That completely gutted me. But it was to get even worse, because the way they went about carving up the Bridgend and Pontypridd teams into one regional outfit was, quite frankly, brutal. We had only been lumped together in the first place because there had been such an outcry over Cardiff linking up with Pontypridd. Cardiff wanted to stand alone, but the idea of a link-up with their bitter city rivals was sheer hell on earth to many people involved with Ponty.

There was no particular rhyme or reason to a Bridgend–Pontypridd amalgamation, and the most galling aspect of it was that we ended up being the only clubs who had to cope with a completely new identity. There was no part of either the Bridgend or Ponty names in the Celtic Warriors – no, it

was new team, new badge, new kit, new concept. There wasn't even any real geographical reason for us coming together and no history of special closeness between the two clubs. It all felt like an experiment to me, and I never believed we would get the support we would need or the backing from the public that would make it work. What's more, I was not prepared to waste a year of my career finding out whether I was right or wrong.

So there we were at the end of the 2002–03 season, still Bridgend players when push came to shove, standing outside Allan Lewis's office at the Brewery Field waiting to hear our fate. We had been told there was to be a 50–50 split of players from both clubs in the new team, and that obviously meant the scrapheap for many of us. That some of us weren't wanted from a playing point of view was a bitter enough pill to swallow, but the fact that these were real people with families who depended on their livelihood from rugby to pay mortgages brought the whole thing into sharper focus.

Anyway, Allan was calling us in one by one and simply saying either 'we want you' or 'we don't want you'. It was savage, but in fairness to Allan there was no other way. But that made it no easier to watch teammates walk through a door and come out again in total and utter dejection.

That day we all got together afterwards and went down to Porthcawl for a

drink. We knew it was the last time this Bridgend team would be together. That was it, the last day, and it had come and gone in the blink of an eye. It felt cold and heartless.

I don't blame Bridgend. It was the Welsh Rugby Union who had let it come to this. And while I'm not saying they took any pleasure out of it, the bottom line was that we found ourselves being herded together like cattle who were either going to be sent to the slaughterhouse or given a stay of execution. As I said, I was convinced that regional rugby was not going to work, and I also had grave doubts about the idea of this particular merger.

When Allan pulled me in, he said that the Warriors wanted me but that my contract was null and void because of the transition from Bridgend to the Warriors. Subsequently, I was free to go if I wanted to. I told him of my reservations and said, 'Sorry, Al, but I'm going to join Cardiff Blues.' I had sorted out a move back to what was my old club in all but name with their head coach and my former Cardiff and Wales teammate Dai Young. As far as I was concerned, I was on my way back to the Arms Park. Allan knew this anyway, because I had spoken to him about my approach from the Blues before, and he respected my decision, wishing me all the best. The contract with the Blues was for a lot less money than I could have been on at the Warriors, where the chairman Leighton Samuel was prepared to continue with

the terms of my old Bridgend contract, just under a new team name. But within an hour, something happened that changed everything.

I received a telephone call from Steve Hansen. He said, 'I'm coming down to see you.'

I said, 'Why? What's the matter?'

He replied, 'Well, I've just heard you're going to Cardiff.' We left it there, and I waited for him to arrive.

By that point, I was 100 per cent fixed in my mind about what I was going to do. But anyone who knows him will tell you that Steve has a way of talking you round, even if you think that you will never be for turning. Within 20 minutes of him speaking to me, I was back in Allan Lewis's office, telling him, 'I'm staying.'

Steve had worked his spell on me, saying that I should stick it out where I was. He didn't want too many of the Wales players concentrated in one region. Instead, he wanted a spread so as to ensure everybody got as much game time as possible. (Although if there was a big concentration of Wales players anywhere, it was surely at the Warriors.) In his overall plan for the regions, my part was not with Cardiff. He said, 'You're going to be captain down here, and this is where I want you to be.' And, like I said, Steve had a way of talking to you that was just so convincing. I told Allan I was sorry to mess him around, but he was happy with my U-turn, and I never even had to speak to Dai, because

Steve insisted on doing that for me, telling him my reasons, which he and the Blues accepted.

But the bitter irony turned out to be that after going through all this, the Warriors only lasted one season before being culled by the Welsh Rugby Union. As far as I was concerned, they had killed off the best squad out of the five, a squad that had it been allowed to continue would have gone on to become a major force at the very highest level of the European game.

Without doubt we had the strongest squad of all the Welsh regions with strength in every department. Among the backs, we had me and boys such as Neil Jenkins and Ceri Sweeney, the centre Sonny Parker, Gareth Cooper and Sililo Martens vying for the scrum-half role, and the ever-dangerous Gareth Wyatt on the wing. In the forwards, we had guys such as Gethin Jenkins, Robert Sidoli and Brent Cockbain, who would all go on to play pivotal roles in the Wales Grand Slam team of 2005. And despite the reservations I have already expressed about the merger of Bridgend and Pontypridd, there was one thing in its favour: if there were two sides with the same sort of spirit and sense of fun, it was those two.

The hardest thing for me in that first year of playing for the Warriors was that I didn't join up with the team until after the World Cup, which didn't finish for us until early November. It meant that

when I eventually went into training after a little period of rest, I literally didn't have a clue who some of my new teammates were – I didn't even know their names.

I first met up with everyone at the army camp in Sennybridge for a couple of days of training and team bonding. I found myself walking past players who would greet me with, 'All right, Gar?'

All I could say back was, 'All right, mate?' because I basically didn't have a clue who they were, and the fact that I am terrible with names didn't help my cause. I knew the situation couldn't go on. I had to find someone I did know from Ponty and ask them to put names to faces for me. It wasn't as if I expected people to know who I was, but it would have been ignorant on my part if I had started going up to individuals and saying, 'Hi, mate, I'm Alfie. Who the hell are you?' I wanted to find out who the lads were from someone else and then the next time I bumped into them in a corridor I could address them by their proper names and make out as if I had known them all my life. That's what I did, and I felt much more comfortable doing that, even if it did take me ages to learn all the names.

Adding to the great shame of our eventual break-up was the fact that we had a cracking little training set-up at the Pencoed Agricultural College just down the road from Bridgend. We had a decent full-size pitch on which to train, we had a lovely team room, a great little gym with weights and an area for basketball, and a common room, where we could relax and play a bit of pool. It really was a top environment to work in every day.

There is, however, one thing I do not miss from my Warriors days: the monthly saga surrounding how we were paid our salaries. Looking back, I'm sure that any one of us could have walked away from our contracts whenever we liked, because we were practically never paid on time, and when we did receive payment it was by the rather antiquated method of a cheque instead of the sum being paid directly into our accounts. The poor Warriors secretary used to have a hell of a time, because come pay day every month we'd be on to the poor girl saying, 'Where's our cheques, where's our cheques?' Invariably, they were not there.

And if you didn't pay your cheque into the bank on the day you received it, you ran the risk of not getting the funds cleared, because it seemed that only a certain amount was put into the account from which the wages were drawn, and a lot of time it seemed that it wasn't enough to cover everybody. A typical scenario would see us issued with our cheques on say the fifth of the month, when we were supposed to be paid on the first, and then it would be like something out of *Wacky Races* with us all jumping into our cars to get to the bank for fear that if we were among the last three or four to pay the cheque in it would bounce.

We would then all burst through the doors of the bank, trying to win the race to the next available cashier. It was farcical.

One of my cheques did bounce once, and it just meant that I had to go cap in hand to Leighton and ask for another cheque. When this happened, he would usually say that it was because he had not received what the Warriors were due from the WRU.

On pay day, if I was training, I would get Jemma to ring the secretary and ask if the cheques were ready. If they were, she would have to leave work in her lunch hour, drive to the college, pick up the cheque and take it to the bank.

As funny as this may sound, there was a serious side to it, because a lot of the boys found that the funds were not there to cover their mortgage payments coming out of their accounts, so they fell behind. Jemma and I found ourselves having to take out a £5,000 overdraft to cover us in case the cheque was late, which, in all seriousness, just wasn't good enough. Our mortgage payment came out on the first of each month, which meant that even if we were paid as we should have been on the first we would then have to wait the four days it took for the cheque to clear. Sometimes, it was getting on for the middle of the month before our money was in our accounts ready to be used, and it got more common as time went on.

• • •

The coaching partnership at the Warriors – Lynn Howells and Allan Lewis – was a match made in heaven as far as I was concerned. As a duo, they complemented each other perfectly. Lynn was as passionate a coach as I have ever known, and Allan was the epitome of control and calculating calm. It was great. We needed a shouter and a bawler as well as an analyser, and in these two we had that mix.

Lynn and Allan had the most difficult coaching job in Welsh rugby at the time; in fact, I would doubt there has ever been a tougher task with a more peculiar set of demands. Lynn and Allan first had to pick 50 per cent of players from two teams, not just on the basis of ability but on personality as well. If it came down to a shoot-out between two players and it was felt that one would have trouble buying into the Warriors concept, even if he maybe shaded it in terms of ability, that was definitely taken into account.

Anyway, they must have done a good job, because although we didn't win any silverware, we did enough in our one and only season to suggest that we had the makings of a great side – and being the only team to beat Wasps in the Heineken Cup in the year that they went on to win it, beating Toulouse in the final at Twickenham, said it all.

We went up to High Wycombe on a dreadful day with it pouring with rain and beat them 14–9, scoring the only try of the game in the second half. We had laid down a marker of what we might

We proved what the Warriors were capable of by beating Wasps away in the Heineken Cup.

be capable of by pushing Perpignan all the way at their feared Stade Aimé Giral ground earlier in the pool stages, before only going down 26–19, and that was when it really began to click together for us. Up until then, we had been so disrupted by the World Cup that it had taken us four games or so to get properly into our stride.

I recall our first game in the Heineken Cup that year was against Calvisano at Bridgend, and we were terrible, even though we gained a 34–25 bonus-point win. Then came the Perpignan game followed by the classic at Wasps. That win meant we got a full house for the return game against the English side at the Brewery Field a week later, and to see 10,000 or so people crammed into the old ground again meant a hell of a lot to me in particular.

It was just a shame that we went down 17–12 to Wasps on a night when, to be fair to them, they came and did a bit of a number on us, showing great mental strength to shut out our crowd and keep their shape and discipline in a match they knew they had to win to stay in the competition. But the evening was far from a disgrace for us, and we showed our mettle by bouncing back in the next match at home to Perpignan,

whom we edged out 16–15, meaning that we went into the last weekend with an outside chance of qualifying for the quarter-finals if we beat Calvisano away and other results went our way.

We kept our part of the bargain by claiming a 28–26 bonus-point success in Italy, but elsewhere the gods were not with us. The hard thing to swallow was that Edinburgh went through instead of us, going on to play Toulouse in the last eight, and I was convinced we were a far better team than the Scots.

So, there was to be no glory for us, but the more relevant point for me was that here was a team that, in their first season together and with only a handful of games under their belt, could go to a place like Wasps and win. You would have had to be blind not to believe that the Warriors could go on to become brilliant – but in the final analysis it was to count for nothing.

The break-up of the Celtic Warriors has to be the shabbiest rugby episode I have ever had the misfortune to be involved in. I was luckier than the rest of the lads, because by the time it came down to the nitty-gritty I had already secured my move to Toulouse. But that didn't mean I wasn't affected by it all. I was – deeply. And as captain, I did all I could to help my teammates at the height of what was an extraordinary turn of events.

I had been through it all once before when the Warriors had been formed, having to watch teammates reduced to devastation at being told to sling their hooks. Now it was happening again, only this time it was not because of a merger but because the axe was coming down on the team altogether. We were being killed off because the Welsh Rugby Union no longer deemed the region financially viable and wanted to reduce to four teams, the number most people wanted in the first place and would have got had it not been for the wrangling over Cardiff and Llanelli standing alone.

I'm not going to try to mount an argument on the basis of economics or politics. I'm not qualified to do that and never will be. But I am qualified to speak about the total devastation our break-up had on players who at the very least saw a season of their careers just ripped up, thrown in the bin and rendered meaningless. But, of course, it was more serious than that. We were now back into the territory of livelihoods, paying mortgages and the ability to put food on the table for families.

In the end, as I understood it all, it boiled down to Leighton Samuel selling his share of the region back to the WRU, which then saw fit to liquidate us. Leighton always argued that the sale had gone through only on the condition that the Warriors would not be scrapped, and that particular bone of contention became the subject of legal proceedings. I can only say that Leighton told us about this condition from the outset and in numerous team meetings throughout the whole saga, and, on reflection, I do

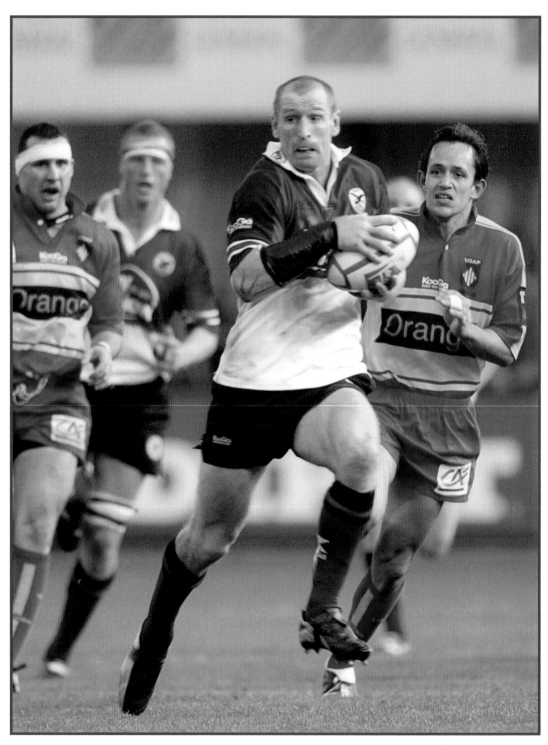

On the charge for the Warriors against Perpignan.

not disbelieve him. I was unsure at the time, but now my personal belief is that he was telling us the truth.

After agreeing my move to Toulouse, I recall that Leighton asked me to promise to go back to the Warriors if it did not work out. He also wanted a £100,000-compensation payment from Toulouse and a game against the French side from which the Warriors would collect the gate receipts. Why would he bother asking for these things, I have since asked myself, if he was set on selling to the WRU? Or maybe he thought differently on the day we met, because he seemed to change his mind on the issue fairly regularly.

I can remember that the first time we were aware that anything whatsoever was going on was when we were called to a meeting with the WRU general manager Steve Lewis and the union's solicitors. We were simply told that the WRU had taken over the Warriors, but that we would just be carrying on as normal.

Then, soon afterwards, and completely out of the blue, we were told by the WRU that we were being closed down. Naturally, we immediately turned to Leighton for answers, and he insisted to us that there was no way this could happen, because the WRU had given him written assurances that the Warriors would be kept going. But we had been told by the union that we were owned by them and that from the following

day the Warriors would no longer be in existence. It was in a meeting with the WRU's solicitor up at the indoor barn at the Vale of Glamorgan Hotel that we found out our final fate. 'As of 12 noon tomorrow, Celtic Warriors will cease to trade,' was the most significant sentence to come from his mouth.

Straight away, the boys had a million and one questions. But there was also a complete numbness in the room. It was not something that you ever expect to happen to you if you are a professional rugby player. Factory and office workers have to contend with their companies going bust, but surely not rugby players?

There was utter shock, especially for the ones who had been through it already at Bridgend and Pontypridd. 'How can this be happening again?' we asked ourselves. I felt a bit differently, because my future was mapped out with a move to France, but I hope the boys remember that I stood full-square behind them when the crap was flying.

What really annoyed me was the cattle auction that had gone on behind the players' backs among Wales's other regions as soon as it became apparent that the Warriors were in their death throes. It seemed like every other person involved in the Welsh game knew what was going on apart from us. Players were divvied out among the four surviving sides with a bit of haggling here and there over selected individuals. The other four regions had been told what everyone was

earning. Once the teams had agreed who was going where, the Warriors players were stuffed, not being in a fair position to negotiate their contracts. Lads went in to see Steve Lewis one by one and were told, for instance, that Llanelli Scarlets wanted them and were willing to pay X amount a year. From then on, there was no good them going to the Blues, Dragons or Ospreys looking for improved terms, because the other teams were all under instructions not to better what the Scarlets were offering in exchange for reciprocal treatment with other players. The whole thing stank to high heaven, to tell you the truth – the players were completely over a barrel, their rights stripped away from them.

On the day this happened, I made sure that I stayed around until the last person left, for moral support if nothing else. A lot of the boys, the Wales hooker Mefin Davies being one, were told quite simply that nobody wanted them and that there was no prospect of their contracts being paid off, because the Warriors had 'ceased trading'. It made me sick, and even if the Toulouse move had not been arranged I for one would not have played for any of the other regions under those circumstances. No, I would have found myself a contract in England or even Ireland before doing that, because at that point Welsh rugby had broken me. The way the other regions had clubbed together to take away the players' bargaining power enraged me more than anything.

If Steve Lewis had called me in that day and said Cardiff Blues were offering me £80,000 a year to play for them, I would have looked him in the eye and said, 'Tell Cardiff Blues, the Scarlets, the Dragons and the Ospreys to stick it up their arses. I'm off to play in England.' The players had been reduced to pieces of meat, with people talking about us and our prices as if we had no say at all in our futures. And the players were kept in the dark most of all. We had to pick up the newspapers to read about what was going on, and the Warriors boys were being sent from Leighton Samuel's Décor Frame factory to the WRU delegations at the Vale of Glamorgan Hotel to be told different things every time.

I also felt for the coaches Lynn and Allan, not just the players. I remember Allan saying at one meeting that if the players had to go through all of this then let them, but why could we not keep the Warriors as a development side that could be built up from scratch with a new influx of up-and-coming youngsters. The bottom line, he argued, was that top-flight rugby could not be allowed to be lost to the Bridgend, Pontypridd and Valleys areas. But his wise words fell on deaf ears, and what we are left with now is a great Brewery Field ground, extensively redeveloped by Leighton, reduced to a white elephant.

I can't speak for Pontypridd and the Valleys, but to me Bridgend is like a ghost town without the top-flight rugby

there. It is like somebody has ripped the soul out of the place. In Ponty, it must feel the same. I remember some of the great Heineken Cup nights they had at Sardis Road when the likes of Brive, Bath and Leicester were all beaten. Now there is nothing. It's all gone – it's history.

As for Bridgend, although we never got really big crowds on a regular basis, a town like that with such rugby tradition not having a proper rugby team to follow is just plain wrong in my opinion. Bridgend has now been placed under the umbrella of the Ospreys region. Does that mean that former Bridgend fans are supposed to immediately start following the Ospreys? My team now, the Blues, have faced a similar battle in the Valleys and Pontypridd, which now fall under their umbrella.

Both regions are trying to spread their appeal, and if you put the question to them, I'm sure they would come back quoting all the successful schemes they have started in those areas. But there is surely still a long way to go. You are talking about trying to convert people, mind, body and soul, and it's tremendously difficult. When I played for Cardiff up at Ponty, they hated us with a fervency I have rarely experienced elsewhere. There will always be plenty of their followers who wouldn't follow the Blues if they were the last rugby team on earth.

Looking back, I will always take pride in what we had at the Warriors, as short-lived as it ultimately turned out to be. It gladdens my heart to recall not just what we achieved on the pitch, but that we were a trusting and tight-knit unit off it as well. We went through so much in such a short space of time, and although the team looked good on paper, I believe we had the potential to be even better on the field. I reckon it would only have taken three or four top-quality signings that summer and we would have gone on to pull up a few major trees in the Heineken Cup the following year.

But others decreed that it wasn't to be. We had no choice but to accept it and move on. And there came a time when I had to focus my mind on what was going to be without a doubt the biggest challenge of my career and probably of my entire life. Toulouse, the Real Madrid of European rugby, had come calling. I was leaving for a new life in France.

8

TOULOUSE

During the 2004 Six Nations, at which time the Warriors were still very much in existence, I began to receive text messages from an agent called Peter Underhill. He had got my number off Colin Charvis, whom he represented. Basically, he was telling me that he needed to meet with me because there was a club 'interested' in me. As we were in the midst of a Six Nations campaign and I had so much to think about already, I didn't even respond to the messages at first. The agent was also speaking to the Wales centre Mark Taylor at the time about a club that was supposedly interested in him, and when I eventually spoke to Underhill he would only confirm that a club was interested in me and the money was great – but that he couldn't say who the club was.

A little while later, I agreed to meet him at a hotel near Bridgend, but it took me ages to find out just who the club was. Then one day he blurted out that it was Toulouse. Of course, I raised my eyebrows when he told me, but it wasn't as if I was already having visions of sunbathing by the pool at some villa in the south of France. Far from it, in fact.

In the life of a rugby player, there are numerous occasions when you hear of interest from other clubs, and most of the time you have to be realistic enough to accept that it's likely to go no further than rumour, or at the most a preliminary discussion. To me, 'interest' could have meant anything, and I had no idea just how firm this Toulouse 'interest' was.

My gut instinct was to be scared. I realised it could potentially be a great opportunity and decided to play along with Underhill for the time being, but deep down a part of me was already hoping that the move didn't come off. My biggest fear was that it would inevitably mean leaving Wales, and I wasn't sure if I would be able to handle that. I told Underhill to carry on with his negotiations and to go back to Toulouse

with the message that I was very much interested and that I wanted to know more about the deal. Gradually, we got further and further down the road towards actually agreeing a contract when specific terms started to be put on the table, and I soon started to worry that it was actually going to happen! I say worry because as you will recall from earlier chapters I have always been wary of being removed from my comfort zone, which was what Welsh rugby had become for me.

The crunch day came when I went to see Allan Lewis. I didn't want to mess him around in any way, and I didn't want to piss about with agents. I wanted him to hear what I had to say about the matter face-to-face. 'Look, Al. Toulouse have come in with an offer for me to go and play there,' I said to him.

I could immediately see that he was genuinely happy for me. He said, 'As coach of this team, I obviously want you to stay, but this is not just a career opportunity, it is a life opportunity, and you cannot turn away from it. On that basis, I would love you to go.' It was typical of Allan to see it like that, and those words coming from a guy I respected so much gave me a new resolve to indeed push ahead and go for it.

The next day, Peter Underhill went to see Leighton Samuel, Allan Lewis and the former Bridgend chairman and then Warriors board member Derek King – whose view on the matter was the same as Allan's – while I sat waiting in the car park of Leighton's factory in Bridgend. Leighton, it seemed, was the only one we would have to convince, and Allan assured me that he would be telling him that there was no way they could block the move, even though he did not want me to go from a playing point of view.

After about half an hour or so, Derek came down and walked across to the car. I could see from the smile on his face that everything had gone OK, and he asked me to go up to the meeting. I walked into the room, and Leighton said that if Toulouse agreed to a £100,000-compensation payment as well as a friendly game from which the Warriors could collect the gate receipts, I was free to go.

Then I really started quaking in my boots, because that was the moment I knew it was happening. Things had moved to the point that it was really out of my hands – there was no going back. Yet even then, I still thought that something might happen that would put the mockers on the whole thing. It seemed that might actually happen when the WRU threatened to scupper the deal because they had not received the £100,000 they said was now due to them because they had taken ownership of the region before killing it off. Thankfully, the matter didn't stand in my way, and I eventually signed for Toulouse at the Wales team headquarters at the Vale of Glamorgan Hotel in June 2004, but not without a last-minute piece of drama that bordered on the farcical.

I was playing for Wales against the Barbarians in Bristol and had been due to sign for Toulouse before the game. But the French delegation's flight was delayed, and so I went into the match still having not signed.

Anyway, the one thing I didn't want to happen to me happened – I got injured. Thankfully, it turned out not to be serious, but it gave me one hell of a scare and looked dreadful to the Toulouse people who arrived five minutes into the match to be greeted by the sight of me being stretchered off. And to think that one of the reasons they signed me in the first place was because they had loads of injuries at the club! As it turned out, I had done nothing more than turn my ankle badly, but because I had heard a crack when I did it, I was frantic with worry while I was on the stretcher that I had done something really nasty that was going to keep me out for months.

I sat in the changing-room and called Jemma almost immediately to tell her that I didn't think it was too serious. Next, I took a telephone call from an agent who was with Jean-Marie Rancoule, Toulouse's general manager. 'Jean-Marie is flapping like hell,' he said. 'We've just arrived in the ground to see you being carried off!' I told him to meet me back at the Vale of Glamorgan Hotel that night and that we would take it from there.

When Jean-Marie turned up, I told him straight away that there was no real problem. 'I need to hear that from your doctor,' he said with a somewhat suspicious tone in his voice. So I dived into a room with our team physio Mark Davies and said, 'Look, butt. Whatever you do, tell him I'm all right!'

So Mark went out and said, 'He's fine. It's just a little thing with his ankle.' He also gave the thumbs up to get over any language barrier. That appeared to be enough to satisfy Jean-Marie, and everything was rosy. I signed the contract at the Vale in front of the media the next morning, and that was that.

Even though there was the spat over the £100,000 still lurking in the background, I was made up to have finally got the deal done. And, to be honest, because of the mood I was in at the time, I just wanted out of Wales. I was still bitter at the way my former teammates had been treated during the Warriors saga and wanted to make a clean break of it. I was also upset that the WRU appeared to be prepared to jeopardise such a huge opportunity for me in order to recoup £100,000, a relatively little sum that was hardly a matter of life and death to such an organisation, even if they did have money worries. It was a wrangle that went on for many more months but eventually fizzled out, although, to this day, I'm not exactly sure how. I'm certainly not aware that Toulouse paid the money, and if I'm honest, the fact that they didn't at first took pressure off my shoulders in the early days.

While I was gutted that the Warriors were no longer in existence, the fact

that Toulouse did not have to fork out a substantial sum to buy out my contract gladdened me immensely. At the time, there were all kinds of daft figures being quoted in the Welsh and French media about what I was supposedly going to be earning. One Toulouse newspaper reckoned I was to be paid 500,000 euros a year (around £350,000), which was just plainly ridiculous. But the fact that there appeared to be so much interest in my salary meant that I was relieved not to have people thinking any more money had to be shelled out on me. It was tough enough for me to be going there in the first place without that kind of millstone hanging around my neck.

Before actually signing, I obviously had to get myself over to France to check the place out and ensure that it was an environment I was going to like. The first time I went over to Toulouse was Easter weekend 2004 when the club was playing Edinburgh in the Heineken Cup. I travelled with Shane Williams, who was attracting interest from Castres, and we went very much on the understanding that we should not be seen out there together. The last thing anyone wanted was it getting into the press, particularly as there was a glut of stories appearing about a so-called exodus of top Wales players to French rugby at that time.

After touching down, Shane and I went our separate ways – him with the fellow from Castres and me with René Bouscatel, the chief executive of

Toulouse who wanted to meet me on one-to-one terms. But as for me and Shane going on some secret mission, well, let's just say MI5 won't be tracking us down for our services.

That evening René took me out for a meal. As we took our tables in a restaurant in the centre of Toulouse, who should be sitting three tables down from us? Yes, Shane and his Castres pal! Everybody in the entire restaurant knew what was going on, and by last orders half the city was probably in on it.

For Shane, things had not panned out, and it was already clear that he would be staying in Wales. For me, it was different. I liked everything I heard from René and was over there again a couple of weeks later when Jemma and I met up with him and Guy Novès, the coach who is like the godfather of the club. Not only that, but I also met some of the players for the first time, and Jemma and I were generally treated like royalty. We were put up in a top hotel and given everything we could want – nothing was too much trouble. It was a case of 'Where do you want to go?' and 'What do you want to eat?'

I had still not signed at that point, and even after I had put pen to paper at the Vale there was still something holding me back from actually packing my bags and making the break. We only got on the plane in the end because Jemma was pushing. If it had been left to me, we would have waited until we got a phone call from Toulouse asking where I was.

It was around about the third week in July before we actually went, by which time we had sent over most of our furniture. I remember walking around our house in the village of St Brides Major in the Vale of Glamorgan on the day we left, for some reason thinking that it would be the last time I saw the place again. It didn't register that in a matter of a few short months I would be back because of Wales commitments. I went around all the rooms, looking in every corner, walking around the garden and getting what I thought were final pictures embedded in my mind so that I would never forget what the place looked like.

When we got to France, we had a house already arranged, and we went straight there after one night in a hotel. However, the first few weeks of my time there were not what would be normal in the future. I had been told by the Irish second row Trevor Brennan, who would go on to become one of my closest friends in the game during my time in France, that there was little point going over at that time of the year because there was hardly anyone at the club due to it being the holiday season. We went all the same, and, if I'm honest, it suited me that there was nobody about during those very first few weeks. I went down to the club every morning with a sense of relief that I would be on my own. In a way, it was precisely the wrong way to feel, because if I was going to spend the next three years of my life there,

it obviously would have been better to meet my new teammates as soon as possible and throw myself into getting to know everybody. But it was easier to hide away for as long as I could get away with it.

Every time a door opened or I heard a bit of movement when I was down at the club gym, the first thought that would enter my head was, 'Oh no, it's a player. I'm going to have to meet someone. What will I say? What will I do?'

The first player I did meet face-to-face after moving over permanently was Xavier Garbajosa, which was lucky because he spoke the best English of all the Toulouse players. He was brilliant. 'Welcome, welcome. Is everything OK?' he said, beaming at me before we started to talk about all things rugby.

Xavier was recovering from an injury and so needed to put in some work during the off-season. Once I discovered that he came in at around 9 a.m. every day, I began to make sure I went in earlier or later, just to avoid seeing him. Daft, isn't it? I just didn't feel comfortable in his company, and it would have been the same had he been any member of the Toulouse squad.

Gradually, I started meeting other players in the gym or at the track. They were all as nice as pie to me and very polite, but I just wasn't happy being around them, and it wasn't because of the language barrier. The way I saw it, the longer I could be on my own, the longer the move to Toulouse would

remain, in a way, unreal. On my own, I could pretend I was still in Wales, back in my comfort zone. Also, training had not really started, and I had it in my mind that when I eventually had to meet the players I would rather meet them all at once. That way I would not have to be in a one-on-one situation. I would be able to go around the changing-room, say hello to everyone and have done with it. I wouldn't have to say hello and then stick around and make conversation.

It also took me a little while to master the route home from the stadium. The first time I headed to the Stade Ernest-Wallon, I got there no problem – getting back to my house was where I came unstuck. I took the route I thought was correct, but before long something didn't seem right, and I frantically rang home to see if Jemma could get me out of the mess I was in. 'Where are you? What do the signs say?' she asked, barely having got any bearings herself since the move.

'I'm not being funny, but I'm on my way to Paris,' I replied in desperation. And I was as well. I was in a dedicated lane for the French capital and feared I would have to go at least a couple of hundred kilometres north before I got the chance to turn around. I was lost and scared on a motorway with hundreds of mad French drivers who were in no mood to make any allowances for a Welshman disorientated in a foreign country and dithering about behind the

wheel. Thankfully, there was a chap at the house fitting our television, and he was able to guide me back to the gate of our driveway before I caught sight of the Eiffel Tower!

When the day finally came and the whole squad came back for the first day of pre-season training, I was like a kid on his first day at a new school and nervous as hell. Trevor came in with me and introduced me in French, which made it a bit easier, and the fact that everyone knew I was coming anyway took the sting out of the situation a little. But what I didn't realise is that in France when you walk into a room of people, the polite and expected thing is that you walk around and shake hands with every individual by way of greeting them. Instead, I just walked up to my locker and sat down. I then had the entire squad come across to me to shake my hand; fortunately, I think they figured out that I didn't know the custom.

Having thought about the custom and seen it done so many times, I now have complete respect for it. In Wales, we tend to just walk into a room full of friends or colleagues, shout out a quick 'Hello everyone' and that's it. When you stop and think about it, that's not much of a greeting, really, is it? To go around and shake hands carries far more meaning. It's much more personal, and it shows much more effort on your part. In my view, there is a lot to be said for it.

Then, of course, if a bloke is introduced to a woman in France, he is expected to kiss her. Because I got used to doing that, I have found myself continuing to do it when I am back in Wales at times, where some women are aghast to be kissed by somebody they have only just met. But, as I say, it's just a difference in culture. What is regarded as the norm in France is sometimes considered very unusual in the UK.

Within about half an hour of us being on the training ground on the first morning, the Toulouse guys were taking the mickey out of me, and it felt brilliant to be getting in amongst my new teammates. It was still the height of summer and was absolutely roasting hot, and we were running up and down the field passing and going through set moves. Well, as you can imagine, I didn't have a clue what was going on, so I just started running all over the place, hardly ever getting the ball. But what was amusing the Toulouse lads more than anything else was that my delicate fair Welsh skin was slowly starting to get redder and redder under the heat of a baking south of France sun. What's more, the only shade on the pitch was next to a tackle bag beneath the posts, which meant that every time there was a break in the action I would make for this bag and cower in the tiny piece of shade it afforded me. All the other boys were there with their tops off, sporting deep

golden French tans and laughing at the poor Welsh boy who didn't even have sunscreen on.

It was the last time I made that mistake. The next day I was plastered in factor 30 and also wore a baseball hat to protect my exposed scalp, even though it fell off a couple of times when we were doing tackling! Rather than laughing with me, the boys had been laughing at me, but I didn't mind that because it meant I was slowly starting to break into the team spirit and slowly starting to find my niche in the squad.

But it wasn't long before something they were doing started to piss me off a little. Because my name was obviously unusual to them, they began calling me 'Garat', which was just the way they pronounced Gareth. One day I told them straight, in a jokey type of way, to either call me Gareth and say it as it would be said in Wales or call me nothing at all. The outcome? They decided to call me 'Chariot', which I was chuffed about at first, because I thought it was due to my long bounding legs or my speed hurtling down the wing. On top of that, they kept holding out their arms in front of them when they said it, and I thought they were alluding to a Roman gladiator riding his chariot. 'Yes, I like that,' I said. 'You can call me Chariot. Brilliant!' They laughed like hell, and for months afterwards called me Chariot. I soon discovered I had got the wrong end of the stick completely.

Running out for my first game for Toulouse.

One day, when one of the boys called me by my nickname, I decided to ask him what they actually meant by it. I then found out that 'chariot' in French meant shopping trolley. For months on end, I had been going around proud as punch to be called a shopping trolley! To this day, I don't know why they saw fit to call me that, but I do know that it was their way of taking the mickey. They finally got round to calling me Alfie, which I obviously would have preferred from day one. But fair play to the Toulouse lads – they really made a big effort with me and tried their hardest to make me feel part of things so that I could settle in as quickly as possible.

It was still tough, though. And the language barrier played a big part in that, because it meant there were many times when I found myself in my own little bubble, and there was nothing I could do to break out of it. Don't get me wrong, the lads were as helpful as anyone could have expected them to be, and I did become much better with the language. It got to the stage that I could understand just about everything that was being said. But understanding what is being said and being able to join in a normal conversation in French are two entirely different things.

I'll give you an example of the difficulties I had. Some mornings, the

137

boys liked to arrive early and have a coffee and a good chat before training started. A lot of the time, I was just left sitting there in my own little world, not part of the conversation. And I knew that I could not become a part of it, because then it would all have to go at my pace and would cease to be, in effect, a proper conversation.

I found that terribly difficult to deal with. The social side of rugby is a big, big thing to me. I love talking and joking with teammates – always have done, always will do. So, to be in a position in which I could not do something that I have taken for granted my whole career was just so tough to handle.

There were other times I felt totally cut off. Say, for instance, we had an away game and Trevor Brennan wasn't playing. Well, the only other native English-speakers in the squad were the Kiwi Maka brothers, Isitolo and Finau, and they barely spoke to one another let alone anyone else. Subsequently, I often found myself on the bus with my headphones on in my own little world. Every now and again, one of the boys would come up to me and start talking in French. I appreciated the effort to try and involve me, but there were also times when I just couldn't be bothered to make the effort myself. And that is just not natural for me.

I found the hardest part of the whole Toulouse package the language, and it didn't help that I had to come back and forth to Wales all the time. That just meant that every time I then went back to France I found myself almost having to start over again with the language. I did go to a tutor, who was brilliant, but there were times when I just couldn't see her. In the winter, for example, no sooner had I finished going back and forth to Wales for the autumn internationals and Christmas than the Six Nations was upon us, which was yet another period that took me away from it all.

The sheer intensity of being a professional rugby player in France was another tough element of life in that country. For the rest of my days, I will have the utmost respect for French players and the way they get through their careers. The French Championship is so incredibly intense, physically and mentally. The sides go at each other hammer and tongs in every game, and the matches just roll on thick and fast.

I remember going to a Wales squad meeting early in 2006. The Llanelli Scarlets players had just beaten Bath in the semi-final of the Powergen Cup and then faced a Test match against Italy the week after. The Scarlets boys were all commenting on how getting themselves up physically for an international was a struggle, having just played such an intense game against an English club side. The aches and pains were worse than normal, they said, and were taking longer than usual to go away. Well, I'm not trying to make myself out to be some kind of superhero, but that's the situation

I faced every week of the year playing for Toulouse. Not only that, there were numerous times when I had to play in a white-hot French Championship match for Toulouse against, say, Biarritz and then board a plane back to Wales for a Test match six or seven days later. And all the travelling involved barely made it any easier.

It's not just the matches in France that are difficult, it's the training, too. On Mondays, we would do weights followed by a flat-out fitness session. On Tuesdays, it would be the full monty: backs on backs, smashing the living daylights out of each another, completely no holds barred. Wednesdays were a day from hell, because you would do team-on-team preparation for two hours in the morning and maybe an hour in the afternoon. We wound down a little bit on Thursdays and Fridays with the game approaching, but they were still intense.

The French philosophy is that training is a means of preparing for games, so you should train as you play. In other words, you hold nothing back, not even 1 per cent. In a way, I have been converted to the philosophy and agree with the principle, because you can set up a situation and go through it in a fake kind of way and think you are prepared to deal with it in a match situation, but that is not the case. It is never going to be as plastic as that in a game, so it doesn't mean anything.

As a result, the boys went down like flies some weeks in training. In fact, there were days when the field resembled a scene from the film *Platoon*. But there was no way that Guy Novès would change anything.

Some days, the first team had sessions against the Toulouse second team. They were just youngsters but keen as mustard, and there was no pussyfooting around with them whatsoever. They were all out to make a name for themselves. And if you made a mistake in training, it was sometimes worse than making a mistake in a match. Guy Novès thought nothing of stopping a session when he spotted a blunder and ripping shreds out of you in front of everyone. He would say something like, 'These are only youngsters. What do you think you are doing? You are an international rugby player!' Thankfully, he never did that to me, probably because he knew I wouldn't understand a word he said!

Everybody respects Guy Novès at Toulouse. There's just something about him. If you get to know him, you have to respect him. He is one of those people who just exudes an air of authority. Some people have that look about them. I don't know – it's something in their eyes. I knew I would never question him – nobody would. Whatever the X-factor that all coaches need is, Guy Novès has got it in spades.

If there was one person who was the difference between me getting through the Toulouse experience and preventing

me from going home early with my tail between my legs, it was Trevor Brennan. Trevor and I hit it off as soon as we met up. I think we both realised very quickly that we were the same type of bloke and thought the same way on most things. The fact that he spoke English was obviously a factor, but our friendship ran far deeper than that. Our two families got to know each other extremely well, because we were always in each other's houses for meals, drinks, etc. Trevor became like a kindred spirit to me and was always a shoulder to cry on in tough times.

He knew I had a bit of a reputation for liking a drink when I arrived in France, and one of the first things he suggested was that we both hit a couple of bars in the town and sample a pitcher or two of the local brew. I had been there eight weeks by that time. The weather had been boiling hot, and I had done nothing other than train with barely a drop of alcohol passing my lips. On top of that, my 30th birthday was approaching, so what better way to celebrate than downing a few jars in the town which had become my home for the time being?

Trevor took me out, and in keeping with the very best Welsh and Irish rugby relations we began to bolt jugs of strong lager like there was no tomorrow. We were even starting to drink out of the jugs themselves as the alcohol took effect. A short while later, after swapping shirts with the barman, I stumbled out of the pub, unbeknown to Trevor, who

began to ring my phone over and over again, worried about where I had got to. I was oblivious to the ringing by that stage, but I did manage to dial Jemma at 4 a.m., even though she had told me that she was going to have a drink at home with her parents, who were visiting that evening, so I would have to get a taxi. 'Can you pick me up?' I slurred down the line to her.

'Where are you?' she asked.

'Pont St Pierre,' I told her – a bridge in the centre of the town near to the bar Trevor and I had all but drunk dry.

As Jemma approached the bridge in the car about 20 minutes later, I was lying on a ledge just off the road in a black 'Pub St Pierre' T-shirt. I staggered into the car and hung my head out of the window all the way home, as Jemma drove through some of the narrowest streets in the old town. It was a wonder I wasn't decapitated before we reached the house.

Of course, we didn't make a habit of such antics. In any case, the socialising culture in France is completely different from Wales. It's more sedate and not about gangs of lads going out and throwing beer down their necks until they can barely stand and then having curry and chips on the way home. Trevor and I both made an effort to go out with the other Toulouse players for meals, etc., which were always enjoyable.

But that night was in many ways typical of the rapport Trevor and I had with one

another. We constantly had fun together. We were always having a laugh and a joke, and he was really the only person at the club I would take the mickey out of. That was largely because I saw that the repercussions could be pretty severe, to say the least, when you messed with the other boys. Almost on a par, actually, with some of the shenanigans that went on during my early days with Bridgend.

Trevor, for example, once played a trick of some sort on the fly-half Freddie Michalak. The consequences were not pleasant – a few days later, he found a bag in his locker containing something that should be deposited down a toilet! But that was mild compared with the revenge Michalak served on Xavier Garbajosa, hooker Yannick Bru and centre Yannick Jauzion after they once conspired to leave the same deposit in his kit bag. Now, Freddie's dad is a builder, so later in the week he went out with his old man's tools and materials under the cover of darkness and built a five-foot wall right outside the front door of Garbajosa's house, and I'm talking proper bricks and mortar. He then progressed to the residence of Bru, who is nicknamed Gobi. Bru had just had the entire outside of his house painted, and Michalak took great delight in daubing 'Gobi' in enormous letters across the front of the building. Next, it was on to Jauzion's place, where Freddie jacked up the centre's car, pinched the wheels and left it suspended on bricks at the side of the street. So, you can

understand why I steered clear of any funny stuff when it came to these guys, Freddie especially.

Trevor and I were always together. If someone was looking for Trevor, they were also looking for me, even though we had trouble understanding each other's accents at first. I can't emphasise it enough: Trevor was a saviour for me in Toulouse and the reason I lasted there three seasons. I am sure I would have left at various points had it not been for him, because I was down on many occasions.

I have never said this publicly before, because I have always wanted people to think I was the type of person who would stick something out, but there were plenty of occasions when I was ready to get on the plane and go back to Wales for good. In fact, I really struggled in my first season over in France. It was just a completely different way of playing rugby, and I felt on many occasions that the lads were deliberately not passing me the ball because they didn't think I was any good. I would go through some games without touching the ball, without getting a decent pass, and it got me down. I was always the one who seemed to be the dummy runner, the one who would end up not getting the ball in his hands, and so I thought that nobody rated me.

This was at its worst in the first half of the first season, and it didn't help that I was quite often not making the team, having to be content with a place

My new Toulouse teammates decided to inflict this haircut on me.
I doubt it will catch on!

on the bench. At that early stage, it was lost on me that you simply cannot expect to make the starting line-up week in, week out in France, because the domestic programme is just so intense. As far as I was concerned, if I wasn't in the starting XV, it was because I wasn't good enough, and that pissed me off, because I am from the Welsh culture in which the traditional thinking, especially before the days of big regional squads, was very much that you play your best team every week. People would say to me, 'That's just the way things are out here,' but it took a while for it to sink in.

There was a time, about three months into my first season, that I was dreadfully down about everything and must have been miserable as sin to live with. To be fair, Jemma reminded me that I could just give it up as a bad job and go home if I wanted to. But there was never a moment when I was prepared to actually go ahead and do that, even though the thought did cross my mind. No matter how bad it got – and things thankfully ended up getting better – I would never have gone home before completing one season. There was no other way of properly finding out what it was like to play in France. And I knew that I might have to go through some bad times to get to the good ones. I knew it wasn't going to be a total bed of roses from start to finish. I also knew that one year was the minimum length of time I had to spend in France for me to be happy

with myself, and if it was going to prove to be a painful and character-building period, then so be it.

The other thing that used to niggle away at me was the sheer number of class youngsters that were at the club, guys who were in the second team but who were so silky, skilful, fast and athletic when you faced them in training that I was certain that they would be considered better than me in a few months, and I would be out on my arse. It wasn't so much an inferiority complex, but it is jolting to see the depth of quality that they have ready to come through the ranks at an institution like Toulouse. Again, it took me a little while to accept that is just the way it is.

It wasn't until the second season that I truly began to find my feet a bit more and accept the way things were done at the club. By that time, I had a Heineken Cup-winner's medal in my locker – only the eighth Welshman ever to get his hands on one – though I had also come round to the French way of thinking that the domestic championship meant so much more. Yes, there's no doubt about it, although everyone in Wales sees the Heineken Cup as the premier competition, it's not at all like that in France. The reason is largely because French rugby considers itself to be vastly superior to that in any other country, so to win the French championship is seen as the ultimate test, something that

demands you beat the best collection of teams in the world on a consistent basis over the course of a long season that runs from August through to the following June. The Heineken Cup, on the other hand, is seen as more luck of the draw, a tournament in which you might only play against two French teams in the entire programme. Therefore, it is not seen as such a test, despite the fact that English, Welsh, Irish, Italian and Scottish sides are involved.

When we won the Heineken Cup by beating Stade Français 18–12 after extra time in an unbelievably tense final at Murrayfield in 2005, it was, don't get me wrong, an awesome feeling. It was still seen as a huge achievement in Toulouse. The town square was packed as the game played on a big screen, and there was utter jubilation when we came through. I missed out on a great homecoming for the team the following day because I had to be in Cardiff, where the British Lions were playing a warm-up Test against Argentina. The team paraded on a bus to packed streets in the centre of the town, and I was gutted not to be involved.

But none of what I missed lessened the feeling of elation that I had. After the game, I remember sitting down holding the medal and thinking to myself, 'I can't believe I have this winner's medal. I cannot believe it has happened to me.'

Then our hooker William Servat came up to me and said, 'Yes, it is real. It is yours.'

I simply thought, 'Yes, it is.'

It had been a monumentally tight game with neither side able to score a try, leaving us level at 12–12 come the end of 80 minutes of normal time. It is easy to say this in hindsight, but for all that Stade are a massively powerful side I knew as we gathered together before extra time that we were not going to lose. That was because I was hearing Guy Novès and some of the other lads speak like I had never heard them speak before. Of course, I didn't understand some of what was being said, but the tone of their voices told me all I needed to know. Everyone was gathered into the huddle: the coaches, the XV who were out there at the time, all the replacements and the guys who had gone off injured. It had been totally even up to then, but from that moment on I knew it was ours. I had never seen some of our guys pumped up like that.

'Come on. Twenty more minutes of work and we have done it,' was the gist of what they were saying. It really hit home to me, because up to that point it had struck me that players in French rugby did not go round head-butting doors, shouting and working themselves up in to a frenzy like I had seen in Wales. That was because they believed that rugby players needed clear minds to execute their skills. The motto was very much 'save the aggression for on the field'.

Not this time, though. Some of the players were going crazy. It meant so much to see this through. Even though we had just played 80 minutes and were exhausted, those scenes lifted everybody, and a penalty and a drop goal from Michalak in time added on was enough for us.

The only thing that marred the day was what happened to Guy Novès at the final whistle when he was marched away by police officers after a misunderstanding that led to a mild altercation. In my opinion, the Scottish Rugby Union needed a kick up the backside for the way they allowed our moment of triumph to be spoiled by letting every Tom, Dick and Harry onto the pitch.

After we won, I was really looking forward to our moment of glory on our own on the special platform on the Murrayfield pitch. And after that, I hoped we would be able to walk around the ground showing everyone the cup. As it turned out, there were more people on the field than in the stands come the presentation – everybody had just been allowed to pile onto the pitch.

I remember when we actually received the cup, I thought that Trevor was standing next to me and began jumping up and down next to him only to find out that it wasn't Trevor at all but some Scottish bloke from the crowd who himself was shouting 'yes, yes' as if he had played in the game and scored the winning try! Not only that, but people were trying to touch our medals and grab the cup. It was ludicrous.

All Guy had been trying to do was get

his family down to the pitch so that they could be close to him and the team, and the police were stopping him. He quite rightly began to complain about the number of ordinary punters who were on the pitch and how it was ridiculous that the people who mattered could not be there as well. Then someone put an arm on his shoulder, so he turned around to smack them away, but it was a policeman! That was it. They led him away and chucked him in a wagon, and it wasn't until everyone's tempers had cooled and Guy had apologised that they let him go. The boys were actually pissing themselves laughing about it – behind Guy's back, of course.

So with all that nonsense and me missing out on the homecoming to Toulouse, I felt I had missed the boat in terms of really savouring the achievement. But when we lost 17–12 in the French Championship semi-final to Stade Français at Bordeaux a week later, the sense of devastation was so acute that you realised what you had just missed out on was ten times bigger than the Heineken Cup. Even though some of the boys were saying that we had still enjoyed a good year and should not take it too badly, the changing-room after the defeat was utterly distraught.

What made it all worse was that in the dying seconds of the game our centre Florian Fritz had broken through, but instead of running the easiest angle to the try line he tried to be greedy and headed for the posts. He was subsequently ankle-tapped by a last-ditch lunge by one of the Stade players and spilled the ball as he fell. It was a real choker, because he seemed to be home and dry; in fact, I can remember having my arms aloft in the air as he went through, celebrating the score before he had dotted down, so certain was I that he had done enough. I didn't see much of the reaction in Toulouse afterwards, because I headed off to New Zealand on British Lions duty, but apparently Florian was ripped to pieces by the local newspaper, which was harsh but not surprising considering what the championship means to the people of the town.

The second season at Toulouse was a hell of a lot easier for me, simply because I was far more familiar with not only my new surroundings and a different country but with how I fitted into the team and my place in the grand scheme of things. Because the club is so big, it's noticeable that there is a huge emphasis on togetherness at Toulouse, on being tight-knit, of being, if you like, a family. On that score, when you join them you feel that you have to try really hard to be accepted by that family so that they will close ranks and protect you when you need them to. Well, luckily, I felt I reached that stage.

It's always difficult when you go to a club for the first time, but going into the second season things could not have been more different. I got off to a real flier, scoring tries for fun. I was playing

on the wing, at both centre berths and at full-back. It seemed that I was playing in a different position every week, but that was great because when you only play in one spot you will normally go three weeks or so and then have a rest; instead, other players were being dropped to create a place for me.

Subsequently, I felt I had really settled and began to feel proud of myself. I had proved I was good enough, and my worries that the boys were not using me in their moves in the first year had gone full circle – now I began to feel like I was the focal point of everything we were trying to do. It made me feel like the main man – that people had confidence in me. Pressure came with that, but I was dealing with it, which made it all the better.

When I am on the rugby field, I am always comfortable, as it is somewhere that I will always know what to do. But I was also used to the different social culture in France by then. In Wales, I got used to playing a game and then going to get pissed with the boys. In France, we would play a game on a Saturday at, say, 5 p.m., then go home for a couple of hours before going out again at around 10 p.m. for a meal and just a couple of glasses of wine with the other players. I found that extremely strange at first, then I began to enjoy it. I took it as it came, went with the flow and just enjoyed the chat and the banter.

Sometimes in the first year, it was a real challenge just to go down to the shop and buy a loaf of bread, something I took for granted in Wales. But I became far more confident in everything I did and also with the language. People would stop me in the street, and I was capable of speaking to them rather than just keeping my head down, putting my bobble hat over my face and hoping people didn't recognise me. Yet the latter is something I still do when I am at home. I still have a kind of in-built desire not to be recognised when I'm out and about or in a social environment. I'm not pretending that I am so famous that everyone the length and breadth of the country will instantly know who I am – not at all. But trying to cover up who I am in public is something that is born not so much out of a fear of being recognised, as a fear of not being recognised.

It is difficult to put this into words, but sometimes when I am out with friends I find that people seem to think that they have to pretend they don't know me out of a need to bring me down a peg or two. It's as if they don't want me to feel that I am special, even though I don't for one minute feel like that anyway. The truth is that nothing would give me greater pleasure than for them to genuinely not know me, but there are times when I am introduced by a mate, and he will say, 'You know who this is, don't you?'

'No,' they will reply, when I know full well that they do and that they just feel they have to make a point. It is nonsensical situations like that which

I seek to avoid, although I admit I am oversensitive about all this.

For a long time, I have had this thing about keeping my head down in everyday life, although it's probably unnecessary a lot of the time. When I am out somewhere like a pub, I make a real point of doing just that, so I don't notice if people are staring at me. I feel I can't look around and make eye contact with people because then everyone is going to be watching me. Whether that is actually the case or not doesn't matter – it is what I fear.

I want to be just another bloke in the pub, but I realise that there are always going to be people who recognise me in Wales because of what I have done in rugby. Don't get me wrong, on the whole it is great to be in that position, and nine times out of ten I can use it to my advantage. But it is a double-edged sword.

I am lucky where I live in Wales in the Vale of Glamorgan, because it is an area where even if I am recognised the locals know who I am and just let me get on with doing what everyone else does. If I'm in a country pub with mates on a Sunday afternoon having a quiet pint, I can be myself and not worry, and that is why my home means so much to me.

9

THE HIGHEST HONOUR

By the second half of 2004, the Wales team was entering a new era. Mike Ruddock had been appointed as successor to head coach Steve Hansen, and we had already enjoyed a relatively successful tour of Argentina under his leadership in the summer of that year. I missed both Tests because of the ankle injury I picked up in the Barbarians match the day before I signed for Toulouse, but we won one and lost one against the Pumas and were heading towards the autumn campaign with justified optimism. But, as is so often the case in professional sport, a new coach automatically led to the question of there being a new captain. And it soon became clear that Mike wanted a fresh start on that front; in other words, someone to take over from Colin Charvis.

Now, as much as everyone loves to hate Charvy in Wales, at the time he was a good captain. He always spoke up for the players, and he never shirked his responsibilities. Consequently, I felt he was doing a good job, and so it must have been tough for him to accept that Mike was all of a sudden pulling in five or six of us to be interviewed for the captaincy. Interviewed? Yes, that was the way Mike wanted to do it, and so he told the likes of me, Michael Owen, Martyn Williams, Stephen Jones and Charvy that he wanted us all to put in for it and go through an interview with the management.

When I actually sat down and thought about it, I realised that in any walk of life when you are asked to reapply for a job, as Colin was being asked to do, nine times out of ten you don't get it. So it was clear that there was going to be a new man, which hardened my resolve to go for it, because even though I rated Charvy as a leader of the team, I knew he wasn't going to be doing the job any more. No matter what happened, somebody else was going to be the top man, and so why shouldn't it be me?

I spoke to Jemma about it, and we

Alfie!

'What makes a good leader? Anything?'

talked about how it would mean added responsibility and added pressures if I were to get it. But she was right behind me and told me to go into it being myself. 'Don't give them the answers you think they want to hear,' she said. 'Give them the answers you want to give them. Be yourself. Don't try to be someone you are not.' That way, she argued, I would get the job on my own terms, and I knew she was spot on.

Anyway, I turned up at the team's Vale of Glamorgan Hotel headquarters one day for my interview. I had dressed casually so was shocked to find Martyn Williams in a shirt and tie, and I gave him no end of stick. I was only surprised he didn't have a briefcase stuffed with old newspapers and a bowler hat on his head!

I went into the interview room with some trepidation, but it proved to be a really interesting experience. Mike, the defence coach Clive Griffiths, Scott Johnson, Alan Phillips and Andrew Hore were on the panel – it was just the sort of situation I suppose you might expect to find in any other interview situation in other walks of life. My initial thought was that even if I didn't get the job, the interview process would be a useful thing to go through for the future. My only taste of an interview before that was in my early years when I used to go to the jobcentre, arrange an interview, speak to the boss of whatever

firm it was and then wait five minutes to find out whether I was wanted or not. Now here I was on my own in front of five big cheeses, feeling very conscious of myself and not being prepared in the slightest for what I was going to be asked.

They fired a number of questions at me, which I suppose were very relevant to my suitability for the job. One was what would I do in a match situation if we were two points down with a minute to go and had won a penalty on the touchline? 'A message has come down from the coach that he thinks you should go for goal. What do you do? Do you kick for goal or do you go with your instinct?' they asked me. I said that I would go with my instinct, because that is what I felt would have been the right thing to do. Thereafter, almost everything I said was along similar lines. I just spoke from the heart, didn't try to bullshit and called everything precisely as I saw it. I left the room thinking that I had come across quite well and had stayed true to myself in the process. I was also happy that I had made it clear that whatever happened my personality would not change.

They had asked me how I thought the players might receive my appointment given my reputation as a bit of a joker. I replied, fairly bluntly, that I would not be changing for anybody. I wouldn't be altering a single thing about my character. I said that I had got to where I was by being me, and if I was to go any

further, I would do so by being myself. If that meant staying where I was, then so be it.

A couple of days later, Mike rang me in France to tell me that I had got the job. I took the call in my house in Toulouse and was incredibly chuffed. After the decision had been made, Alan Phillips told me that as soon as I had left the room at the Vale hotel Mike had said, 'We must have him in the job now. Let's do it straight away. Let's tell him he's got it.' In the final outcome, Mike bided his time, managing to keep a lid on his enthusiasm, but to hear something like that made me swell with pride. And whatever people would later think of my relationship with Mike, I will always be grateful to him for being the guy who believed in my ability to do the job, for being the guy who saw that I was capable of captaining Wales and placing his faith in me.

To have been handed the job obviously made me feel unbelievably privileged. I was happy with where I had got to as a player and with the strides I had made since deciding to buck up my ideas a couple of years earlier. But now here was a chance to push myself to the absolute limit. Of course, in doing so, I was leaving yet another one of my comfort zones and going into uncharted waters. And you've guessed it, I was as apprehensive as I had been at other times in my career, such as when I had first been called into the Wales team, about what might lie ahead. By now, though,

Celebrating becoming Wales captain by opening the sponsor's product.

I had the maturity to deal with it and meet the challenge head on.

Throughout the selection process, I had told myself that it was unlikely I would get the job. I even thought about not actually turning up to the interview. The point being that I was full of negative thoughts, and then all of a sudden I had the captaincy in my lap, the biggest challenge of my career. But there was no time to wallow in self-congratulation. The 2004 autumn series was looming, and we faced two of the world's best in South Africa and New Zealand. Talk about a baptism of fire!

I remember going into camp at the start of the week leading up to the first match of that autumn series against South Africa. As much as I had promised to carry on behaving as I had always done, it wasn't quite that simple. In fact, it was nothing like as simple. I had always been the one laughing and having a joke, but as the week progressed I began thinking to myself, 'Oh God. At some stage, I am going to have to address the boys for the first time as skipper.' I had spoken out in front of them many times before, but never as captain, and I certainly didn't count the one time I had led the side in the warm-up international in Dublin just before the 2003 World Cup. That didn't come into it. So, I fretted about what angle I was going to take with them and whether they would just laugh at me when I pulled them together. Moreover, would they ever be able to take me seriously as their leader given my track record for playing the fool?

In short, I didn't know how the hell I was going to approach things. Perhaps I was worrying unnecessarily, because up to that stage the boys had been great and had greeted me exactly as I would have wanted them to. Instead of taking the mickey out of me, they were all genuine in their congratulations, and from the outset there didn't appear to be any problems with them possibly seeing me as a bit of a joke skipper.

Colin Charvis was outstanding with me as well. Even though I had replaced him as captain, there was never any hint of bitterness. I had rung Charvy as soon as I got the job to let him know that even though I was chuffed to get the

nod, I would always hold him in high regard for the way he had led us. He was brilliant in his response, promising me that I would get his full backing, and never once after that was there the slightest awkwardness between us.

It wasn't until the Wednesday before the South Africa game after Mike had announced the team that I made my big move to talk to the players for the first time. Up to that point, I had been in a bit of a quandary, asking myself, 'What do I do? What do I say?' I had pledged not to change my personality, but no sooner had I initiated a bit of a joke or joined in with a bit of banter in training than I would think to myself, 'Should I be saying this now that I'm skipper?' I was unsure of what was appropriate any more, but it soon fell into place.

On the Wednesday morning that Mike announced the team, we all jogged down to the bottom of the training pitch, and I pulled everyone together for the first time. I did not have a message to the team as such, but a message to everyone who was and wasn't playing. I simply said that I knew it was tough for all the boys who were not selected but that their presence and support was valued immensely. I continued that from then on it would be about us all sticking together, and although my little speech was hardly of Winston Churchill proportions, it was enough for me.

I don't know why, but from then on I knew everything would be all right for me in my captaincy role. It had only been

a small step, but it was a small step in the right direction. What's more, I had laid down a precedent at that moment, which was that under my leadership the Wales set-up was never going to be just about the first XV or the 22 players in the squad, it was going to be about all of us. It is easy to keep 15 or 22 guys happy; it is keeping happy the boys who are asked to report for training on a Monday and then told to get on their bike back to their regions on the Wednesday because they haven't been chosen that is the main challenge. And it was a challenge that I was determined to meet head on.

From my little moment on the Wednesday up until the kick-off before the South Africa game on the Saturday afternoon, I was fine. I kept myself busy. I did my media duty and was buzzing about here, there and everywhere. It is surprising just how much busier you are in the build-up to a Test match when you are captain. There are quite a few little extra duties that all add up. For instance, I now make sure that I know precisely who the mascot is, having been caught out on the day of the South Africa match.

With it being my first match as captain at the Millennium Stadium, I was simply unaware that it was my job to take the mascot under my wing, and when we arrived at the ground I walked straight past the little lad, not having a clue who he was. A few moments later, the poor little chap had to approach me and say,

'Hello, I'm the mascot for today.' My heart melted for him, and I knew that from then on the same thing could not happen again. I have since made it my business before every Test to find out everything about the mascot: his or her name, age, school and what team he or she supports – basically, as much as my brain will allow me to remember. That means I can walk up to the mascot as soon as I see them and put them at ease, making them feel at home and as if they are the most important part of the whole afternoon. And you should see the look on their faces when I say their names. I can see them thinking, 'How on earth do you know my name?' It's a small part of the captain's role, but one I now take very seriously.

But back to the Springbok game. I didn't do much in the build-up to kick-off apart from checking that the buzz among the boys was there. It is something that is difficult to quantify, but you instinctively know whether it is right or wrong, and on this day it was definitely right. However, there was a moment just before we left the changing-room for the start of the match that left me choked with emotion.

I never prepare speeches to give to the boys before matches. I would never sit up in bed the night before writing thoughts down on paper, and the biggest reason for that is that I am a huge believer in spontaneity. What you may feel is right the night before in the quiet of your bedroom might not be right come the here and now of a charged dressing-room minutes before a Test match. For me, the best thing for a captain to do is to pick up on the precise atmosphere of the time and then just go for it with whatever feels right to say.

The night before the game against South Africa, I worried about how to go about my team talk the next day. Should I indeed put some thoughts down on paper? What if I miss out a couple of important words, though? Then I just threw the pen and paper aside and vowed to do it off the cuff, not just for the Springbok game but for the rest of my time in the job. So what if I cocked up when I was speaking. At least I would be talking from the heart and in the moment. And you know what? It has worked every time since. Not once in all the games I have captained the team have I ever been lost for words – something always comes to me.

We were seconds away from going through the dressing-room doors to meet the Boks, and I gathered everyone together in a huddle. 'Boys,' I said, 'I am just asking you to stand with me for 80 minutes. Stand tall with me for the anthem, and then stand tall with me for 80 minutes. Bollocks to the result. Bollocks to the scoreboard. Just stand with me for 80 minutes. Be proud that we are together and that we have this opportunity to play together. Puff your chest out. Stand tall with me.'

I was choked up to the eyeballs and only just managed to keep it together.

I had bottled everything up all week, and now it was starting to flow out of me, the emotion of being charged with the responsibility of not just leading my country, but leading a bunch of lads – not into battle, because sport is not a battle and it is not a war – but into something that most people can only dream about.

People have often said to me that it must be the most precious moment possible when I am standing on the pitch listening to the anthem as captain of Wales because of the pride and honour. Well, great moment though it undoubtedly is, for me it will never beat the final moment that you have with your team in the privacy of the dressing-room just before you take the field. You look into the boys' eyes, and they are bulging as if about to pop out, like rabbits caught in headlights.

What makes it all the more special is the circle that you form together. There is something about a circle that engenders as powerful a feeling of 'us against the world' as possible. A circle is complete. It feels like it is impenetrable. All that you have is inside, and all that you do not need is outside. It doesn't matter which member of the squad you are standing next to, you are all connected in some way. You are able to look into the faces of your teammates and see their expressions, their eyes. There is an intimacy that you just do not feel when you are standing in a straight line.

What's more, when you are out on the pitch singing the anthem, you are sharing the moment with 75,000 others who have all paid to watch you perform. And great though it is to have that kind of support, the circle in the dressing-room is a precious moment just for the team. It is personal. It is for nobody else in the whole world, which for me makes it hands down the ultimate time.

I also felt I had to preside over a key psychological shift when I took on the captaincy. During Steve Hansen's time as head coach, he had continually emphasised that it was performances, and not results, that mattered. Such reasoning drove some people, and sections of the press, absolutely potty. Nothing, they argued, could ever be more important than putting wins on the board. But they were blind to the realities of where we were in the game at that time.

Steve thought that we were at a stage in our development when the pressure of having to deliver results could only inhibit us. I suppose his thinking was that he wanted to keep that pressure away from us and that dampening down the importance of the scoreboard might actually enable him to get more out of us. In any case, you can't win if the performance isn't good, he argued. Well, I wouldn't say that is strictly true, because the best teams have a knack of winning when playing badly, and there have been plenty of times when I have lost in a Wales jersey feeling that we

had played the better rugby. But I think Steve was playing mind games with us all anyway.

Whatever the rights and wrongs of it, our displays in the 2003 World Cup and the 2004 Six Nations saw us push the very best teams – New Zealand, England and France – to the brink of defeat, so when I took the armband I felt that there was nothing left to be gained from gallant defeats against the top sides. I just thought to myself, 'It's time we started winning against these sides.' And I believed in the team so much that I was convinced that was exactly what we were ready to do. That line had been crossed.

Despite losing to South Africa by just two points – 38–36 – in my first game as captain, we never really looked like winning, because we only got to within one score of them at a time when we knew the referee was about to blow his whistle. The score, don't get me wrong, was great for us, as it was far closer than we had got to them for years. But the last thing I wanted to see in the newspapers the next day was Welsh back-slapping and quotes about how brilliantly we all thought we had done in defeat. At the end of the day, we had lost, and I wanted everyone involved to get away from going along with the public perception, which was that we had done OK and could never have expected to win anyway. Instead, the gist of my post-match remarks was that the defeat was not acceptable in any way

and that winning the game had been all that mattered. And they were 100 per cent genuine sentiments.

I wasn't playing a game, and I hope the acquaintances I have in the media realise that I have never been dishonest with them. It's strange but when I think back to only a few years ago, I was hopeless with the press. But having increased the amount of work I do with them after being made captain, I have found it a helpful part of the job. I have learned – or at least I hope I have – how to express myself better in public. I have learned how to speak my mind in an open forum in the company of a room full of journalists as well as doing one-to-ones. Being in front of the cameras doesn't bother me either, and all this has added up to me feeling almost as though I have learned a new trade. Through dealing with the media, I have come out of my shell, and, yes, I have become a different person. I knew when I took the captaincy that media duties, especially in Wales, were a massive part of the job, and I feel proud of myself for the way I have gone about them.

For all that the South Africa game had been monumental, it was by no means *the* match of the 2004 autumn series for one obvious reason. How could it have been when we had New Zealand coming to town for the final match of the programme? And they were led by Messrs Henry and Hansen, just to add a large pinch of extra spice. A few

of the newspapers were already billing it as some kind of revenge match and a chance for me to put one over on Henry. But, to be honest, I was far more concerned about catching up with Steve again and concentrating my energies on helping Wales win, rather than focusing on a personal battle between me and my old sparring partner.

We lost the match 25–24, but we should have won, and I will probably go to my grave regretting that we did not. In the career of a Welsh rugby player, there are very few chances to register a win against the All Blacks. It used to be that you had a crack at them for your club side, but in the professional era touring international sides have done away with playing against non-Test sides – although the Ospreys did get a crack at Australia last season. But my point is that touring has become less about actual touring and more about flying into town and concentrating everything you have on a one-off Test match.

Our loftier status in the world game these days allows us a crack at New Zealand once a year if we are lucky. So, when the chance comes along, you really feel you have to grab it. And 20 November 2004 might have been the best I will ever get.

We played really well that day. Either side could have won, but if we had done so, we would have fully deserved it. Because I had just begun to place all the emphasis on winning, it would have been an outstanding way to start an era

of concentrating on that outlook. It was not because I was captain and wanted us to be immortalised as a Wales team that had beaten the All Blacks, like the 1953 and 1905 teams have been. No, what motivated me more was the thought that as a team we would have remembered each other far more for the special reason of having beaten New Zealand.

Again, all I tried to get across after the game was that we could not afford to be happy with a near miss. 'We've played our guts out and performed well. We can still walk tall and be proud, but let's also have a bit of hurt inside as well,' I told the lads. 'Because if we don't hurt after losing, then we are never going to win.'

The atmosphere in the dressing-room afterwards was half and half. We were not distraught, because we knew we could not have given any more. I didn't mind that, but I also made sure that we didn't take too much credit from losing. To this day, I regret not winning that game.

When I was appointed captain of Wales, I didn't for a moment want any of my family to treat me any differently, that's for sure – and none of them has. As much as I didn't want to change because of the title, I didn't want other people's opinions of me to change either. It was so important to me that everyone close to me knew that, and I think they have always known that I would never have taken the captaincy just because it would

put me on a pedestal or because I would be able to call myself an ex-captain of Wales in the future.

Obviously, my family and close friends were proud, but no prouder than they had been when I had first played for Wales, and the reason for that is that they know me better than anyone else. I had gone from being a postman in Bridgend who liked a game of rugby at the weekend and then going out on the piss with the boys to being captain of Wales. Let me tell you, I regard this as proof that dreams can be achieved, no matter how far-fetched you think they are. If someone like me can do something like that, there must be hundreds, thousands even, out there who could do something similar and achieve something they have always believed to be completely out of their reach. It just goes to show, you should never dismiss your dreams as dreams. I should know. Not only had one dream come true when I was appointed captain of my country, another one was just around the corner.

10

GRAND SLAM

As we headed towards the 2005 Six Nations, I could tell that we were just about on the brink of peaking as a team. Having come so close against New Zealand, there was a real sense that we had arrived at the point when a big result would be ours. The team was firing on all cylinders, everything we were doing in training had an edge to it and Mike Ruddock was still more or less in his honeymoon period as head coach.

Mike got one thing spot on from the start: he didn't come into the job looking to rip up everything Steve Hansen had done. He didn't come in with a new broom and an attitude that he had to stamp a whole new mark on the team and take ownership of it by sweeping away the remnants of the previous regime. Mike knew that we had found a way of playing that suited us, and more importantly that it was a style that brought the best out of the abilities of the squad. We played an enterprising, high-tempo game, which was too much for many teams on the international circuit. In fact, we were becoming world renowned for it.

There was no way we would have got anywhere if we had attempted to play, say, a set-piece-orientated game based around the forwards. We just didn't have the bulk to do that. But we did have good rugby brains, pace to burn and high skill levels, which nobody had done more to improve than Scott Johnson. Mike let us go with it on the basis that if it ain't broke, don't fix it.

That said, I did not in my wildest dreams expect us to win the Grand Slam, and I think if every other person in Wales was honest with themselves, they would say the same thing. I think a couple of my more optimistic mates put £20 on us at 66–1 to win it after the New Zealand game in the autumn before, but I think even they were just having a flutter with no real expectation of a return on their investment. Don't get me wrong. I knew we were growing as a team, and I knew we were going to

It's not illegal to smile.

be competitive in the 2005 Six Nations. But win the Slam? Forget about it.

Then came the biggest ice-breaker of our careers: the victory that pushed us onto a whole new plane; the win that unlocked the door to the Promised Land, if you like.

5 FEBRUARY 2005
WALES 11, ENGLAND 9

We had narrowly lost to South Africa and narrowly lost to New Zealand. Now

was the time to take a major scalp. Not in a month's time; not in a week's time. Now.

England were the world champions, but they arrived in Cardiff under the leadership of a new coach in Andy Robinson after the departure of Clive Woodward, and they were also bedevilled by injuries to key players. It was similar to what Wales went through in the 2006 Six Nations in terms of absentees, though not as bad, and there were also some players in their ranks who we felt were nearing their sell-by dates. Add to this

the way the respective sides were playing at the time – England were robotic and a little boring, whereas we were playing in a style that was fast becoming branded 'Total Rugby' by the media – and all the ingredients were in place for us to go and do it. And that is before you even take into account the spirit and togetherness we had among the whole squad. There were no superstars in our ranks, and the emphasis on nobody being bigger than the group itself was then at its strongest. It wasn't about who scored the tries or who kicked the kicks. That was irrelevant. It was about all of us working hard together. If there had been a hint of anyone having a bad attitude, we would have brought it to the table and dealt with it. But there was no such thing.

In fact, the way I was thinking when I woke up on the morning of the game was basically that we *had* to do it. If it was ever going to happen for us against England, I thought to myself – and God knows I have been on the wrong end of some real tunings against the old enemy – it was going to happen that day. In hindsight, I realise that it is ironic that while it did happen for us, it happened despite the fact that we played badly on the day. Afterwards, we knew as much, and, to be honest, it dampened down a lot of the euphoria.

In the dressing-room, I remember Scott Johnson saying, 'Hey, boys, wind your necks in. We may have won, but we played terribly.' And we all knew that

he was right – we had been awful. Even though we had scored the only try of the match through Shane Williams in the first half, we realised when we looked at the video the following day that we had squandered four or five gilt-edged chances to cross their line through our own poor execution.

Of course, the match will always be remembered for Gavin Henson's magnificent last-minute penalty from long range that secured us the three points we needed to win the game. But the truth is that we should have been out of sight by then. How we were trailing to three Charlie Hodgson penalties, I will never know, because if we had been poor, England had been even worse. But because the game was so tight, as the New Zealand game had been, I knew it was there for the taking, even when we were 9–8 down in the closing stages, and looking back I truly believe we deserved to win. We were the better team.

Apart from the fact that it had been far from a vintage performance, I had another reason for not being entirely happy with myself after the game. During the first half, the giant English lock Danny Grewcock – who I discovered on the 2005 British Lions tour is a really top guy – stepped over a ruck and raked his studs in the face of scrum-half Dwayne Peel. Now, as I say, Grewcock is a gentleman off the field, but on it he plays hard – very hard. He is one of those fellows who you really want on your team and not among the opposition.

But when I saw his enormous boot come over the top and catch Peely, I saw red, big time, immediately thinking to myself, 'You cheap-shot bastard.'

To this day, I do not regret intervening in the way I did. Peely is a good mate of mine, and all I saw was a guy who I would run through a brick wall for getting a boot in his face. To me, the fact that I stepped in is another example of what our boys mean to each another. But I do have two regrets about the incident. The first is the rather girly couple of slaps I administered to Grewcock, who probably barely felt them caressing his grizzled face. 'If you're going to get sin-binned,' I thought to myself, 'at least chuck a couple of punches that are worthy of the punishment.' I couldn't believe it the next day when I read in one newspaper that I had received a yellow card for 'punching Danny Grewcock twice in the head'. I had, in fact, caught him once, and, as I explained to the press afterwards, I have probably been sent to my bedroom by my mother for doing worse. The second regret is more obvious: the ten minutes I spent off the field – even though Grewcock got his marching orders as well – could have proved really costly to the team.

Grewcock was the first to be shown yellow, and Martyn Williams immediately came over to me all excited, saying that we should kick the penalty to touch and take advantage of his absence in the lineout. I was secretly hoping I had got away with my misdemeanour and started walking away from the incident. Then I heard the dreaded word from the referee: 'Fifteen!'

'Oh bollocks,' I thought to myself, and then that was it: I was in the bin.

As I sat there watching the action, all I could think was what a great opportunity it would have been for us if we could have had 15 against 14 out there; in other words, if I had been able to keep a lid on my temper. The fear that I would end up costing us the game was all-embracing, and it had all been for a pathetic slap barely worthy of a primary-school playground. But thankfully that didn't happen.

What can I say about Gavin Henson's match-winning intervention? Well, for a start, you cannot argue with what he did under such intense pressure. I know this can be a bit of a tired cliché, but it really was the type of moment we all dream about as kids: a last-minute penalty to win a rugby match for Wales against England, and the most difficult of chances at that. Gav looked lifelong ignominy in the eye and didn't blink, writing himself into the history books in the process. And hats off to him for doing so.

I know Gavin has talked a lot about what actually happened from the moment we were awarded the penalty, but let me share with you my recollections. As soon as it became clear we had the penalty, I went over to Stephen Jones, who was, and still is, our front-line goal kicker.

'Can you kick it?' I asked Stephen.

He stood at the spot from which the kick would have to be taken and said, without much hesitation, 'No, give it to Gav.'

Fair play to Stephen for doing that. Fair play to him for saying no when he was the one who had first option on being the hero. Typically, though, he put the team before personal glory. It could have been the penalty that changed his life, but he was man enough to admit that it was probably out of his range.

Gav had already come over to us by that point and seemed to be itching to be given the nod, which was also great to see, so I gave him the ball and asked him to kick it. I strolled away and took up a position immediately behind the line of the kick. I watched the whole thing except for the ball actually going over the posts – but I didn't need to. I just had to listen to the roar go up, and what a roar it was. By then, I knew the game was ours. There was no coming back for England.

After the match, all the boys wanted to go into central Cardiff and celebrate the victory, which was understandable. But Andrew Hore came up to me and said, 'Would we go out if we had lost?' It immediately got me thinking. I wasn't sure of the answer to the question, but Horey's message was, 'Hey, let's not get carried away.' He asked what the point of beating England would be if we then went out to Italy the following week and lost? Crucially, we only had a seven-day turnaround, so a heavy night

Nice one, Gav! Henson and I savour our 2005 win against England that set us on the road to the Grand Slam.

on the booze would eat into precious preparation time on the Sunday. And we were not so well advanced as a team as to be able to just dismiss that. I totally agreed with Horey, and the fact that we had not played well in beating England only served to hammer it home.

As it turned out, I think some of the boys did venture into town, Gavin included, but the key was that nobody took advantage and got bladdered. The lads all thought too much of the team to do that. As I have explained earlier, the attitude that it was OK to get pissed and perform poorly in training the next

day was a thing of the past. By then, everyone had too much respect for the group.

After the game, I remember going from the Millennium Stadium to the Hilton Hotel, where the post-match reception was to be held. The whole city, it seemed, had gone mental. It took our coach the best part of an hour to snake a distance of no more than 600 yards. There were fans banging the bus, standing in front of it and just generally shouting and bawling their heads off in delirious celebration. The England coach followed and took some serious abuse by all accounts. Some guy even head-butted it and split his scalp open in the process.

Both coaches ended up arriving at the hotel at roughly the same time, and the English guys, I have to say, were outstanding in defeat. Jason Robinson stood up to make his captain's speech and graciously conceded that the best team had won, which was brilliant. For me, that was the mark of that England team as a bunch of individuals. In my time as captain, I have always impressed on the players the need to be magnanimous in defeat, and I think that how you handle adversity says a lot about a team. To a man, England were gentlemanly, humble and accepting of the reverse without making any excuses, even though they were world champions at the time.

A week later, we had cleared the second hurdle in our clean sweep.

12 FEBRUARY 2005
ITALY 8, WALES 38

Sports people are always lambasted for talking about the need to 'take each game as it comes'. But there are times when you are almost left with no choice, because it is simply the way you must look at things. And adopting that approach, as well as actually adhering to it, was one of the reasons why we were successful. We never allowed ourselves to look too far ahead at what could be achieved if we kept our heads.

The fear of ruining everything we had done against England underpinned everything we did, and we tweaked quite a few things after deeper analysis of the video of that match. Fortunately, our homework paid off, because it all clicked together for us against Italy at the Stadio Flaminio in pretty impressive fashion. This time, the performance was something to celebrate. We ran in six tries, and there was never any looking back after Martyn Williams was awarded a contested touchdown on the stroke of half-time. The way we carved open the Azzurri sent out a real warning to the rest of the Six Nations teams. We ran riot. The ball was going to hand every time, on some occasions from the most ambitious passes, and in many ways that game on its own summed up what we did throughout the entire campaign. It was Harlem Globetrotters stuff at times. It seemed nothing we tried could go wrong.

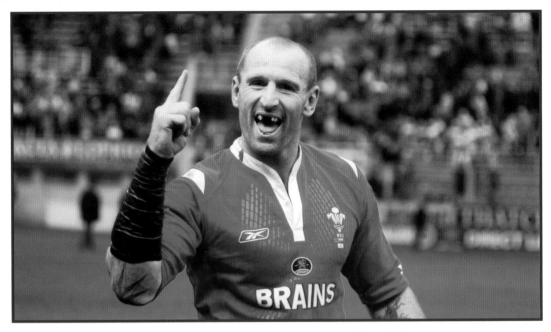

Get in there! Another notch on the road to Grand Slam success
– this time beating Italy in Rome.

I have to say that in the aftermath of the win in Rome there was a very real sense of having avoided a potential banana skin. That probably sounds patronising to Italian rugby, especially in the light of the improvement they showed in the 2006 tournament when they got a draw against us at the Millennium Stadium and in beating us and Scotland in 2007. But despite that, it is still the case that you can never really win against Italy, because victory is expected, and I do not mean any disrespect in saying that. All Italy represents is a potential cock-up. That is how the match against them is always viewed by the spectators, and if that changes in the future – and there are definite signs that it could – then all well and good.

But if what had happened against Italy had merely kept the dream alive, what occurred next in Paris has since been seen by many, even accounting for the win against England, as quite simply our finest hour.

26 FEBRUARY 2005
FRANCE 18, WALES 24

If there was one match in which the Grand Slam was truly won, it was this one on a bitterly cold Paris afternoon. If the Slam was seen as a remote possibility going into the game, it was considered to be a probability when we came out the other side. In golfing terms, Paris was our Amen Corner, the toughest challenge at the apex of our long campaign – and we came

through it. But you would never have predicted a Welsh victory judging by the sheer one-sidedness of the first half.

What can I tell you about that wretched first half other than it was raining French jerseys down upon me in my full-back position. It felt like we had disturbed an ants' nest of French players. They were darting and bolting from everywhere, and if we stopped one, another one would be there to carry the fight to us again.

Their scrum-half Dimitri Yachvili scored early on, and Aurélien Rougerie blitzed over a little while later. It looked like total carnage was on the cards. But when I went off at half-time, I took a sneaky look at the scoreboard – something I rarely bother doing – and was staggered to see that we were only 15–6 behind. Stephen Jones had kicked a crucial penalty before we went in, and at nine points adrift I realised that we were still very much in the game.

Granted, it didn't look great for us, and most people in the crowd were probably just debating whether or not France would run up a half-century of points. But after being completely battered by them, we were still very much in with a sniff of a comeback. However, by the time we trooped off after 40 minutes, it was not just game over for me, but championship over. I had broken my thumb, and while I tried to pretend it wasn't true, there came a moment during the interval when I just had to admit defeat – and it absolutely destroyed me.

I remember that I made a tackle in the corner towards the end of the first half. It wasn't a big hit by any means, and I thought nothing of it at the time. Then I suddenly became conscious that something was wrong with the thumb on my right hand. Every time I moved it, it was audibly clicking. I wasn't worried at first, because I could move it, and I told myself that had to be a good sign. But the clicking was very pronounced indeed.

Play stopped for a French scrum, and just before it restarted our physio Mark Davies, Carcus as we call him, ran onto the field to check out my thumb. He was pressing it and playing around with it, and then he said, 'Alf, it's broken.'

'It's not fucking broken!' I yelled at him, desperately unwilling to accept my fate. 'Now leave me alone and fuck off.'

As play resumed, he had no choice but to do just that, and, stupidly in hindsight, I ran off in the vain hope of being able to play on. Moments later, I received the ball and passed it. That was the moment I knew it was futile trying to deny it any longer: my thumb was seriously damaged – it was actually broken in five places – and by then it had begun to throb. In fact, the pain was starting to really kick in.

Back in the changing-room, the team doctor came over to me and pressed the exact spot where the primary break had occurred. It went crunch, and he looked up at me and said, 'Alf, it's gone.' I can remember those words hitting me like

a thunderbolt to this day. As soon as I heard them, a lump started forming in my throat. While the rest of the boys carried on listening to whatever was being said to them as we plotted how we could get back into the game, I stood up and walked out on my own to an empty room around the corner, where there was one of those big baths. Sitting down on the steps in the silence, I cried and cried. I must have been there for about 15 minutes, sobbing for all I was worth. It wasn't just my thumb that was broken, it was my heart, too, because I knew that was it for me. I would play no further part in the 2005 Six Nations. And all the while, those words were echoing in the back of my mind, 'Alf, it's broken. Alf, it's broken.'

Until now, I have never told a soul about my despair in the emptiness of that room. The only person who saw me in that state was Professor John Williams, who came in to hand me a couple of painkillers. The professor could see my distress – I was still bawling at that point – and that I was in no mood to talk, so he just handed me the pills and left. I eventually composed myself, and the first thing our medical boys said was, 'Right, let's go to the hospital.'

'No way,' I replied. 'I'm staying to see the end of this game if I die doing it.' I put on some warmer clothes and began to make my way back out into the stadium around three or four minutes after the lads had returned to the field. As I made my way down the tunnel, the crowd began screaming and shouting. I looked at the doctor, and we both assumed that France had added to their lead. I cursed to myself, only to get out into the open and see Martyn Williams being congratulated by our boys. My heart leapt, and I made my way to my seat like a kid on Christmas morning.

I sat and watched the rest of the game, witnessing a comeback that will go down as one of the all-time greats by any international side. To turn the match around in the manner that we did is something I think even a team like New Zealand would have struggled to do. I was, of course, going through the full range of emotions: ecstatic one minute as we claimed another few points; devastated the next as I remembered my own unfortunate plight. But if France had blitzed us in the first half, it was us doing the blitzing in the second.

Yet for all our heroics, we had to withstand a breathtaking assault on our line by a desperate French team trying to claw the game back in the final minutes. We held on, although our hearts were in our mouths at the end when Stephen belted the ball dead thinking that time was up. It was, but for some reason the New Zealander Paul Honiss delayed for a second before putting us all out of our misery.

I bounded down the steps from my seat and headed straight down the tunnel for the changing-room. I didn't want to do the lap of honour with the rest of the boys, because although I was chuffed

After victory in France, I managed to still do the ayatollah with a broken thumb.

that we had won, I was also upset, and I didn't want my mood spoiling the atmosphere. It was then that I got a message that the rest of the lads were refusing to go around the pitch until I had joined them. I could barely believe it. This was what we meant to each other. We had just secured a momentous win, and the most important thing to the lads was that there were only 21 Wales players out there when there should have been 22, because all 22 deserved that moment. On hearing that, I went back out, thinking, 'I may be injured, but this team is still a part of me.' I ran around the pitch, instinctively trying to clap, although my shattered thumb was preventing me from doing so. It was

an amazing feeling and a day I will not forget as long as I live.

Back in the dressing-room when we had eventually left the field, I gathered the boys in a huddle again as I prepared to go to hospital. 'This is the last time this season I will be able to speak to you like this. For your effort in the games we have had so far, I just want to say thanks. Thanks for your commitment and thanks for your support.' I had more I wanted to say, but my voice began to crack with the emotion, and I cut it short there, rather than break down in front of the boys. Then it was off to the hospital, where I had the thumb put in a bandage in readiness for an operation by a top hand surgeon back in Wales.

I share a joke with a policeman on our return from Paris to Cardiff, even though I know I'm out for the rest of the tournament.

We arrived home the next day, and I did my media duties. It was tough, because something like a broken bone is so final. You know that there is a set amount of time you are going to be out, and that is the end of it. But when everything else around you is going so brilliantly well, it leaves you with an excruciating mix of feelings.

That evening, I sat down with Scott Johnson and told him that even though I was out for the rest of the Six Nations, I wanted to stay around the camp. I asked if that was OK and even said I was willing to pay my own way if need be. But Johnno said that they expected me to stay with them anyway, and, injury aside, I was still as much a part of the team as I had ever been. It meant the world to me to hear that.

If Paris had been the day of a lifetime, our next assignment was to prove almost as unique.

. . . .
13 MARCH 2005
SCOTLAND 22, WALES 46
. . . .

The match against Scotland was as one-sided a victory for Wales at Murrayfield as you are ever likely to see in the modern era. At one point in the game, in which I was of course not playing, we led 43–3. The Scots were woeful and clearly capitulating under the leadership of the Australian Matt Williams. But the

fact that I could not play because of my thumb put me in a position I had never encountered before.

I was in camp every day during the week leading up to the game, not really doing much, just the odd bit of analysis and chipping in with a bit of banter every now and again. Hopefully, the lads valued the humour I brought to the camp, something which has always been important. We have always said that there must be times when we switch off from the game, otherwise we run the risk of burning out mentally, and I have a hell of a lot of time for that school of thought. In short, I was doing what I always did, except I wasn't taking part in training. I felt at times like somebody who had won a prize to spend a week with the Wales team in a spot-the-ball competition! But at no time did I feel like a spare part, even though my presence was not what it normally was, and the boys helped in that respect by doing their best to include me in everything they possibly could.

Come the day of the game, I was on the bench at the side of the pitch. I had been in the dressing-room beforehand going around some of the boys individually and offering a few quiet words of encouragement. But I felt it was Michael Owen's job to be the main motivator of the team, so there was no question of me making a speech.

When the game began, it really was a cakewalk. The boys put together some majestic stuff based on wonderful running angles and silky-smooth skills. It was 38–3 at the interval with Scotland in total disarray, and I remember turning to Mark Taylor, who was with me on the bench, and remarking that there were 50 points there for the taking.

Scotland rallied after the break as we stepped off the gas, and it all finished on a bit of a damp note for us given the start we had made. But if you had offered us 46–22 at the start of the game, we'd have bitten your hand off. We had set up a day the like of which Cardiff had not seen since 1988 when Jonathan Davies's Triple Crown team had played France for the Grand Slam. And we knew that we had the chance to do something no Wales team had managed for 27 years.

. . . .
19 MARCH 2005
WALES 32, IRELAND 10
. . . .

What should have been the day of my life turned out not to be. Instead, I struggled dreadfully with my emotions, and you could say that it was the best and the worst day of my rugby life rolled into one. I stayed with the team, and I remember going downstairs at the hotel on the morning of the game and suddenly beginning to notice things that just pass you by when you are playing. For example, I was struck by the number of fans who had gathered at the hotel. When you know you have a game, you find you want to avoid getting caught up with them all, because

you are trying to focus and don't want to allow the atmosphere to have any negative effect on you. But this time I was very conscious of the hubbub that surrounded us and the people milling around, all wide-eyed with expectation.

As soon as I had opened my eyes in my hotel bedroom that morning, I saw that the sky was blue, the sun was shining and that it would be a glorious early spring day in Cardiff. I turned on the television, and the match was there. I turned on the radio, and the match was there. Everyone, it seemed, was talking about the game and how the team had a chance to do something that no Wales side had done for 27 years. There would never be a day like it, they were claiming. Then it came crashing down upon me that this was the day I had waited for all my life, and I was not going to be a part of it. Oh, I was there all right. I was with the lads, and I'd be with them on the team bus, at the ground and in the dressing-room – but I wouldn't be able to do a damn thing. I would not be lacing up my boots. I would not be feeling the number-15 jersey sliding down my back. I would not be gathering the boys together in a huddle before we left for the tunnel. I would not be leading them out onto the field as 74,500 fans went delirious. I would not be standing tall at the top of our team line for the anthem. I would not be playing.

I never thought that I would get the chance to win the Grand Slam for Wales in front of our own fans, but that chance should have been there for me that day. It wasn't, and the realisation was ruining me. I subsequently spent the day being false. I was very conscious that I could not in any way allow my personal anguish to be picked up on by the rest of the boys. I might have been missing out, but they still had the mother of all jobs to complete against an Irish team chasing the Triple Crown. My teammates also had every right to savour the experience and did not deserve to have my mood dragging them down. So I put on the most convincing front I could, trying to smile and be myself as much as possible, even though I wanted to curl up in a ball and die.

Part of me was wishing away every minute of what should have been the biggest day of my life, and I was trying to be somebody else. Fortunately, I must have done a pretty good job, because not once did any of the boys come up and feel the need to commiserate with me. In any case, the times when I was around the boys were the easiest, because I could get involved with the banter and the conversation. Then, for a few precious moments, I would forget that I wasn't playing and that I had a hand in plaster. Ten minutes later, it would all come crashing down around me again. The moments when I was on my own were the worst. I got through it all somehow, but my mood affected everything I did, from the moment I woke up to when my head hit the pillow that night.

Grand Slam!

I did receive the trophy with Michael Owen on the pitch at the end of the game, but that was not how I had wanted it. Instead, from the moment my hand had gone into plaster after the France game, I had hatched a plan for what I wanted to happen if it came down to us winning the Grand Slam and there was to be a trophy presented to us in front of the crowd – and it certainly did not involve me taking the glory. No, I viewed that moment as the ultimate opportunity for us to show the rest of the world what we were about – that we were first and foremost a team, not a collection of individuals.

The way to do that, I was convinced, was to get someone who had turned up to squad training every Monday and had then been sent back to their region on the Wednesday having been told they were not selected for the forthcoming match to go up and collect the trophy on our behalf. And the man to do it in my eyes was the Newport Gwent Dragons hooker Steve 'Jabba' Jones. He was a guy who had been in exactly that position, and I was of the opinion that this was our chance to show everyone that somebody like him was as important to us as anyone else in the squad.

I know this will sound ridiculous to a lot of people and some would have considered it silly if it had happened. But it was what I wanted, and it was important to me.

I told Alan Phillips, our team manager, that if and when we won, I wanted all 30 players, including the guys who had not figured in that day's squad of 22 and were in shirts and ties watching the game up in a hospitality box, to be down on the podium with the team getting the credit they deserved in their rightful place. However, when I told Martyn Williams what I wanted, he shook his head. 'Alf, you've deserved this,' he said. 'You have earned the right to go up there and receive that trophy, so get yourself up there.'

I didn't even speak to Steve Jones about my idea, but I think that if I had played and been in my kit, I would have insisted that he get up there and receive the trophy. Without a doubt, I would have foregone the pleasure of lifting the trophy as captain in order to send a message to the world about what we stood for. It had been my little master plan from the start.

I didn't want to do it to court controversy, just to ensure that people knew we had won the Grand Slam because of the efforts of 30 players, not 15 or 22. Guys like Steve Jones, as far as I was concerned, had won us the tournament. But, in the end, my plan never materialised.

I'm not sure how many of the others wanted it done like that, and because I had not been captain that day I didn't feel I could force the issue too much. These guys had just sweated blood for 80 minutes, and the last thing I felt they would have wanted was someone who hadn't played coming onto the pitch and laying down the law. And so me and Michael Owen went up and lifted the pot between us, with some woman from the BBC trying to interview the two of us as we all went nuts with champagne flying everywhere.

That evening, all the boys were understandably chucking the ale down their necks, and they deserved it. Me? I had a couple of half-hearted drinks in the Hilton Hotel where the post-match reception had been and then went on with the rest of them to a little private pub just inside the grounds of the Brains Brewery in Cardiff. By this time, the lads were steaming, and I was pretending to be the same, but in truth I had been sipping my drinks all night and leaving most of them in little corners about the place.

My mates have since asked why I didn't just throw myself into it, get a load of beers down me and basically drink away the pain of having missed out on the big day. But that was the problem. I knew from experience that drink would have made it all ten times worse. Normally, if I'm pissed, I act like I'm the happiest man alive, but if I have an issue, something niggling away in my mind, the drink makes it worse. On top of that, I knew we had a massive day of drinking planned for the next day, so I was content to save myself for that.

The get-together the next day was a fitting way for us to finish things off – all

I check everything is in order before an Eden Park photo shoot.

together relaxing and savouring what might turn out to be a once-in-a-lifetime experience in the upstairs of The Yard pub in the centre of Cardiff. The only one who by his own public admission did not exactly cover himself in glory was Gavin Henson, who stumbled away from us before the end of the day in a completely paralytic state of drunkenness. Unfortunately, Gav ended up putting something of a dampener on things, because by the time he made his early exit, it was all the boys were talking about, and the issue sort of took over the rest of the proceedings.

Most of the boys were already nursing rather severe hangovers when the Sunday drinking began in earnest, and whatever Gav

had consumed the night before and then that day obviously didn't agree with him. But by that time, I had managed to shake off a lot of my dark mood and was ready to have one last blast to see out what had been a great tournament. And remember, I've always been a Sunday drinker!

We pushed a load of tables together and all sat around with me taking charge. 'Come on then, guys,' I said. 'Let's play some games. Let's get some drink down ourselves. Right, jugs and glasses up here. Jugs and glasses in the middle, and jugs and glasses down there. If you mess up in any of the games, you bolt half a glass down you, and that's that.'

It didn't help Gav's cause that he came off worst in some of these games,

Jumping for joy. Me, Shane, Stephen and Gav on an Eden Park photo shoot.

and soon it was all over for him. We all carried on from there, going across the road to The Walkabout bar in Cardiff's St Mary's Street, but Gav's early departure took the wind out of our sails.

I've already set my watch waiting for some people to condemn our drinking. Well, on a general level I would never actively encourage anyone to drink more than they chose to. But you have to understand the dynamics of a rugby team, especially in the wake of such success following a prolonged period of intense pressure. What can I say other than it goes on among rugby teams the length and breadth of the globe: always has done; always will do.

For me and a large proportion of the lads, that Sunday was not the start of a long time apart. Just three weeks later, the British Lions squad to tour New Zealand was announced. I was in for what would be my first and last chance to play for the Lions. We had conquered one Everest in winning the Grand Slam – now another one lay in front of us.

11

LIONS BLACKOUT

Whenever a Lions tour looms, you can't find peace and quiet anywhere for people talking about likely squads, likely Test teams, a likely captain, sometimes as early as 18 months before it is due to start. I remember when Graham Henry led the 2001 expedition to Australia when he was still Wales coach, I was secretly hoping I might be in with an outside shout of going. Don't get me wrong, I didn't expect the call – nothing like it, actually. But if your chances are slim, there is always a part of you that hopes against hope.

I missed out that year, which in all honesty left me disappointed for all of ten seconds. And, in hindsight, I am glad I did not go on that particular trip for two reasons. The first is that I have heard so many horror stories from players who went about what it was like and how they didn't enjoy it. The second is that because of the type of guy I was at that time, I probably would have either got myself kicked off the tour or got myself a really bad name on it. I really don't think I could have coped that long under Henry's command in a tour environment, day after day being made to feel inferior and as if I didn't have a cat in hell's chance of making the Test team. I would have ended up waking up every morning barely being able to wait to go back to sleep at night.

But as the 2005 tour approached, it felt like we had been through the longest build-up to a series in the history of the game. In that time, everyone who was close to me was, as usual, telling me that I would be selected, but all along I knew that their opinions were not going to count. But it wasn't as if I was getting myself worked up about it. I have always said that nothing can ever top captaining my country. I said it before I became a British Lion, when perhaps it was easier to make such a remark, and I said it after I became a British Lion.

There are so many people in the

How can something mean so much, then so little?

game who harp on about the Lions being the ultimate accolade. I'm sorry, but I cannot agree. To me, playing and captaining Wales cannot be topped, even though the Lions is an amalgamation of the cream of Wales, England, Scotland and Ireland. That is just the way I see it. When I was a kid playing rugby on the local field, I was never Willie John McBride; I was always Gareth Edwards or J.P.R. Williams. And the clincher for me is that Lions tours only come around every four years, so when they do they are very much hit and miss for all players. So much of it is about being in the right place at the right time and whether you happened to have had a good Six Nations immediately prior to a tour. Injuries are another factor. How many great players down the years have been prevented from touring or gone and tried to get through not fully fit?

For these reasons, to set your stall out and place the Lions at the pinnacle of what a player can achieve does not make sense to me. Surely, what someone has given their own country over a long period of time is a more justifiable benchmark. Some people say that to be a rugby legend you have to be a Lion. I disagree completely. In saying that, I don't in any way intend to be disrespectful to the Lions concept, but to me a rugby legend is someone who has played 500 games for their club and maybe 50 times for their country, who has been at the coal face over a sustained period, who has travelled on a bus for hours playing club matches and put their body on the line over and over again.

For me, the 2005 Lions experience was different right from the start, because I knew that I was in with a better chance of going than ever before. Not only was I playing well for Wales and Toulouse, but I also felt that I was far more of an established player and character in the game. I felt I had something to offer over and above playing. I was no longer someone who would sit at the back of team briefings and daydream. I was now someone who was willing to stand up and take responsibility in a team environment. And if that meant getting up and speaking my mind in front of the best players the British Isles had to offer, then fine.

I did not for a minute take selection for granted, though. What's more, on the day that the squad was announced, I went through a good two hours or so of believing that I had not been picked. The reason was that we had all been told to expect to hear any good news by text on our mobile phones at 11 a.m., with the official announcement due to be made to the media at about noon. Well, back in Toulouse, I didn't receive a bleep, so there I was with Trevor Brennan thinking to myself, 'Oh well, if it's not to be, it's not to be.' All the Toulouse boys knew that we were both in the shake-up to go and were asking every five minutes whether we were in

or not. Then, I took a call from Jemma, who told me that she was watching Sky Sports News and that I was in, so there must have been some cock-up or other over the plan to text us all.

Rather than a day of unbridled celebration, though, it was bittersweet for me because of the non-selection of Trevor. Even though he had not featured in the Irish side for a while for reasons other than his form, we both really believed he had a great chance. In Ireland, in particular, he had been built up by the media as a genuine prospect and was seen in the same way as Lawrence Dallaglio at that time – a player who was still capable of distinguishing himself in a Lions jersey, even though he was no longer playing Test rugby. I think that had prompted Trevor to start believing that there was a strong chance of him going, but he didn't make the cut and was gutted about it, asking why he had been so strongly tipped only to be discarded in the final analysis.

So, Trevor was trying to bury his disappointment and be pleased for me, whereas I was trying to stifle my excitement and show sympathy to him – and I did genuinely feel for him. But it just meant that we ended up killing the moment for each other. We did go for a meal together that night with our wives, and we had a couple of glasses of champagne to celebrate, but the whole evening never really took off.

No sooner had I been selected than I found myself embroiled in a situation that could have ruined my chances of winning a Lions Test cap before I even had a chance to get on the plane. The French season goes right the way to the beginning of June for teams who make it to the play-off final. And with the Lions leaving in mid-May, I knew that I would have to deal with a clash of interests. I also knew that if Toulouse's season carried on to the very end, my chances of making the team for the first Lions Test would be next to zero, because I just would not have had the time on tour to acclimatise and press my case for selection.

I was getting pressurised by the Lions manager John Feehan to get some clarification on the matter. But I had actually already dealt with the situation head-on from the start, before I had even been selected for the Lions. I had gone to see Guy Novès and told him that if it came down to a choice between the two because the Lions had insisted that I go with them right from the start, then my first commitment would be to the club. I wanted him to know before I even knew whether I was going that there would be no battle for my services, because Toulouse had already won it.

Trevor told me that I was silly to take that stance, because a Lions tour was a once-in-a-lifetime opportunity that had to be grabbed at all costs. But I was not for turning on the matter. I had given it a lot of thought, and my gut feeling was

that the club deserved my commitment. In any case, I always had the captaincy of Wales to fall back on should the Lions react badly to my decision. Again, in my eyes nothing could top captaining my country.

Guy was naturally pleased, because there had been a lot of speculation in the French press about what I would do, but it was not an exercise in arse-licking. It was just me doing what I felt was right. In the end, I just about got away with it anyway, because although I was late joining up with the squad in New Zealand, I got there just in time to make a case for Test inclusion, having left France after we were beaten by Stade Français in the play-off semi-finals.

I have to say that Clive Woodward was brilliant throughout the whole episode. I made sure I kept him informed, and although he could have been awkward about it all, he merely told me how impressed he was with my commitment to Toulouse. 'Just promise me you will bring that commitment with you when you join us,' he said.

I got on really well with Clive. I didn't pretend to be anything other than myself in my dealings with him, even though he is a knight of the realm and, in comparison with me, speaks with a posh accent. I was Alfie, no more, no less, and there were times when I spoke my mind to him. On more than one occasion, I was blunt, saying that I didn't think things were going well in training or that our game patterns were not right.

His response was to say, 'Well, I'm really glad you're letting me know rather than going along with it for the sake of it.'

I was honest with him from the off, and I think he appreciated that. And because I had put my marker down from the word go by speaking my mind, Clive knew what to expect. He knew that what he saw was what he would get. Playing it straight with people by speaking your mind and letting them know where you are coming from is, in my view, the healthiest base from which to form any kind of relationship, socially or in a working environment. That is what I did with Clive.

I was exhausted when I first arrived in New Zealand after a horror flight around the world that I literally thought was never going to end. Half the trouble was that I was on my own and subsequently bored out of my brain. But the sheer length of the journey would have tested the most experienced of travellers. I had to fly from Toulouse to Paris, Paris to Heathrow, Heathrow to Bangkok, Bangkok to Sydney, Sydney to Auckland and then Auckland to Wellington. It was a shocker, and it took me a week to recover from searing jet lag. It meant I had one game, against Wellington at the 'Cake Tin' stadium, to make my mark, and to be fair I felt I did that in a good victory that saw me score a chip-and-chase try in the second half.

I felt really into the whole thing, but coming late to a touring party brought

with it its problems, because I had missed so much of the build-up and preparation. Not only that, but I barely knew anyone other than the Welsh boys, and it was difficult to see them bantering with the Irish, English and Scots when I was still 'Billy No Mates'. But that resolved itself soon enough as I integrated with a great set of lads.

Looking back, I can honestly say that there is not a single member of the party whom I dislike, and I will be eternally grateful for having the chance to get to know the guys from the other nations. For instance, someone like Matt Dawson, now retired, is a friend for life. I would guess that the impression a lot of Welsh supporters have of him is of a rather cocksure English upstart. Well, I can assure you that if he was like that, I wouldn't give him the time of day. But he isn't at all. Daws is one hell of a bloke and was a real favourite with all the Welsh guys, not just for his character but for his competitive nature and ferocious will to win. He may not have been one of the most physically imposing rugby players on the planet, but I'd rather have played with him than against him any day. He had such a fierce will to win and loved getting stuck in.

I wasn't long in New Zealand before the drama of selection for the first Test arrived. I say drama because when it came to making the announcement, you would have thought that the entire population of the world was hanging on the choices. In fact, it was embarrassing. It was like some kind of stage show. The team all had to walk into the room with pictures of them coming up on screens and a DJ in the corner. And the media . . . well, you had to see to believe how many of them were there.

When the team had been named earlier to the players in the team room, there were actually no great surprises. We had pretty much all worked out what it would be from the training and matches prior to this. Personally, I knew I was playing, and I knew I was playing on the wing. But afterwards when we had to go and speak to the media, I just had no appetite for it whatsoever. For all my experience in dealing with the press up to that point, I wasn't ready for the sheer number of journalists. I was well out of my comfort zone. Don't get me wrong, I can handle talking to the Welsh press and the rugby lads from the English national titles, but there were about 70 or 80 journalists thronging around all looking for an angle and watching every move we were making.

However, I look back on that day and laugh because of one episode, which, in hindsight, was absolutely comical. I was sitting down with about ten press guys milling around me and two other fellows, who I also assumed were media men, sitting either side of me. It struck me that the two of them seemed a bit weird because they were not asking me any questions, their eyes looked a little glazed over and they were both reeking

of booze. Now, I know journalists are traditionally meant to be fond of a drink or two, but this pair smelled as though they had been on a fortnight's bender. Anyway, I answered all the questions that came my way, and the press lads gradually filed away as they got what they were after, leaving me sitting there with these two blokes. Thinking that they too were press boys, I said, 'All right, lads, are we done?'

'Oh, we're not journalists,' one of them said in a Welsh accent. 'We're just a couple of pissheads who have come along to meet you!' They had just strolled into the room in our Christchurch hotel, not having been asked for any identification, and sat next to me as I spoke to the press. 'Anyway, all the best,' one of them said, and with that they just walked off! I got up and walked away chuckling to myself. It was a rare moment of light relief in a country where I found it very difficult to switch off from rugby and relax for even the briefest of moments.

In New Zealand, you can't get away from rugby – anywhere. Everywhere you go, it is all people want to talk about. In fact, the only place it was possible to get away from it was the team room, where there would often be players who wanted to talk about other things and rest their minds from the intensity of it all.

When I'm overseas, I like to go out and about every now and then, for a meal or to see the sights. But in New Zealand we couldn't. It just seemed like there was nowhere for us to go and

nothing to do. There are only so many frames of snooker or games of table tennis you can play before you cross your boredom threshold and feel like you are going out of your mind. I met up with Steve Hansen, who was, of course, the assistant coach to Graham Henry at that time, on occasion, hooking up for a coffee and a chat. But those moments were all too rare.

As for the playing side of the tour, well, I guess we will not be judged favourably by history. In the build-up to the first Test, there were several occasions when I thought, 'What the hell are we doing?' One of the problems we had was that Clive had clearly gone there not just to win the Test series but to win over the hearts and minds of the New Zealand nation as well. His argument was, 'Let's get them on our side.' That was the way he insisted we could beat them. But it meant that on what were supposed to be our days off during the week, we found ourselves doing community work. We were doing something every day. We never had any time to switch off.

Some days, again when we were supposed to be off, we were having to get up early and travel for two or three hours on a bus just to take some session at some far-flung school. OK, there is always a certain amount of that stuff that you have to do, but it got to the point that we all began to feel we were doing more community work than rugby training.

Then, when this had become clear, Clive stopped it – and the result was a backlash from the New Zealand public who accused us of neglecting our duties and breaking promises. But the fact was that we had reached a position at which we just could not prepare properly. There was always something that had been pre-booked, and we were finding that there just weren't enough hours in the day.

Looking back, a big part of me thinks that Clive should have said from the start, 'Sod the lot of you. We've come here to win, and we don't care what any of you think.' I really felt all this hindered us. Although it is easy to judge in hindsight, I feel we should have gone there to play rugby first and foremost, with winning friends some way down the list of priorities.

But this wasn't the only situation that we discovered had greatly offended the Kiwi people. No, if there was a fuss made about us cancelling day visits, there was an even bigger rumpus when our reaction to the haka in the first Test apparently struck a chord with their sensibilities. We had received a letter from a Maori dignitary some time before the game informing us of how we were supposed to accept the haka in line with tradition. It detailed how the youngest member of our tribe was meant to stand in front of the leader, with the rest forming a semicircle behind him. Then when the opposition finished the haka with the usual jump, the young one was supposed to pick up a piece of grass and throw it. That, we were told, was a form of pulling the rug from underneath the opposition and thus accepting their challenge.

So, that was precisely what we did. But guess what? We discovered afterwards that it wasn't good enough for the Kiwis. Yes, apparently our well-intentioned actions had in some way or another offended them. In trying to make an effort to dignify their haka as far as we could and do what we thought was right, we had, it seemed, only annoyed them. Exactly what you are supposed to do in response to it, I still don't know – and I can't say I particularly care. But I had absolutely no time for their complaining.

To tell you the truth, I was pissed off we were making the effort in the first place. As far as I was concerned, we should have just stood in a line and watched them get on with it like every other team in the world does. From a respect point of view, that would have sufficed, as long as none of us sloped off to our own line in the way David Campese had infamously done at the 1991 World Cup.

Of course, the big story ahead of the first Test was the omission of Gavin Henson, but I can't say I was particularly surprised, and I don't mean that in any inflammatory way. In fact, I don't think it was much of a shock to any of the players. I think that because of who

Gavin was, because of his personality, it was made into big news when from an out-and-out playing point of view it wasn't. In all honesty, it was rare to see Gavin out of his room on tour. He hid himself away, which was fine if that was what he wanted. As far as I was concerned, Clive's plan for his first team had been in his head long before we left the UK.

It took me about four days from when I arrived before I registered my concerns to him. I had spoken to all the Welsh boys and got their feedback on how things were going, and Clive had clearly adopted captains from all four of the home nations. At that time, Wales were playing the best rugby of all the nations, and our lads felt we were playing too physical a game with not enough flair. I pulled Clive aside and told him the way we were feeling. 'This is the general feeling of the Welsh boys,' I said. 'We would like to be able to express ourselves a bit more and play a bit more rugby.'

Again, he was receptive. 'I'm not saying I will do it,' he replied, 'but thanks for coming to me and telling me.'

By the same token, I'm not saying that the opinions of the Welsh boys were necessarily right. Actually, looking back, perhaps we might have had more success if we had played even more of a power game and utilised the strength of the English forwards a bit more. Who knows?

• • •

The first Test was not just a hugely disappointing experience, it was a weird one, going down 21–3 in depressing fashion as we did. In the changing-room beforehand, I wasn't even that pumped up for it. Why, I couldn't precisely say. The atmosphere was strange. Everyone was really trying to get things going, but it was as if we were entering the beginning of the end of a long, hard season, and for me it just wasn't happening between us. The vibe wasn't there, as hard as we tried to get it going. Amazingly, for the size of the occasion, there was no oomph there – some days, that oomph just won't come. It's not down to any one individual or a lack of effort. Personally, I didn't know what to expect, because it wasn't the Test environment that I was used to with Wales. But it definitely didn't work for me, and I stress again that it was nobody's fault in particular.

We then ran onto the field with the crowd whistling and baying, formed a circle and Brian O'Driscoll began talking to us. 'There are all these people who have come to watch us. They have travelled thousands of miles to watch us, and we cannot let them down,' was the gist of Brian's message.

Then, even though I wasn't captain, I decided to pipe up with my own thoughts. 'It's not for them, it's for us,' I said, contradicting the skipper. 'It is for us in the circle. This is for the boys I am looking at right here, right now. That is why I am doing this. We are the ones who have smashed each other week

183

I launch what was a rare attack for the Lions against New Zealand.

in, week out. We are the ones who have earned the right to wear this jersey, and so we will do it for ourselves.'

I didn't cut across Brian; I waited for him to finish what he was saying. And I didn't feel for a moment that I had undermined him in any way. It felt right to speak and, as I have stressed earlier, such situations demand spontaneity. I respect Brian O'Driscoll as a player and as a captain, and in no way would I ever be derogatory towards him. But at the time I thought, 'Sod it. I'm only going to be a British Lion once in my life. I say this now, or I never say it. If I cock it up, so what? At least I will have had a go.' What's more, I felt that what I said was well received by the lads, and I have never for a moment sensed that Brian resented what I did.

Unfortunately, though, Brian's contribution as captain and to the tour itself was to end in disgraceful circumstances just seconds after kick-off. At a breakdown in play, he was lifted up by New Zealand captain Tana Umaga and hooker Keven Mealamu and dumped head first into the turf. He could have broken his neck rather than the collarbone that he did, and the protestations of innocence from the New Zealand camp were made to look very silly when the camera footage emerged later.

My early try in the second Test gave us hope, but it soon evaporated.

I was right next to the incident, although by the time Brian landed I had one eye on him and one eye on the play carrying on around me, having run off to fulfil my defensive duties. But if you look at the footage, you will see the pair of them have one or two goes at lifting Brian before they manage to actually get him airborne. What irks me to this day is that I clearly heard the linesman, who had walked onto the field at that stage, shout, 'Leave him alone, leave him alone,' as they were trying to scoop him up. The problem was that they didn't leave him alone.

Meanwhile, I carried on until the ball went dead, and then I sprinted across to the linesman as Brian lay on the deck in agony. 'Oi, you said leave him alone, and then they picked him up and chucked him,' I ranted at the top of my voice, pointing at him. 'What are you going to do about that?' But nothing was done. Nothing.

We went on to lose, and although we made an appeal about something that was as clear as day, nothing was done about it by the officials or the citing commissioner. The whole business was appalling, and of course all we got from the New Zealanders were the predictable accusations of sour grapes in defeat.

I really felt for Brian. He was done good and proper, and done illegally in

my view. And neither the linesman nor the citing commissioner had the balls to do anything about it. When he was carted off on the stretcher, it was more or less clear that his tour was over, even if the players weren't 100 per cent sure at the time.

After that, it just went downhill for us, and we ended up slumping to defeat with just a Jonny Wilkinson penalty to show for our efforts. We couldn't complain. We had been totally outclassed by a New Zealand team that not only carried far more potency in their back line, but also gave us something of an unexpectedly torrid time up front. It was hugely deflating, especially as we knew that claiming the first Test was so important in terms of a series victory.

The one thing I remember more than anything about the game was that by the end of it I was probably as cold as I have ever been in my rugby-playing life. There were hailstones coming down that felt as though they were the size of tennis balls. I had been moved to full-back by the closing stages, and I recall thinking that if a high ball went up I would be done for because I was reaching the stage at which I couldn't feel my hands. In short, it was one of those games in which you just find yourself counting down the clock. And to think that this was the first Test of my one-and-only British Lions tour. But that was just the way the game was. From start to finish, it didn't happen for us, and maybe the roots of our poor performance were in

the lack of atmosphere generated among us beforehand.

Some people suggested that the Lions party was too large, but I don't think so. I think it was proved by the number of injuries that we suffered that taking so many players was necessary. One of the arguments against the size of Clive's squad was that it didn't allow individuals to get into the groove and hit top gear for the Test matches. But I'm not entirely convinced by that. I had played 50 games by the time I arrived on tour, so the last thing I felt I personally needed was loads of matches before the Tests, for which I hoped to be fresh and ready to roar. Yes, you need a big squad, and, yes, that big squad needs time to be whittled down into an effective team. But you cannot come in from a hectic season and do it all.

Of course, with the first Test done with and Brian O'Driscoll done for, the question of finding a new captain had to be addressed – and quickly given that there was only a week to go before the second Test.

The day after the defeat, Clive called me over to him at breakfast. I had just assumed that the Irish second row Paul O'Connell would be asked, but seconds later I heard the unexpected coming from Clive's mouth. 'Look, obviously Brian is out, so I want you to take over the captaincy,' he said. 'Would you like to think about it?'

'I don't need to think about it,' I

replied. 'I'll do it, just so long as I can do it my way, the way I think is right.'

'You do it whichever way you think is best,' Clive said.

I couldn't believe it. I was very excited and immediately set about texting Jemma and my parents to tell them.

Of course, the most pressing challenge for me was to get the players behind me, and while achieving that with Wales was one thing, doing the same with guys from the other nations, some of whom were legends of the game in their own right, was clearly not something I could take for granted. But I didn't change my leadership methods. I said to the lads that I didn't care what nationality they were or whether they were worth a million pounds, they were all the same in my eyes.

What I felt was needed at that time was humour. Not only had we lost the first Test, but the drudgery of being on tour was starting to wear everyone down as well. I sensed that the Irish, Scots and English were not having that much fun in their respective national camps at that time. Everything they did seemed very drilled and serious, and the attitude seemed to be that you couldn't possibly be working if you were having a laugh. My attitude, though, has always been that if you can have a laugh and work at the same time, then you work better. So, I tried to make a few jokes here and there, and attempted to lighten the mood.

I also went to see Clive and told him

that I wanted to pick a vice-captain. He asked me who I thought it should be and suggested that I might want to consider the English flanker Martin Corry. But with respect to Martin, who I think is a great player and person, I didn't want him as my deputy. I wanted someone who I felt could bring a bit more fun to the role, and with that in mind there was only one fellow for the job – Steve Thompson, England's hooker and another who has since hung up his boots.

'He's a great bloke,' I told Clive. 'All the boys really like him, and he is great fun to be around. What's more, he will work hard.' That was it: Thommo was my vice-captain, and I was chuffed, because I considered us to be on the same wavelength. So, the mantra going into the second Test was, 'Let's train hard, and let's work hard, but let's have some fun while we're at it.'

I didn't really do that much talking for the rest of the week, although there was one, now infamous, little speech that I did make. The English boys still talk about it with me when we meet up in the Six Nations. It came the day before the second Test, while we were on the training ground in a huddle.

'Look, boys,' I said. 'I've got just two words that sum up our situation at present: "Don't fucking panic!"' We all stood there for a split second looking at each other before I broke the silence by saying, 'Oh, that's three words, isn't it!' Everyone collapsed with laughter, and it

The captains are called to book.

broke all the tension in one fell swoop.

My language is bad enough as it is, but when I'm around the boys it tends to degenerate even more, and I can't say I'm particularly proud of that. But that little incident summed up my first week as captain of the British Lions – we had worked hard, but we had had fun doing so. What's more, I felt as though the boys came with me, got behind me and respected me. I have always stressed that I was not the initial captain of the Lions and that all I was doing was taking over from Brian in respect of leading the side. But the game is nothing without enjoyment, and that message was at the heart of everything I tried to do. I was new to a lot of the guys, and I hope they found my approach different.

After taking over as skipper, I was dealing more and more with Alistair Campbell, our press officer, whose inclusion in the party drew derision from the media corps who deemed him an obstructive and totally unnecessary presence. But I found him to be a top man, and we had many great laughs. Because of his history working as a spin doctor at the highest level of government, we were all fascinated to know the truth behind certain episodes that had gone on while he was bounding around the corridors of power as one of Tony Blair's henchmen. The lads picked on various so-called scandals and demanded he tell them the truth – though I don't think he ever did! However, he did confess to us that he had once had a problem with

drink. We asked him whether the death of Princess Diana had been an inside job and what George Bush and Bill Clinton were like. More often than not, he would try to answer us as honestly as he could without betraying any official secrets. Also, he was willing to have the mickey taken out of him, which we did mercilessly. That said, I have to agree with the doubts expressed about him needing to be there in the first place. And there was one occasion when something he did dropped me right in it.

If you recall, Campbell took a hell of a lot of stick for putting out made-up quotes from Gavin Henson after his omission from the first Test team and then arranging for a photographer to release pictures of Gavin and Clive looking like the best of buddies, even though the pair of them didn't have a clue that the shots were being taken. The critics argued that this type of spin doctoring had no place in rugby. And they had a point.

I was even more ready to sympathise with Campbell's detractors later on when he released 'quotes' from me ahead of the second Test. Apparently, I believed that what had happened to Brian O'Driscoll in the first Test would fire us up like never before. Now, even if I did privately believe that there was a small percentage of that terrible incident that we could use to our benefit, I would never have entertained saying so publicly for fear of motivating the All Blacks.

I was very annoyed when I learned of

the release, and I pulled our press man up on it. 'Oi, Campbell,' I said. 'This is rugby, not bloody politics. I probably know more about the rugby press than you ever will. I didn't say a word of this. You've just given New Zealand a bloody team talk.'

'Oh, yes, I suppose . . .' was his rather mealy-mouthed response. But the horse had bolted.

For all his experience in government, I think Campbell was learning as he went along when it came to rugby. I say again, he was an outstanding bloke. He was not someone I would normally meet, but he was prepared to be one of the boys.

When the day of the second Test arrived – our last chance to save the series and the entire tour – I was wound up a treat and absolutely mad for it. I felt completely different from how I had felt a week earlier. I cannot explain why that was or whether it was simply because I was captain, but sometimes as a rugby player you get these warm, positive feelings enveloping you about two days before a match. And this was one of those occasions. 'This is going to be brilliant,' I said to myself, and I couldn't wait for kick-off to arrive.

Then I put something into my body that sent me into overdrive. If I had merely felt wound up beforehand, now I felt as though I could run the one-hundred metres in five seconds. It was nothing illegal, I stress. No, I drank an energy drink called Focus, which was

a favourite among the English boys. Moments after it had gone down, I felt as if I had taken some drug that was making me go crazy. For some reason, it had a huge effect on me. I took to the field that evening with my eyes bulging, ready to go at the All Blacks like some crazed wild dog. But although I glided underneath the posts for a try early on, it was to prove a false dawn for us, because we then proceeded to take the heaviest of all the Test defeats, losing 48–18 after completely losing our way for most of the rest of the match.

Yet it wasn't really about how bad we were. The fact was that we were never allowed into it by a New Zealand team that I am convinced would have thrashed any side in the world at that time. They were that good. Not only did they have a potent back line with their outstanding fly-half Danny Carter pulling the strings, but they stood up to us in the forwards as well, which was a department we had hoped to get the better of. On top of that, Graham Henry, Steve Hansen and Wayne Smith had them supremely well drilled.

So, the series was gone. There was disappointment, sure, but I don't look back on it and remember it as a time when I felt real devastation. We hadn't been good enough, simple as that, and no amount of dwelling on the reasons why was going to change anything. As a player and stand-in captain, I knew I had given everything I had, but it always came back to the difference between the

two sides out on the park. Had we played them ten times, I'm not sure we'd have got the better of them.

However, what followed that night was something that I regretted for the rest of the tour. Even though the game had finished, my body was still feeling the effects of the energy drink I had taken beforehand. I couldn't sit still in the changing-room, and when I looked in the mirror, my pupils were like dinner plates. I could barely stop talking, and instead of arriving back in the changing-room and slumping in a corner, devastated by what was a humbling defeat, I was still supercharged. And, unfortunately, I was still supercharged when I got to the post-match function at the hotel in Auckland.

I am glad that it did not affect the speech I made, and after I delivered it I felt pleased with everything I had said. I hadn't said anything out of the ordinary, but the words had flowed, and the sentiment of me being proud to have led the Lions, proud of the whole squad and willing to give credit where it was due to New Zealand was more or less on the money as far as I was concerned. It couldn't have been too bad, because Raewyn Henry, Graham's wife, came up to me afterwards and congratulated me on what I had said and how I had said it.

But things sort of took a downward turn after that. I began drinking bottles of the New Zealand brew Steinlager with Stephen Jones and Steve Hansen,

and they were going down like there was no tomorrow. It was turning into one of those nights when there was never a moment when I didn't have a bottle on the go. No sooner had I drained one than I was lifting the top off the next one. Goodness knows how many I'd sunk by the end of the function, by which time Stephen and I had been so caught up in our drinking that the team bus had left us behind.

It didn't really matter, though, because we knew where the boys had gone to continue the evening – a club in downtown Auckland – and we made our own way there. The drinking continued at a fierce pace, and I was fast getting out of control. The club was packed full with not just the Lions but most of the New Zealand squad as well, and I was completely out of it, dancing the night away, wearing a pair of shades and one of those headband things with two metal springs sticking up from it like a pair of antennae.

At one stage, Tom Shanklin appeared next to me with a tray of shorts – about 12 to 14 shot glasses full to the brim with some spirit or other that I presume he had bought for the boys. I picked up every single glass and knocked it back. Just to make even more of an exhibition of myself, I was jumping up into the DJ pulpit every now and then, pretending to scratch records like some street rapper and shouting into the microphone. The other players could barely believe what they were seeing, and Steve Hansen later

told me that the All Black flanker Richie McCaw had made a remark about what a nutcase I was. I can't say that I blame him on the evidence of what he saw that night. But I was to pay a heavy price for my exuberance.

In many ways, the next morning was the calm before the storm, because I was still drunk from the night before. I managed to get through a bit of pool recovery and then headed back to bed. It was then that the full extent of what I had poured into my body the night before started to take its revenge. To this day, I am convinced that I had alcohol poisoning – I was that rough. My hangover raged for two days, during which time I could barely lift myself out of bed and couldn't face a thing to eat. As for training, it was all I could do to walk to the toilet, never mind run around a field.

Because of my self-inflicted state, I had left myself vulnerable to picking up an infection, and I duly did just that. Whatever it was, it hit me for six, and I spent most of the week unable to contribute to the preparation for the last Test and more or less convinced that I would not be able to play. As it turned out, I did somehow manage to get through the match, but I can assure you that I took to the field feeling far from fit. In fact, I dragged myself through it, having only begun to feel reasonably well the day before.

We took another sound beating at the hands of the All Blacks. They were never going to be content with a series victory that saw us claim the dead-rubber third Test as a consolation. No, they wanted to rub our noses in it, and the 3–0 result meant they did just that, even if we did acquit ourselves better than we had done in the previous two encounters.

After the game, I delved into my bag and found a packet of fags. How they got there, I couldn't say! I strolled into the physio's room, sat on the couch and lit up. It was the end of a long season. Some of the players walked past, most of them trying to wave the smoke away, and then the tour manager Bill Beaumont walked in. 'Alfie, it's nice to see someone doing it the old-fashioned way,' he said. I smiled and inhaled another drag.

Clive said a few words of thanks to us that night, and most of the squad headed out on the town for the night to celebrate the end of a long and often arduous tour. Not me, though. I'd learned my lesson of a week before and wasn't silly enough to go through it all again. I just stayed in the hotel for a quiet night, chatting with whoever was around and consoling myself with the brilliant thought that the next day I would be heading home.

And that was more or less it. There was no goodbye ceremony or any kind of big fuss on our departure. We all kind of went our own way, with the party being split on different planes.

When I look back on my first and last Lions experience, I will most likely view it as something which could have been

so good but failed emphatically to live up to the best expectations that I had. Becoming a British Lion and getting the chance to be captain will remain milestones of which I am very proud and are things that can never be taken away. They are boxes that have been ticked and will remain ticked for ever. I will harbour proud memories; I will recall moments fondly. But as a general package, it will never really occupy a place close to my heart.

12

JUSTICE? WHAT JUSTICE?

Many people believe that what happens in life depends a lot on simply being in the right place at the right time. Unfortunately, I have learned to my cost that the opposite also applies – you can be in the wrong place at the wrong time, and it can leave you wishing you could turn back the clock.

How many times do we read the same story in the newspapers these days? You know, 'Famous sportsman involved in nightclub bust-up'. They have become ten a penny. I don't claim to know the truth about each one, but I know the truth about what happened when I was inadvertently caught up in an incident back in October 2002.

It was more than three years before I was able to put it behind me. And even now, while I hardly ever think about it, I still carry a raging sense of injustice at the comical way in which so-called justice was meted out by a French court – it had to be experienced to be believed. I did nothing illegal throughout the whole sorry incident, yet I now have an affray charge on my record, a fine of 1,500 euros hanging over me and, most disturbing of all, it briefly led to me being branded a thug in the press and even to my little niece being bullied in school.

Before I go any further, let me say that while I am no angel and have made mistakes in my earlier days, I am not a thug and never will be.

I was in my second spell at Bridgend in the autumn of 2002 when we travelled to south-west France to take on Pau in a European Challenge Cup game, otherwise known as the Shield. It wasn't even a particularly big encounter. I've no wish to denigrate any competition, but the Shield has always been seen as the second-string European tournament, the one in which all the teams who have failed to qualify for the Heineken Cup scrap over a consolation prize.

Pau were a really handy team at that

time, boasting players such as the French international centre Damien Traille and the number 8 Imanol Harinordoquy. We ended up losing the game, but it had been a close affair, and we were not too downhearted as we headed back to our hotel in the town after the game, because we still had to face them at home.

We had a couple of drinks in the hotel bar, but there was a nightclub across the road that was run by the sponsors of the Pau club, and they invited us over. Up to that point, we had just been having a beer or two and a sing-song. That may sound a bit old-fashioned, but if there was one thing our coach Allan Lewis was brilliant at, it was rounding everyone up after a game and getting a good sing-song going, and all the boys loved it.

As time went on, we soon decided to take the sponsors up on their offer and head over to the club. Even J.P.R. Williams, who was with us, came over. By the time we got there, a couple of the lads were getting a little bit loud and boisterous, but it was all harmless stuff. There wasn't any trace of a sinister mood in the air. Then a local handball team came into the club – and that was when things started to go downhill. The team consisted of blokes and girls, and most of them were small, wiry people. Anyway, they had a buffet laid on for them, and they invited us to share some of their food with them.

We then headed upstairs to another room in the club, and that was where the actions of our prop Phil Booth began to drag us all towards what was to become a dangerous zone. Boothy is renowned for being a bit of a showman when he's drunk, and sure enough it wasn't long before he was doing handstands. He had already been kicking it all off downstairs, standing on the bar with his trousers down and what have you, but everyone was taking it in good spirits, and there was a lot of laughter. As he was doing another handstand, he started to topple over. Just at that moment, our club doctor Tony Gray, a small bloke, walked past. Boothy wiped him out, feet first. Tony looked hurt, so we all went over to check he was OK.

As the doc came round from the blow, Boothy made his way over to the stairs, where he confronted another group of people, including a girl who was later to allege that he had grabbed her. I remember looking up and seeing a scrawny bloke take a swing at Boothy. Next, Boothy was running downstairs with the group of people after him, so we decided to follow, just to ensure that things didn't get too out of hand.

When we got downstairs, there was barely any disturbance. It wasn't as if punches were being thrown or anything, but there was a little melee, at the centre of which was a girl and some of her friends, all of whom were screaming at Boothy. The bouncers were there by that point, and everyone was blabbering on at a million miles an hour in French. Then, all of a sudden, the guy who had

swung at Boothy decided to leg it out of the bar.

We had all had a few to drink by that stage, and we thought that he was trying to escape the scene, so Andy Moore said, 'Get him, Alf, he's running away.' I chased after the bloke into the street, with a bellyful of beer inside me, but I got hardly anywhere. I couldn't have gone more than 50 yards before I stumbled and fell into the side of a parked car.

The fellow had got away, and I am glad I got nowhere near to catching him, because who knows what I might have been accused of doing. So, I picked myself up and headed back to the club. By then, those of us who were outside were worried about our guys left inside and were trying to go in and shepherd them out of there. But the bouncers were having none of it, although there was no physical stuff whatsoever at that point. We left it there, and that was it – or so we thought.

A week or so after getting back to Bridgend, we were informed that a letter had arrived at the club from France saying that they were pressing charges. John Samuel, the brother of chairman Leighton Samuel, called a few of us to a meeting and wanted to know who had been fighting. We assured him of the truth, but even though there had been loads of us in the nightclub, Boothy, Andy Moore, Richard Webster and I had been singled out as the ones to blame for the disturbance.

I can understand why Boothy was singled out, but Webby had not even been at the club. He had stayed at the hotel, and Andy Moore and I had certainly done nothing wrong. As far as we were concerned, it was as if they had selected us at random. Our solicitor believed that while Boothy had been an obvious target, the rest of us were singled out because two of us were current Wales players and the other a former Wales international and British Lion. As higher-profile personalities, he explained, we were likely to be viewed as the ones who had more money.

Our initial reaction was to dismiss it as the nonsense it was and assume that it would all blow over. But it wouldn't go away. For the next two years, we found ourselves hopping back and forth to France for meetings with a judge in Pau.

Throughout this process, our accusers' stories were changing. On one visit, Andy Moore was accused of having smacked the girl in the face, which was clearly a complete and utter lie. On another, Boothy, who would later be charged with sexual assault, was alleged to have punched her in the back.

Meanwhile, I had not been accused of anything and nor had Richard Webster, which understandably led us to ask why we were there at all. We made representations to the judge, saying that the rate at which they were changing their story was clearly ridiculous, but our pleas fell on deaf ears. Because it seemed like the whole thing just wasn't

going to go away and the French authorities were doing nothing to help us, we decided enough was enough and that we just wanted it all to end. So even though we were 100 per cent innocent, we decided to give them the only thing they had wanted from us in the first place – money. We decided to bite the bullet and pay them off.

Having lived in France for more than two years, let me enlighten you as to what is happening in their legal system with alarming regularity. It appears that a significant group of people, largely foreign immigrants from places like Morocco – and I say this without a hint of racism – are seeking to claw money out of people by pursuing compensation claims through the courts for the most ludicrously minor things, most of which are invented anyway. It's got to the stage that you only have to look at them in a funny way and you're up in front of a judge. This, it seems, is the fate that had befallen us.

It was an easy way for these people to get money out of us, which is why we just wanted done with it all. But we found we couldn't even do that. Apparently, the case was going through the police files to court, and there was no way we could stop it. My attitude was, 'Fine, let it go to court.' I knew I had done nothing wrong and was convinced that the truth would come out.

After two years of going back and forth to France, even the judge who was dealing with us in the run-up to the

case told us that she could barely believe that it had gone this far. In one meeting, she even put her cards on the table by admitting that as rugby players – me in particular because of my Toulouse association – we were being made an example of. The case, she confessed, would have been thrown out a long time ago had we been ordinary people, and she admitted that these types of legal actions, in which people just wanted money, were becoming a real menace in the French judicial system.

Up to that point, I had had to swallow a load of negative press coverage in Wales and France, which placed me, as the best-known player, at the head of the whole mess. The tone of every report was 'Gareth Thomas and his teammates involved in sexual-assault incident', 'Gareth Thomas this' and 'Gareth Thomas that'. Reading some of it, you would have thought I was some kind of serial killer! But as soon as the judge had been honest enough to tell us the truth, we knew we were going to have to face the music in court regardless.

So, we decided to front it up – or at least three of us did. Richard Webster, Andy Moore and I turned up on the day of the trial, more than three years later in November 2005, but Phil Booth, fearing he would be locked up if found guilty, decided not to go. That meant they tried him in his absence, but the fact that he did not show up did not reflect well on any of us.

From the off, the case was pathetic, an absolute joke. I was made to stand up in a public court – which because of who we were had been packed out by every tramp off the streets and quite frankly stank terribly – and talk about so many things that were irrelevant to the incident, including my wages at Toulouse. The line of questioning I faced from our accusers' lawyer was farcical, only proving that rugby itself was on trial rather than the three of us for anything we had done that night. He proceeded to make a mockery of justice with inquiries like, 'Do you think rugby is a sport played by hooligans?' I stood there, embarrassed for him as much as anything, wondering what on earth such a question had to do with what we were in court for. It was to get even more laughable.

'How many GCSEs and A Levels have you got?' he asked. Incredibly, they got away with this, and moments later came the absolute classic: 'What does J.P.R. Williams think of all this?' I stood there for a moment, dumbstruck.

'Excuse me? J.P.R.? What on God's earth does J.P.R. have to do with all this?' I wondered. Apparently, because J.P.R. was linked to Bridgend and still revered in France thanks to his exploits for Wales in the 1970s, his feelings about the matter were somehow relevant, according to this buffoon.

Then, just to heap even more ridicule on the whole process, he began to list the number of disorderly incidents that had occurred in the French Championship in the previous four weeks. 'There have been five brawls, two red cards and ten yellow cards,' he said. 'What do you think about that?' Again, the idiocy of the question left me lost for words. But that was it, more or less – a trial of the sport of rugby rather than us as individuals.

The eagerly awaited prosecution summing up was next. The accusers' lawyer's appalling argument was that we should be made examples of not because his clients wanted money but because the sport of rugby needed to be cleaned up.

Our solicitors, whom we had brought over from Wales, were brilliant throughout. On more than one occasion, they revealed the case for what it was, saying that it was a total joke. They pointed out that if the case had been heard in the UK and these kinds of questions had been asked, it would have been laughed out of court before it even got off the ground. Furthermore, it would never have approached the trial stage, because it was so blatantly obvious that these people were just after money.

In the end, Webby was cleared, although he was still saddled with legal and travelling costs, while Boothy was fined 3,000 euros and given a suspended six-month jail sentence. Andy Moore and I were, unbelievably, found guilty of affray and fined 1,500 euros, but there was one last priceless piece of French justice to be handed out. It transpired

that Andy, Boothy and I were each responsible for the others' fines. In other words, the judge told me that because I was the only one who lived in France, they would make me pay all of the fines if Boothy or Andy failed to pay up! We can't get the money off Phil Booth ourselves, so we're going to leave it up to you to get it, was the incredible message. It took quite a bit of believing. It was like something out of the Middle Ages.

Throughout all of this, I wasn't really afraid, because my conscience was clear, and I hoped – naively as it turned out – that justice would be done. I have always been brought up to believe that if you have done nothing wrong, then you have nothing to fear. I know Jemma was a little bit afraid, largely because we had to live in France. And as I awaited my sentence after the trial, there was always the thought that if things could be this farcical up to this point, what on earth might lie in store for us further down the line.

The photographs of the victim's so-called injuries, which he had gone to the police station to have taken, did nothing to put me on edge either. The bloke was claiming to have been knocked around by rugby boys, but all he had was a small burn on his back and one above his eye, one of which he had clearly picked at to make worse. He had played handball that day, and these minor burn injuries were exactly the sort of thing he could have sustained in the course of playing a game on an indoor surface.

If I had been guilty, it would have been obvious. For example, if any one of us had hit that scrawny guy with even 50 per cent of our force, his injuries would have been all too apparent. Instead, save for those two little burns, there wasn't a scratch on him.

When we stood up in court next to him, we were, almost literally, twice the size of him, and one of our lawyer's arguments was that if the bloke had been in a brawl with the likes of us, he would be black and blue, rather than just sporting two poxy little burns on his back and eye. So, I had been confident that we would win. That was until our friend started asking his questions about J.P.R.

Three judges, two women and a man, heard the case. One of the women nearly fell asleep in the middle of the proceedings, and the other was tutting with disdain every time I said anything, as if she had made up her mind that I was lying through my teeth. Looking back, I am convinced that we were guilty in their eyes before a question had even been asked.

When it ended, I was just relieved it was all over. The pathetic nature of it all meant that there was no point in wishing I had not been found guilty – I never stood a chance from the outset. The worst thing about it, though, was being branded a thug by sections of the British press, especially when they did not know the full facts.

As I stated earlier, I rarely think about the whole sorry episode now, but there are times when it enters my mind. One such occasion was when the Welsh Rugby Union's application for me to be honoured with Mike Ruddock was turned down because of my conviction. The truth is, though, I couldn't care two hoots about getting an MBE, OBE or whatever. Stuff like that just doesn't matter to me, and anyone who knows me properly will tell you as much.

I have to say, I was angry that Boothy didn't turn up to face the court. It could have been the other way round: we could have left him high and dry to deal with it on his own, and if we had, he would have been in real trouble, as he was the one up on the most serious charge. But we decided to stick together. Boothy had gone back and forth to France every time before the case, but when it came to the crunch he was nowhere to be seen. Instead, he sent a letter to the court claiming that he could not attend due to 'work commitments'.

It annoyed me that someone like Richard Webster, who was not even present when all this was supposed to have happened, was prepared to stand shoulder to shoulder with us, when Boothy, who had done more than any of us to cause the problems in the first place, could not even bring himself to show up. We were all standing in a court in France because of something Boothy had started, yet he was safely oblivious to it all back in Wales.

Thankfully, Toulouse were very supportive of me. I had told them all about the case before I signed, and they assured me that they knew exactly what went on in the French legal system. It also helped that the president René Bouscatel was an ex-judge who knew the score.

The one thing I was worried about was the way that people would perceive me because I had been in court. For a lot of people, that is enough: they don't care about the actual truth of the case and are just content to label you as a wrong 'un who shouldn't be given the time of day. And it hurt and angered me to see that one local newspaper had put together a misleading headline that placed my name next to the words 'sexual assault'. It did not paint an accurate picture, but, hey, I bet it shifted a few extra copies that week.

I was also branded a thug in some quarters, a truly horrible and damning word. To me, a thug is someone who goes down the pub of an evening and picks a fight for no reason – someone who communicates with their fists first. That is just not what I am about. Things became worse when my niece Carys started to get a hard time from some of the other kids at her school about 'what her uncle had been up to'. My mother complained to the newspaper, and the next week they printed an apology. But that meant nothing to me, because the damage had been done.

On reflection, it was a stage of my life that I would like to forget about, but, in saying that, I have learned from it. From now on, if I am out and about and any kind of fight starts, I will walk away. There are so many people out there who are quick enough to start trouble, and the only thing on their minds is making money out of it. So, perhaps there has been some good to come from all of this. If nothing else, maybe the experience will help me to avoid those wrong places at the wrong times.

13

RUDDOCKGATE

I slammed the door of my parents' car outside the BBC Wales studios in Cardiff, knowing I had just lost my head on television, and a nation enthralled by the saga surrounding Mike Ruddock's shock departure as coach of the Wales team had seen it all. I couldn't even remember what I had said on air, but I was in a hell of a state. All that was on my mind was getting back home to see the programme on television in my own front room. Then I would hopefully discover that I had spoken reasonably well on behalf of the players, and the watching public would understand that any loss of control on my part was down to the passion I had for the team and all that we stood for.

'That was the biggest tuck-up in history,' I mumbled to myself as we sped through the Cardiff night and out towards my home in the Vale of Glamorgan. All the while, I was thinking about how the interview on the *Scrum V* programme – the weekly magazine show

that rounds up the state of Welsh rugby from top to bottom – had gone. I had sat in between Jonathan Davies and Eddie Butler, and taken an artillery of awkward questions about the reasons why Mike had left that I could never have prepared myself for even if I had tried.

At the heart of the matter was the suggestion that the players, led by shop steward and captain Gareth Thomas, had knifed Mike in the back by attending some cloak-and-dagger meeting with the Welsh Rugby Union chief executive Steve Lewis to demand his sacking. I didn't blame Jonathan, Butler or Gareth Lewis, the presenter of the show. Deep down, I knew those fellows were only doing their jobs, although I did feel as though they had already made up their minds and that nothing I could have said would have made a blind bit of difference. But that did little to put me at ease.

Mam and Dad had sat behind the scenes alongside the production team

Whose opinion matters?

I'll always respect Mike Ruddock, but we went through some trying times.

while I did my stuff in the studio and had listened to Nigel Walker, who was head of sport, tell his guys to, 'Pull out, pull out. You look like you're just bullying him now.' They too had been totally unprepared for what had unfolded.

The 30-minute journey from the studios to my home passed me by, as a range of doom-filled thoughts scrambled my mind. Then the driveway to our house was crunching underneath the car wheels. I got out into the dank February air and marched in through the front door. The warmth of the house enveloped me, which was always a source of comfort on a cold winter's night, but I did not appreciate it that evening. I remained in a state of utter agitation.

The plan was for me, Jemma, Mam, Dad, and Compo Greenslade and his wife Cath to watch the show and then go out for a bite to eat. But there were none of my usual smiling greetings as I walked through the door to see some of the people who matter most to me in the world. Instead, my eyes felt as though they were bulging out of my head, my face was hot and I could not sit still. I was pacing around the living room as the programme was about to start.

I quickly ducked upstairs to find my favourite puppet of the cartoon character Alf, as if searching for something to give me comfort. 'Alf will give me good luck,' I thought. I picked him up and held him tight.

I returned to the living room, which had by then filled up with the others, all of whom were eager to see my performance. They had all chosen their seats and were waiting for the programme to start like some Hollywood movie. I still couldn't sit down. Seconds later, the most frightening ordeal of my life began. All week, I had been feeling light-headed, but as I leant against the fireplace just as the *Scrum V* titles began to roll, I started to feel pins and needles down my left arm. I retreated to a chair in the corner of the room underneath an alcove beneath the stairs. I was behind everyone else, and they were all glued to the television. My arm had gone to sleep. I was holding it up in the air as if trying to reach out and grab something, all the time asking myself what on earth was wrong. I also realised that I couldn't really move my neck. I then lost all feeling down my left-hand side, even the sight in my left eye.

As long as I live, I do not think I will ever experience such a terrifying situation. My first thought was, 'I'm having a heart attack, and I cannot believe that rugby has done it to me.' I thought all the stress of the Ruddock business was to blame. 'The one thing outside of my family that I love in life is going to end up killing me,' I told myself.

I shouted, 'No, no,' and then began sliding off the chair onto the floor. I was desperately trying to manoeuvre myself around in a circle so that I could get one last look at all my friends and family

I do battle with Eddie Butler during the infamous *Scrum V* appearance.

On the defensive at Broadcasting House.

before I died. The first words I can remember hearing after I collapsed were those of my mam saying, 'Gareth, stop being so bloody stupid. Stop messing around!' I couldn't blame her. I've cried wolf so many times, usually when playing the fool around my family and friends. Not this time, though. In fact, saying no was my attempt to tell Mam and everybody else that it was not a joke this time – this time it was for real.

I was on the floor, and as far as I knew I only had moments to live. I could make out everyone running around in a blind panic with shouts of 'Turn that bloody telly off' ringing around the room. Just before someone got to the switch, I could hear the dulcet tones of Butler booming out from the set. 'Oh no,' I thought. 'I'm about to die, and the last voice I'm going to hear is Eddie Butler's. I'm going to meet my maker with him shouting, "It was player power, Thomas – and you were to blame!"'

By then, I was flat out on the carpet, gasping for breath, filling my lungs with short bursts of air and clinging desperately to Compo's leg as if my life depended on it. The scariest thing was that the inside of my body was beginning to feel cold and numb, as if it was in the first stages of shutting down. It might sound over the top, but it was then that I really thought I was going to die.

I could still hear Jemma's soothing words. She managed to stay quite calm, sipping from a cup of tea throughout and telling me to 'keep breathing, Alf'.

I could also see my mother running around screaming. She knew what I had been through in the last week, and she too believed that the accusation that I was responsible for Mike's exit was going to send me to an early grave. It was a fair enough assumption to make, because at the time nobody could think of any other reason why such an attack should have happened.

Doctors have since discovered that a bang to the head, which made me fall awkwardly to the floor as I scored a try for Toulouse against Pau the weekend before the Six Nations opener against England, had caused an artery in my neck to become damaged. I had been walking around blissfully unaware of the problem for the best part of two and a half weeks. The attack had been the end result.

Lying on the floor in my home, I squeezed Compo's fingers and tried to trigger the feeling in my left side. I was a desperate, crumpled figure. Then Compo, whose calmness amid the frenzy had been a real help, decided to blow gently into my face. I found it had an incredibly soothing effect on me, and I finally began to recover something like my normal breathing cycle. Eventually, after about ten minutes, I recovered enough feeling in my body and my breathing stabilised sufficiently for me to haul myself up into a chair, though my eyes rolled and my head pounded for all it was worth. My mam cursed everyone who had thrown flak my way

in the past fortnight or so. I told her not to worry about it.

That night, I decided that I was never going to lace up my boots for anybody ever again. Not Wales, not Toulouse, not the Pencoed second XV. And I definitely wasn't going to give the time of day to anyone who didn't know the real me. Because as far as I was concerned, that had been the root of all the trouble – people who didn't know me making snap judgements based on duff information.

When the ambulance arrived, the medics gave me a blood test, monitored my heart and said that the attack had probably been down to sheer exhaustion. At the time, they obviously didn't have a clue about the knock I had taken, and in all the confusion it never occurred to any of us to mention it.

I went in the ambulance to the Princess of Wales Hospital in Bridgend, and it was there that things really hit home. I was only 31 years of age, but I was hooked up to a heart monitor in some hospital. How had it come to this? I still didn't have a clue what the real reasons for my condition were, and the nurse who attended to me told me to come back the next day for a scan, in the meantime only being able to guess at what might have happened. 'I think you could have had a really severe migraine,' she said. But that didn't really stack up, because I had never suffered from a migraine in my life. To be honest, it scared me to think that it could have been a migraine; in other words, something that could

come back intermittently in the future with such severe symptoms as I had just experienced.

A couple of days later, a scan at the BUPA hospital in Cardiff revealed what was wrong – an artery in my neck had ruptured when I took the blow in the French league match. It was a huge relief. The attack had happened because of something very specific, and most importantly of all it was something from which I could recover. From the moment I knew I would be able to play again, I resolved to do just that, and my attitude towards those who had slung mud my way was, 'I'll show the lot of you. If you want a battle, you've got a battle.'

My brush with death, for that is what a ruptured neck artery is, had not been caused by stress, but the doctors admitted that it could hardly have helped. In a way, the episode was a fitting culmination to a period of four months or so during which the glow from our 2005 Grand Slam had faded. That spring afternoon in Cardiff when Wales had ended a 27-year wait for a clean sweep by beating Ireland now seemed a long way off. When the Wales squad met up for the 2005 autumn internationals, I was already concerned that we were slipping into bad habits. And, yes, the role of head coach Mike Ruddock was in my opinion becoming a problem that would eventually need to be addressed if nothing changed.

The secret of our success in winning the Grand Slam was in the attention we paid

to the little things in and around the squad – the way we conducted ourselves from the moment we met up in camp to the time we left the changing-room in the Millennium Stadium after the all-important match. On the training field, for example, if we were doing a drill that required us to attack the middle of the pitch, the point of the attack had to be in line with, say, the right-hand post, not between the two posts. It was the type of thing that Steve Hansen used to hammer us for getting wrong, calling a halt to the session and demanding we start again until we got it right. It used to drive us nuts, but we all came to realise the importance of precision in these situations. Now, though, we were just carrying on with the drill, not worried that our angles might have been slightly out, and it seemed that there was nobody prepared to call us to book over it, no figure of outright authority who would be on us like a ton of bricks if we were sloppy in anything we did.

Other outwardly trivial things were also slipping. For example, when we were running in a line to warm up before training, we were too often fragmented, instead of all being perfectly together and looking like a team that meant business. A little thing, yes, but the little things all added up. And there were rumours that some of the lads had skived off weights sessions. It was so unlike anything that we stood for.

However, it was off the field that the general slackening was arguably most evident. As an international team, we were lucky that almost everything we needed was provided for us, making our lives that little bit more comfortable. One example was bottled water. There was gallons of the stuff at every training session, and the moment you felt any type of thirst coming on you were welcome to go and take a bottle. Ever since we had truly become a team under Steve Hansen, it was an unwritten rule that if you opened a bottle of water and took a few swigs, you didn't then just discard it half-full and go and open another one an hour or so later. Doing so was regarded as taking the mickey and a totally unnecessary waste that showed a disregard for the things that were given to us as a team. But it was starting to happen, and, worse still, the half-empty bottles were being left around the place for someone else to clear up.

Not only that, but the changing-room was also being left in a mess with lads thinking that it was OK to scrape the mud off the base of their boots and just leave it on the floor. Before, it would always have been swept up and put in a designated basket. It was the same for dressings and bandages, which were now just being cut off and dumped for somebody else to clear up. And if you opened a new pair of training shorts, you never just left the wrapping on a bench or on the floor, but that was now happening as well.

After one of the 2005 autumn internationals, I was the last one out of

the home changing-room, and when I looked back over my shoulder I saw that the place was a disgrace – it looked like a bomb had hit it. In the past, we had always considered cleaning up after ourselves to be part of our team ethic. It was a little standard that made us what we were, and now it was disappearing. As unimportant as it might seem to outsiders, what I was seeing was the gradual disappearance of all the little things that had made us a great squad.

That day, I apologised to Viv, the guy who had to clean up the changing-room after us. Yes, it was his job, but the fact that he had to go in and sort out a mess created by us, mess that just a few months before would never have been there in the first place, really riled me. And, let me stress, this is not a case of me having a pop at the rest of the boys, because I was getting caught up in it all as much as any of them. We were all slipping into bad habits without realising it. The showers were constantly left in a mess, and the gym we used at the Vale of Glamorgan was being left in a mess. It just wasn't us. It wasn't us at all.

It also emerged that on the morning after the match some of the boys ordered Cokes from the bar at the hotel and then left without settling their bill. Hardly a hanging offence, I know – the bill would always have been taken care of – but it was yet another unnecessary pain in the arse for whoever was left to deal with it.

We had always had pride in our appearance and respect for the things that surrounded us, not just pride in our performance on the pitch. We wanted people to remark that we'd left the changing-room shipshape, that nothing had been broken and that each and every one of us had been polite no matter whom we had been dealing with. All these little things, some of which were not expected of international teams, were important to us. And, I stress again, they made us what we were. We had come to see this type of mucking in as part of what we were about. As players, we all knew how effective this approach was, and we all knew that on this score we were guilty of dereliction of duty.

The biggest concern for me was that I was convinced that all these lazy little habits were affecting what we were doing on the pitch. The only analogy I could think of to describe how I felt was that of a tower. If you take out one of the blocks at the base, as small as it might be, it causes the whole lot to collapse.

A few of the senior players and I called a meeting during the autumn campaign and spelled out what was happening and how it had to be addressed. There were a lot of new players in the squad who had not been schooled in our ways, and I did not want to come across as some kind of preaching headmaster type. But there were things that needed to be said, so we called everyone together and delivered a few home truths. And for a time, things improved. However, the upturn was only temporary. The bad

habits gradually came back, which was inevitable without a figure of genuine authority to stamp them out.

I didn't really address this issue with Mike, because I did not want to go to him and lay on the line the importance of a type of behaviour that had been hammered into us by his predecessor. I felt all along that there was only a certain amount we could do about it as players. But I hoped our squad meeting would be enough, because sometimes the best people at getting through to players are players themselves. I often disregard comments from outsiders because I know they are ill-informed. But if a player says he is not happy about something, I will always stop in my tracks and listen, because he is someone who stands by my side at the coal face.

In terms of the actual playing side of things, away from the bad habits off the field, I also had major concerns about where we were heading on the pitch and the amount of work that needed to be done to keep us among the leading teams in the world. And we got off to a bad start in the opening game of the 2005 autumn series when we were thrashed 41–3 by the All Blacks.

In hindsight, there were obvious reasons for the one-sidedness of the score. For a start, I personally didn't feel anywhere near as prepared as I should have done going into the game. I had played in the Heineken Cup for Toulouse against Wasps the Sunday before and

had then spent the Monday recovering. We then did a light training session on the Tuesday, had the Wednesday off and then did team runs on the Thursday and Friday. When the full-strength squad had not been together properly for more than six months, it was nowhere near enough to be able to take on and beat the best team in the world.

Don't get me wrong: going into the game we all felt that we were indeed ready and that most bases had been covered – it was only ever going to become apparent to us in hindsight that this was not the case. What I did know going into the encounter was that I couldn't pick up on the vibe I've already mentioned that you always feel as a rugby player when you know your team is really firing on all cylinders. Instead, that extra-special atmosphere, that elusive ingredient that is difficult to put into words, just wasn't there, and there was no way of creating it. I could tell that there was nowhere near the same expectation among the boys of beating the Blacks as there had been the year before when we pushed them to within a single point and should really have beaten them. Consequently, we were handed a lesson by Graham Henry's men, who ran in five tries against us, with their brilliant wing Rico Gear grabbing a hat-trick and the incomparable fly-half Danny Carter amassing a twenty-six-point haul. It was all so unexpectedly easy for them in the end.

We were better against South Africa a week later but still well beaten, the final

scoreboard reading 33–16 in the Boks' favour. And the build-up to that match really sticks in my mind. The key issue of the week was over what defensive system we should use. South Africa were well known for their rigid and suffocating blitz defence, and having watched them cause terrible problems for teams on the international circuit I wanted us to give them a taste of their own medicine rather than sticking with our drift-defence strategy.

To explain, a blitz defence involves the defending back line operating on a man-to-man basis, with defenders sprinting up in straight lines into the faces of their opposite numbers. The way to beat it is with precision mis-passing or little dinks over the top, but if the blitz is done well, it can be a nightmare to outwit. The drift is different in that defenders operate in zones, standing back a little bit more and inviting the opposition to find a gap in their wall, although they obviously still have attackers whom they are responsible for stopping.

I wanted us to go with the blitz and surprise the South Africans, but Mike was reluctant because it was a system that the team had tried in Argentina the summer before and failed to master. He didn't want to return to something that had not worked for us before, but he didn't close the subject altogether. I broached the matter with the senior players and put forward my thoughts. I told them that if we were to go with the blitz, we all had to be 100 per cent

behind the decision. It was made clear to me that everyone was behind it, and when we went back to Mike for approval he agreed to change his mind, given that we all thought it could work. In the event, I suppose you would have to argue that it wasn't successful, not just because of the decisive defeat we suffered, but because the Boks scored four tries to our one, two of which came from the brilliant wing Bryan Habana.

However, the bottom line was that while the players and management team seemed to be reasonably happy with what we had going, other teams had clearly worked us out. The Grand Slam was a distant memory, and we needed someone to grab hold of us and take us to the next level, to take us somewhere none of us had been before. In my mind, Mike was the one and only person to do that. I wanted him to say to us, 'Boys, we have reached this level. Now come with me to an even higher place.' And the change in direction, the new ideas, the move to the next echelon, had to be presided over by him. As head coach, it had to be his master plan. For me, the time had come for Mike to truly take up the reins and lead us to even greater conquests and eventually to a position from which we could go to the 2007 World Cup as contenders to win it.

Things had been relatively easy up to that point, and we had been on a roll. We had been through the donkey work of the Steve Hansen era when so many

of the foundations for what we were now doing had been laid. Then the all-important victory against England in the 2005 Six Nations opener had given us the momentum we needed to crack on and take the Slam. But the fact was that when Mike took charge in the summer of 2004, the team was more or less running itself. It was credit to him that he did not come in and introduce change for change's sake, but it was almost as if there was very little for him to do anyway.

After the win against England, we were in one of those zones in which we were playing some great rugby, but we were also having many things go our way. The Grand Slam had been a whirlwind of success, during which we had barely any time to think about the incredible journey we were on. But now that journey had ended, and there was no point in any of us trying to relive it. Serious questions were starting to be asked of the Grand Slam champions for the first time, and it was clear to me that we needed to find a new path.

After the defeat to South Africa, I returned to France for a fortnight, and we fielded a younger, more experimental side against Fiji, spluttering to an 11–10 win. When I returned to Wales, I detected that nothing had changed in the way that the senior squad was running, so I decided to speak to Mike face-to-face and lay all my concerns – and some of those that had been passed to me by other players – right on the line.

It was the night before the final game of the autumn series against Australia, and I went along to Mike's room at our Vale of Glamorgan Hotel base and knocked on his door. 'Look, Mike, we've taken Welsh rugby to a level nobody thought we could,' I said to him. 'Now we have got here, all the players and I want to be taken a step further. And we want you to take us there.'

It led to a frank discussion between the two of us in which we both put points across. I won't go into too many details, but Mike said that he felt I didn't come to him often enough over a whole range of matters, preferring instead to go through his assistant Scott Johnson. He said I should have been going to see him far more regularly as his captain. I conceded that he had a fair point and explained that it was only because, as a back, I worked more closely with Johnno on the training ground, day in, day out, and as such he seemed the more natural port of call for me. Mike worked largely with the forwards, focusing on the scrum in particular, and he delegated much of the rest of the work: Johnno had developed most of our patterns on the field; Robert Sidoli had taken over the lineout. It was clearly an arrangement that had worked up to a point. But I made it clear to Mike that the team could not stay as it was. It had become a ship that for the first time really needed somebody to guide it. It had been floating merrily along for a while, with everyone taking

it in turns to paddle. Now it needed the captain of the ship – definitely Mike – to take it to another level, somewhere we had never been before.

Nobody can ever question the loyalty I had to Mike. Anything he wanted to do, any path he chose to take us on in his quest for improvement, I would have gone with him. Mike assured me that he agreed with my call for him to really stamp his mark on the team and that he did want to lead us to that new territory. I left his room that evening feeling hugely encouraged that we had aired a lot of things and that from then on there would be real change. I also accepted that this wasn't just down to what Mike did. I knew I had a role to play in it as well, and I resolved to make a big effort to put right the problem he had with me not going to see him directly. I sensed a line had been drawn in the sand, and it was time to look ahead to the Six Nations.

To make things all the better, we beat Australia for the first time in 27 years the next day at the Millennium Stadium. The final score was 24–22, with me combining with Shane Williams to put him in for what would prove to be the winning score in the second half. The gloom had been lifted, it seemed, with a first win against one of the southern-hemisphere big three since we had beaten South Africa just before the World Cup in 1999. We could look forward to the Six Nations opener against England the following February with genuine optimism.

As soon as we met up for the Six Nations, though, I started to get that sinking feeling you get when you expect change and it doesn't arrive. For a start, I felt we were under-prepared again. Leading up to the 2005 tournament, I had been going back and forth to Wales from France for squad training all the time. This time, though, I had not been back at all. When I flew home the week before the England match, it was the first time I had joined the squad since the autumn, and it felt as though we had an awful lot of ground to cover to be ready to face the world champions in their own back yard in less than a fortnight.

Worse than that, though, the little things were once again not there in training. The players were desperately trying to remedy it, and we were actually saying amongst ourselves that we needed to pick it up and that we were not where we should be. But the situation was difficult. Robert Sidoli, a big player for us, had been given the role of taking charge of the lineout, so he was constantly with the forwards working on that. Then you had Mike taking the scrum and Johnno taking the team runs and the backs. The problem was that it was difficult to see the general strategy and at the same time focus on all the little things that had to be right as well. The whole way we were functioning was, to be blunt, confusing.

However, despite this, we were still confident going in against England on 4 February. For all our shortcomings

in training, we still thought that we could successfully get through the game on what we knew we were capable of producing on a good day, on what we had put in place over the course of the previous two years. But it didn't happen, and the way we played at Twickenham said it all about what was missing.

I had wanted us to forget about everything that had gone before and to tear into this Six Nations playing a brand of rugby that maximised our strengths but also contained things that nobody expected. And following my clear-the-air session with Mike just before the Australia game, I was really optimistic that would happen. Yet nothing like that ever materialised.

England ran out 47–13 winners, and, OK, I think even they would admit that the margin of victory flattered them. They deserved their win, but a late cluster of tries made it look more emphatic than it was over the 80 minutes. Our problem, however, was that we only played good rugby in short spells – and I put that down to the fact that all the little things on and off the training field that had come together to make us Grand Slam champions had eroded away. Our bad spells were almost always the result of one of the little things having let us down – I rest my case. We had been a team capable of playing great rugby for 80 minutes; now we were slipping backwards and becoming a team that could only produce the goods in fits and starts.

Our plan had been to run the England pack around the park – let's face it, there was no way we were going to get the better of them in a physical dogfight – and we believed that our fitness would hold sway in the end if we could get our patterns right. But we just weren't able to deliver a standard of play that we had previously been capable of.

Of course, all the critics were wise after the event, saying that we lacked structure and attention to the basics, but as far as I was concerned that had nothing whatsoever to do with the defeat. The sin-binning of Martyn Williams just after half-time, when he was rather harshly adjudged to have obstructed Lewis Moody at a restart, was also held up as a key moment. Again, that didn't tell the half of it – and to pile that on Martyn's shoulders was way out of order. The truth was that we should have been capable of going to Twickenham and beating England playing the style of rugby that we loved playing – the fast and open style – with a selection of new ideas thrown in.

We tried to revert to what we knew we were good at – the high-tempo, skills-led attacking game based on offloading in contact and supporting runners anywhere and everywhere – but what happened just showed how much we had fallen off the pace. There had been no real change of direction; responsibility levels had stayed the same. We were still standing still.

Furthermore, what happened after

the game put an added dampener on the whole weekend. There was a lot of talk among the boys about going into central London that Saturday night to attend an evening that the England scrum-half Matt Dawson – a really popular guy, particularly with the Lions players in our ranks – was arranging. A lot of the lads were really keen to go, me included, but I remembered what Andrew Hore had said to me the year before after we had beaten England in the first game, about how we had another game in a week's time and that to go out on the pop in a big way was not the right thing to do. If we had lost that day a year earlier, we certainly wouldn't have bothered, and yet here we were, having just been defeated heavily by England, planning a fairly major night out with Scotland coming to Cardiff in eight days' time.

I went to our team manager Alan Phillips and told him that a posse of our players, me included, were planning on heading into central London that night, but that even though I was intending to go I did not think it was a particularly good idea. He agreed and said that we had to sort it out. Alan went off to speak to Mike about it and came back with the message that the head coach had agreed that it was not the right thing to do.

'Right,' I said, 'this needs to be done correctly. The boys are pissed off enough as it is, and unless this is dealt with properly there is a danger that they will go behind your back and just scatter across town.' I told Alan that Mike had

to get everybody into the team room and lay it on the line that on no account was anyone to go into central London or have a heavy night out and that he should warn them what the consequences would be if they did. As far as I was concerned, the message had to be conveyed in the strongest terms, and it had to come from Mike and nobody else.

A little while later, Mike came to me and said that he did not want to round the lads up in the team room like schoolboys and would rather give them the message from the front of the bus. I nodded but knew straight away that it would not carry as much weight delivered from the front of the bus, because these situations are all about creating the proper environment and making a point of calling a meeting. I thought that Mike should have faced the boys in a more formal and deliberate setting. The guys would then have been in no doubt that the message was serious and not to be ignored. I knew that on the bus there would be a few of the lads at the back muttering behind chairs that they were going to do as they pleased.

Just before Mike spoke, I told him to use this chance to stamp his authority on the team and do exactly what we had spoken about that night before the Australia game the previous autumn. But he took the microphone and simply said that he didn't think it was a good idea to go to central London, that people were welcome to have a drink at the hotel or locally, but that going to the centre of

town and coming back at all hours of the morning was to be avoided. I wasn't best pleased, because I felt that the message hadn't been properly conveyed. The importance of it had been diluted because of the circumstances of its delivery.

Almost immediately, I was proved right, because as soon as we got back to the hotel I had players moaning to me about not being allowed to go into central London, saying that they were grown men and should be given their freedom. The moment Mike had finished speaking, I knew that this would happen. If everyone had been summoned to the team room to have the call properly explained to them in a forceful manner, it would have been different.

What frustrated me most was that every player with a grievance was coming to me to ask why they weren't allowed out, and I sensed a real readiness in the ranks to simply ignore the coach's call. The fact was that discipline was crumbling because it had been allowed to crumble. Two years earlier, if Steve Hansen had made the call that we weren't to go out, it would have been accepted without a single murmur. And whatever we ended up doing, it would have been done together. Now Mike's authority was being challenged, leaving me to wonder whether he had ever properly exerted it in the first place.

The fact that the squad was falling out of line was evident that night as we began to split into little factions. Some were up

for having a drink with the post-match meal and then going back to the hotel, some wanted to go straight into London and to hell with the meal, others wanted to go to the meal and then into London afterwards. However, there was one common thread: nobody was happy as the bus left the stadium.

I then found myself in the position of having to tell the team not to do something that I myself wanted to do. I took the microphone at the front of the bus when we got back to the hotel and the management team had disembarked, and admitted that I wanted to go into town that night. But I stressed that whatever we did would be done together: one in, all in. I said that because Mike had indicated we shouldn't go into the city centre, we wouldn't, adding that anyone was free to have a good drink that evening at the hotel or nearby if they wanted to. I still had to field questions from some of the boys after that, but I ended by explaining my unhappiness at the position I was in. I hated feeling like it had fallen on me to categorically ensure Mike was not disobeyed. I never saw that as part of the captain's role. As far as I was concerned, whatever the coach had said should have been heeded, without any need for the skipper or anyone else to shore up the message.

As it turned out, we eventually managed to steer around the situation, because we went back and had a great laugh at the post-match dinner. We had a good drink and went back to the hotel

before finishing off at a club just a short walk down the road. It was a really good night, and a night on which none of us went over the top. But I still resented having to stand up and tell the players not to do something I wanted to do myself. I certainly never wanted to have to do it again.

Sometimes, players find it impossible to see the bigger picture after games for the simple reason that we are the ones who have actually played. Finding a release mechanism after the pressure of a Test-match week can take over, and the next game can feel as though it might as well be six months away. That evening, we needed someone who hadn't played to see the bigger picture and make us all see it as well. Mike had said his piece in his own way, but the message hadn't hit home.

To make matters worse, a subplot had unfolded that would erupt the following week into a temporary boycott of press duties by the players. Looking back, it was an episode that probably did more than anything else to make people think that so-called player power had removed Mike from office, because it happened just days before he departed and was admittedly an example of our solidarity. But the fact is that our refusal to carry out our media duties for one day in the presence of one journalist had nothing to do with Mike. No, this problem had far deeper roots.

The legion of issues surrounding Gavin

Henson's book had finally been put to bed by the time we went to Twickenham – or so the players thought. A storm had blown up the moment Gavin's thoughts about our Grand Slam season and the subsequent British Lions tour had been aired in his autobiography *My Grand Slam Year*.

From the point of view of our squad, the key problem was that it contained criticism of several of us and other material that just didn't sit well with the boys. As Gavin had been injured throughout the autumn campaign when the whole business first began, we were able to sweep the problem of him rejoining us under the carpet for the time being. But that wasn't to say that it wasn't a major topic of conversation.

Being in France, the information I had about what he had said in his book was sketchy at first and confined to what I had heard had been serialised in various newspapers. I rang Peter Underhill, Gav's agent, to try to find out exactly what had been printed. 'Don't worry,' he said. 'I've read the bits he's written about you, and he's been quite complimentary.'

'Well that's OK then,' I said and put the phone down. Immediately, I couldn't believe what I had done and how selfish I had been. I couldn't believe that I had been happy just to hear that I was in the clear. The issue that mattered was how the squad had been affected, so the call ended up doing nothing to resolve the problem.

There had been a little bit of talk about it in France, and the Toulouse players thought it was hysterical that Gav had called his book *My Grand Slam Year*. They were taking the meaning a bit too literally, thinking that Gav was claiming the success for himself rather than the team. I tried to explain that it was all getting lost in translation, but I don't think I got through to them.

I took some time to find out exactly what was in the book. I didn't get to read it until I returned to Wales for the autumn games in 2005, a couple of weeks after the book had been published. By then, I had been forced to listen to a lot of complaints from the boys. Many of them were coming up to me and showing me excerpts of what had been written, accompanied with, 'I can't believe he's said this . . .' And when I looked at some of the sections, I too was surprised. There were some fairly derogatory remarks about one or two of the Llanelli boys, Garan Evans in particular, whose inclusion ahead of Gav in Steve Hansen's 2003 World Cup squad had clearly been a source of disgust for the author. There was also a tale about how Martyn Williams had once lost his temper with Gav during a match between Cardiff Blues and the Ospreys. Again, the feeling was that it was an incident that should have stayed among the players, given that they were international teammates.

I remember picking up a newspaper at that time. Under a banner headline, there was a picture of Gareth Jenkins, the then Scarlets coach, and he was quoted as saying that Gav had sold the soul of the game down the river and had lost the dressing-room in the process. I have to say that Gav had indeed lost the Wales dressing-room at that time. Nobody wanted him back in the squad; nobody wanted him around. For that reason, I knew something had to be done.

Gav was saying in the newspapers that he had received no negative feedback from his fellow players and making out as if there was no problem at all. But that definitely wasn't the case. So, we could either let it go on with everyone thinking it was OK, or we could deal with it in a way that allowed us to register our displeasure without airing our dirty linen in public. If we were going to achieve this, we obviously couldn't have individual players speaking out in the press, so we decided to kill the matter in-house and then release a short statement saying that as far as we were concerned the whole business was closed and that nothing would be held against Gav when he returned to the squad. We got hold of Gav and asked him to come to the training camp and see us so that we could thrash it out. He had to be made to face the entire squad, because, at the end of the day, it was the entire squad who had the problem with him.

Before he arrived, I told the lads that the meeting was not intended to be a witch-hunt and that we were not getting

him in so we could all gang up and bully the poor bloke. I told them that they had to give him some credit for being willing to come to the hotel and face us all, which could not have been easy, and I made it clear that I didn't want people shouting comments at him from the floor. I didn't want him treated like a naughty schoolboy. I wanted all those who wished to have their say to have it and for Gav to be able to put his side across in a civilised and grown-up environment.

When Gav arrived, I began by making it clear to him that the rest of us were not happy with what had been written in the book or that he had said in the press that we were OK with it. I told him that every person who was in the room had a problem with the whole episode, so from then on he could never make out otherwise. Then I opened the floor to a few people who were determined to confront him. I'm not prepared to name those individuals or reveal what they said, but suffice to say that a couple of them let him have it with both barrels. Gav's response will stay private, but he must take credit for coming in the first place, and the matter healed itself as time went on. He came back into the squad for the clash away to Ireland in our Six Nations campaign that year, having missed the start of the championship because of suspension, and I'm sure he will have a long and successful Wales career even though he missed the World Cup in 2007.

While we thought that the meeting with Gav represented closure on the subject – I had also issued a press release saying that no player would ever drag it up in the media again – we were to receive a rude awakening when we opened the match programme on the day of the England game. Staring back at us was a piece by Graham Thomas, the journalist who used to present the BBC Wales *Scrum V* programme and who had ghostwritten Gav's autobiography. The gist of it was a staunch defence of Gav's right to say what he wanted in his book, and I suppose he had a point from a freedom of speech point of view. But there was also material in it condemning what Graham Thomas saw as a kind of public-schoolboy mentality among the squad, whereby we had called Gav to account for deviating from some unwritten code of honour among the players.

To me, it was plain nonsense. None of the issues with Gav were about any code, they were purely about trust, which we felt had been broken. Without trust among a group, you have nothing, whether you are an international rugby team or a gang of labourers working on a building site. But quite apart from what the article contained, we were annoyed that it had been written at all, and especially in the programme on the day of our Six Nations opener at Twickenham. Instead of the Gav business being put to bed, here it was again, and I could see the players starting to twig in the changing-

room before the match as we all flicked through the programme, something most of us always made a point of doing. Gradually, we were making eye contact with one another, as if to say, 'Are you reading this stuff as well?'

We had no choice but to put it on the backburner at that stage, but the day after the game I went to see Alan Phillips and made clear the squad's deep unhappiness at the article and its timing. In all our team meetings, Alan had said that if any of us had an issue with something a journalist had written then we would deal with it by approaching that journalist or his organisation and talking it through in a conciliatory manner. That way we hoped any problems could be resolved amicably, bad feeling wouldn't fester and our relations with the media would improve. So, Alan and I met with Nigel Walker to register our concerns.

Nigel agreed to our request not to deal with Graham Thomas for just that week leading up to the Scotland game. It was a stand that the team felt we had to make, and it was very much a decision made by the whole squad, not just by me or any other individual intent on rabble-rousing. And it wasn't as if the BBC would lose out in any way – they had an army of other journalists who could just as easily quiz players in the build-up to the match.

However, on the day of the main media conference ahead of the Scotland game – the Wednesday of the Test-match week – I was sitting in the room ready to go when in walked none other than Graham Thomas. To be fair to him, it wasn't done in defiance, because it transpired that, unbelievably, he had not been told of our temporary refusal to deal with him. But I wasn't to know that at the time, so I got up and walked out. It was barely noticeable, because Mike hadn't even arrived at that point and the conference hadn't begun.

I collared Simon Rimmer, the team media officer, and asked him why Graham Thomas had come despite everything we had spoken about that week. He went off to make a few phone calls, and it soon emerged that the message hadn't been passed to Thomas, who, perhaps understandably, wasn't prepared to go anywhere. As far as I was concerned, that was it. There was no way I was going to speak to the media while he remained in attendance.

And the primary reason was that we had made a stand as a team. I had been part of the decision, but it had not been my decision alone, despite all the suggestions afterwards that I had been the ringleader and that it had become a personal battle between me and one journalist. My team had adopted a stance, and I was going to stand full-square behind it no matter what the circumstances. How would I have looked to them had I just meekly caved in? Weak and unsupportive of their views, that's how. And there was no way I was ever going to head in that direction.

Rimmer and Mike were of the view that we should just go in and get the media conference over with. But I was having none of it. We had made a decision, and the fact that Graham Thomas had turned up was down to the BBC not us. I told them that if I walked into that room, it would make me a poor captain in the eyes of my team. I couldn't have cared less what the press thought of me as a leader, but my team? That was a different matter altogether. I would rather be pilloried by journalists and backed by my teammates than the other way round every single time.

Mike asked Michael Owen to come into the conference instead of me, but he refused for the same reasons that I had given – that we were making a point as a squad. To me, the principle was no different to that of a picket line – you stand together with your colleagues, and you don't cross it just because the boss asks you to. The only player who did speak to the press was the wing Mark Jones, who somehow didn't get the message of what we were doing, and we jokingly called him a 'scab' afterwards! 'I don't know, boys, but everyone wants to talk to me today,' Mark said as he came back from the press conference.

'Yes, you daft sod, because you're not supposed to be in there!' we replied.

I understand that we had a responsibility to deal with the media, and I as captain more than anyone. But standing up for what the team believed in was more important that day, whether people thought we were right or wrong. And I believe it showed what we meant to each other as players.

Little did we know it, but Mike was heading towards his final game in charge. However, the way he behaved didn't offer an inkling of what was to come. In the press conference after we had beaten Scotland 26–18 the following Sunday, I can remember saying that we should be in good fettle to face Ireland because we had the ex-Leinster coach in charge of us. The match against the Scots was not a vintage display by us by any means. They were vastly improved from the previous season, but they were undone by the early sending off of their second row Scott Murray, and I always felt from then on that we would be too strong for them.

The meeting that kept the whole of Wales talking for months after Mike's departure had happened earlier that week. If you believe the conspiracy theorists, I had called summit talks with Welsh Rugby Union chief executive Steve Lewis to demand Mike's sacking in an act of treachery of Judas Iscariot proportions. Sadly for the would-be Hollywood scriptwriters, it was nothing like that. Yes, there was a meeting between senior players and Steve Lewis. Stephen Jones, Martyn Williams, Brent Cockbain – whom we asked to go as someone who was part of the squad but outside it at that present time because of injury – and I met him, just as a

delegation of us had intermittently done ever since he had taken the job.

The main purpose of the meeting was to clarify an insurance issue, which had become a concern to some of the boys after Gareth Cooper had gone off at Twickenham with a damaged shoulder. The aim was to discover exactly what the extent of our cover from the WRU was and what we were entitled to in the event of certain scenarios. I made it clear to Steve that unless we were fully covered for the worst injuries imaginable on a rugby field, then we would consider withdrawing our services.

When I revealed this on the *Scrum V* programme, I was leapt upon by Eddie Butler, who claimed that being prepared to go on strike was further evidence of player power. I countered by pointing out that rugby players are no different from anyone else in the world of work – if we were not adequately insured, there was no way we could be expected to fulfil our duties. I stand by that completely, but our fears were allayed by what Steve told us, so the matter never went any further.

A few more run-of-the-mill issues were discussed, and then I moved on to the subject of Mike Ruddock. I told Steve about my concerns that Mike wasn't taking enough responsibility in the running of the team, considering that he was head coach. Immediately, Steve tried to cut me off, but I had enough time to get a little further, saying that we all wanted Mike to be the one to take

us forward. That wasn't happening at present, though, I continued.

Steve did manage to get a word in, though he was quite abrupt in his response. He told us that if we had any issues, they would have to be between us and Mike, and that as far as the union was concerned the coach would retain their full backing. 'Fair enough,' I thought. But what he didn't seem to realise was that I had already imparted these exact concerns to Mike. I only ever brought it up with Steve because I thought someone else might have more luck than I was having in trying to trigger a bit of change. But I was wasting my time with him on that particular subject. The meeting was called to a rather hasty end, and that was that. But it wasn't.

On the Tuesday after the Scotland game, I received a phone call in Toulouse from Alan Phillips. 'Mike's leaving,' he said. 'There's a press conference being called for 9 p.m. tonight.'

'What d'you mean? Why?' I asked.

'Family reasons,' he said. 'That's all I know at the moment.'

It was a fairly brief call, and for 24 hours or so all I knew about the matter was what I saw on the Welsh news, which I used to get via satellite, and what people back in Wales were telling me over the phone. But it was all conjecture and opinion, speculation and tittle-tattle. That said, the matter was clearly dominating the news agenda. I don't think it would have been knocked off

the front pages had a volcano erupted underneath the Millennium Stadium.

The next day, the players were beginning to be accused of knifing Mike in the back – me more than anybody. One of the most pathetic theories was that we were jealous of Mike for having been awarded an OBE in the New Year's honours list. I actually found that a rare source of amusement throughout it all – you could either laugh or cry at the sheer depth of some people's ignorance. All I can say is that anyone who knows me will confirm that receiving something like an OBE is the sort of thing I will never care two hoots about. For the record, the players have never had a problem with Mike's award and appreciated the fact that he immediately had the good grace to say that he was accepting it on behalf of everyone who had been involved in the Grand Slam effort.

Anyway, in the madcap aftermath of his departure, I sent him a text the day after his exit was formally announced. It read along the lines of, 'Whatever you believe and whatever you think, I feel you should have had the courtesy to tell us to our faces that you were going.' Mike texted me back and asked me to call him. I did. He assured me that he had left because of a breakdown in negotiations with the WRU over the renewal of his contract, which was a matter that had been dragging on in the press for some time, and the details of which I knew absolutely nothing about. He added that the whole business had

reached a stalemate and that this was the reason he had decided enough was enough. I asked him to tell me if our meeting with Steve Lewis had been the reason. He simply replied that as players we would get his full support for the rest of the Six Nations.

The next time I spoke to Mike was the day before I was due to go on *Scrum V*. We chatted amicably and asked each other how our families were coping with the storm. I then asked him to do me a favour. I told him that I was due to go on the programme and asked him to put it in writing that so-called player power was not the reason he had left the job, in order to clear up any confusion and to put an end to the players being solely blamed for his leaving. Mike said that he didn't have a problem doing so, but then five minutes later he phoned me back to say that his solicitor wouldn't allow him to do it.

I realised that if it had reached the point at which solicitors were stepping in, I might as well just let it go. Furthermore, I knew that if this whole episode was now becoming a legal matter, I would be seriously out of my depth. I didn't have a clue what I could or couldn't say from a legal point of view, and I was about to go on a national television show where my every word would be pored over.

I don't claim to be the sharpest tool in the box, and I must admit that I was not looking forward to facing a barrage of questions and then having to tread on eggshells as I answered them. But I

resolved to go through with it anyway. I just wanted to fight the players' corner, and I was determined to tell the truth. In any case, I knew that if I tried to lie, I wouldn't be clever enough to get away with it.

I turned up at the BBC, and the greeting I received immediately alerted me to the fact that things could be about to turn lively. In fairness to the presenter Gareth Lewis, he was upfront with me as I walked in, but his words prompted alarm bells in my head. 'Alf, I like you as a bloke, and please remember that whatever happens out there tonight I'm only doing my job,' he said.

'Oh great,' I thought to myself. 'What does that mean?'

I took my place in the studio, and I remember that before the cameras were due to come on they showed a pre-recorded video of Gwyn Jones interviewing Scott Johnson. I was desperately trying to listen to what Johnno was saying, because having been out of the country for the last week I wanted an update on what had actually happened. But Eddie Butler seemed to be hell-bent on not letting me listen to it. I was trying to listen to Johnno with Butler rabbiting away in my ear about French rugby, but I didn't have the heart to tell him to put a sock in it.

Then it all – rather infamously – kicked off, and it wasn't long before my whole body was tingling. I couldn't get past the fact that I was as passionate about being the Wales captain as any

of my predecessors had been but my motives and, as far as I was concerned, my integrity were being called into question. At times, I honestly felt like I was back in the dock in court with a set of lawyers trying to trip me up on everything I said.

Butler and Lewis were going at it like some two-pronged legal team for the prosecution moving in for the kill. Jonathan Davies was less involved, because I think he knew a bit more about what made me tick, having played in the same side as me in the past. It got to the stage that I felt Butler was flat out accusing me of having knifed Mike in the back without having a shred of proper evidence other than some 'source', which predictably he was refusing to reveal.

What my parents witnessed behind the scenes also left me really disappointed. They had picked me up from the airport so came to the studios with me on the way home, and they were to tell me afterwards that it wasn't just Butler and Lewis who were tearing me to shreds. People backstage were rewinding snippets of what I had said and barking orders to Butler and Lewis, who were wired up to them, to 'get into him on that' and 'grill him on this'. You can imagine how my parents felt listening to things like that having never experienced such an environment.

And they also told me about Nigel Walker's commands to Butler and Lewis to stop bullying me. Those words said

it all for me. The captain of Wales on the nation's prime rugby programme was, in the words of BBC Wales's own head of sport, apparently being bullied. Mam and dad told me that they were disgusted by the whole business.

However, after the show, I was fine with them all. I shook hands with Butler, Jonathan and Lewis, who I respected for having had the decency to put his cards on the table before the whole thing had begun. But I felt that Butler had taken the whole thing personally, and I sensed that he thought he was on a bit of a crusade to get 'justice' for Mike. But that's his business. I cannot say that I dislike the man, because I don't know him. Saying that, after everything that has happened, I will probably never get to know him now. I certainly can't envisage me inviting him around for Sunday lunch in the near future!

As I walked out of there, I didn't have a clue how I had come across, but I obviously had concerns. The one thing I hoped more than anything else, though, was that people would be able to see my

passion. I am passionate about Wales, passionate about rugby and passionate about my upbringing, all of which I thought had been questioned by the panel.

Unfortunately, I fear that if I do a million good things with the rest of my life, the one bad thing that I have been accused of will always stand out. There is little I can do about that. All I can say is that throughout my life, I have only ever tried to be honest with people.

In detailing the most turbulent period of my career in this chapter, I have tried to be objective and avoid any undue criticism of individuals. Above all, I have simply called things as I saw them. I wish Mike Ruddock nothing but the very best in whatever he does in the future. I have the utmost respect for him as a rugby man and a person, and will always remember him as the guy who had the faith to make me captain of Wales. For me, there is no bigger honour in the game, and I will always be grateful to Mike for bestowing it upon me.

14

MY MATE MARADONA

It was the summer of 2006, and I had just come through the most turbulent season of my career; in other words, the so-called 'Ruddockgate' saga and the damaged artery in my neck that could have finished my career. I was back training for the new campaign with Toulouse when my phone rang – it was my old mate Alistair Campbell. 'Have you been watching *Soccer Aid* on the TV?' he asked me.

Well, because I'd been in France, I hadn't, but it seemed that the programme had the nation back home hooked. Pop megastar Robbie Williams was leading a team of England celebrities against a rest of the world team led by the famous chef Gordon Ramsay, all in the name of charity. After a week of training, the two teams would face each other in a showdown at Old Trafford, and it made for a great piece of reality television. Terry Venables and Ruud Gullit were in charge of the sides, and it was really catching people's imagination.

I couldn't answer the phone immediately, but when I listened to the message I heard Alistair mumble something and then say, 'How do you fancy playing at Old Trafford?'

I texted him back: 'Stop taking the piss.'

Then he rang again. 'Seriously,' he said. 'Eddie Irvine has just pulled out. They want a replacement, and I suggested you. I've told them you were captain of the British Lions and that you're a bit of a boy. They've had a show of hands and want you to come along.'

I agreed, and the next thing I knew I was on the phone to some woman who was telling me that the flight had been booked. Then I rang home to Jemma, who was able to tell me just how big this thing was and how the likes of Robbie, etc., were involved.

As I travelled, I began to wonder just what I had got myself into, and fear started to take over. I knew that in terms of my name and fame I was nowhere near

these guys, and, on top of that, my age-old preference for staying in my comfort zone was once again rearing its head.

When I turned up at the Conrad Hotel in Chelsea Harbour, where the teams were based, I was told that the others were all over at Stamford Bridge taking part in a televised quiz and was asked to be on the bus in five minutes. When I climbed aboard, a woman followed me on and said that we'd be off in two minutes but we just had to wait for Brian. I was wondering who Brian was when Brian McFadden, formerly of the band Westlife, walked on. 'Hiya, butt!' I said, giving him my traditional Bridgend greeting. He was really down to earth and was soon talking about his missus, the Australian musician and actor Delta Goodrem.

When we arrived at the quiz, we were ushered past the bouncers and into the room where Chris Evans was conducting matters from the stage. To be fair to them, they all clapped and cheered me in, but I felt like a fish out of water at first. I looked around: there were people from *EastEnders*, Robbie Williams, Gordon Ramsay and famous ex-footballers such as Paul Gascoigne – it really was quite surreal. Not a lot of them knew anything about me or rugby, but to a man they were great with me – really friendly and genuine even though they inhabited a different world.

At one of the first training sessions, a cameraman came up to me and said, 'Sorry to be rude, mate, but who are you?' I could see he was cringing with

embarrassment, but I told him not to worry and that I didn't expect him to know who I was.

'I'm Gareth,' I said.

'Ah, the rugby man,' he replied.

After a day or so at Fulham's training ground getting to know everyone better, I realised that they were all perfectly normal and that there was no need to behave any differently around them. I got on really well with David Ginola and Marcel Desailly, the former French World Cup winner, partly because of the French connection with me living in Toulouse at that time.

By the time the game came around, I didn't expect to play, being the latecomer and all, but Brian was injured, so he told me that he would play for the first two minutes only and then make way for me. So there I was, Gareth Thomas from Bridgend, partnering Marcel Desailly at centre-half at a packed Old Trafford with Peter Schmeichel calling the shots behind us. We treated it as a bit of fun for the first five minutes, but when we went a goal behind and realised that England were taking it more seriously, we picked it up. The likes of Lothar Matthäus, Dunga and Gianfranco Zola may be game for a laugh, but they do not lie down on a football pitch for anyone, and they soon started to play and go into tackles with that little bit more ferocity. The match just flew by, and afterwards we had a great drink together back at the Conrad.

Jemma and both sets of parents came up to join us, and they had a ball. Jemma

had her picture taken with Ant and Dec, and she also collared Robbie. At first, he didn't know who she was and explained that he wouldn't be doing any pictures that night. But when Jemma said that she was Alfie's wife, he changed completely. 'No problem. He's a top bloke,' said Robbie. Things like that made it so memorable.

And then there was Maradona. For some reason, don't ask me why, there seemed to be a connection between us. I sat next to him a couple of times in the changing-rooms, and he was fascinated by the wealth of tattoos that I have had done. 'Your tattoos, your tattoos,' he would say, his eyes wide with amazement.

His people kept telling me that he liked rugby and that he was a friend of the Argentina scrum-half Agustín Pichot. After the match at Old Trafford, Gus Poyet, the former Chelsea and Spurs midfielder who had been helping Ruud Gullit run the side, approached me and said, 'Diego wants your jersey.'

'Tell him he can have it,' I said. 'It's still hanging on the peg.'

'No, no,' Poyet replied, 'not your football jersey. He wants your rugby jersey. Your Wales shirt.' I couldn't have been more delighted or honoured.

Gus told me that I would need to get Maradona's secret address, something he has in order to protect things getting stolen in the post, so after the game Jonathan Owen, my pal from ITV Wales, and I approached him. His people tried to block our path, but he waved us through, as he sat there puffing on a big

fat Cuban cigar. His missus wrote out his false name and address, and I pledged to put the jersey in the mail for him. It was an amazing feeling, because he is one of my all-time sporting heroes.

We had a good *craic* that night. Peter Schmeichel was taking the mickey out of me because I had accidentally broken his finger when I kicked it during the game, and I had several really close chats with a number of the guys, including Robbie and Gazza. I wouldn't reveal what we talked about just to sell this book; suffice to say it was surprising some of the personal stuff we chatted about, given that we had only recently met. Again, that just emphasised to me how normal these fellows were underneath all the showbiz hype.

I felt different from them because my fame was nothing like at the same level. I could walk out of the hotel in London through a screaming throng of girls and none of them would have a clue who I was, let alone want to stop me for an autograph. But making an impression on the other guys, which I felt I did, was enough for me. I wouldn't claim to be able to ring up Robbie Williams of an evening and chat about old times, but if our paths ever did cross again, I'm sure he'd recognise me and say hello. And that would be enough.

Soccer Aid was a wonderful little diversion in my life, and something to cherish before the serious business of resurrecting my rugby career began.

15

THE FIGHTBACK, THEN CONTROVERSY

If you've ever played a contact sport and you have been out for a considerable time with an injury, you will know all about the mental challenge of facing the first collision when you return. It's something that simply has to be confronted if you want to carry on, and for some it can become a bigger barrier than for others.

That was the position I found myself in as the 2006–07 season began. The damaged artery in my neck had healed, and I was ready to start training again with Toulouse, but while doctors had said everything should be fine, they could give me no guarantees. There were nagging worries lurking in the back of my mind – of course there were. After all, we weren't talking about a broken ankle – this was a neck artery, something that you simply couldn't mess about with. Yet rather than dwell on awful things that might never happen, I resolved just to get on with it, because I was always going to carry

on doing what I loved most – playing rugby.

The hardest part, the ultimate test if you like, was going back to training with Toulouse. As I've said earlier, Toulouse train like they play. There is no holding back, and the contact is full-on from the word go. In my first session, I found myself in the second team playing against the first XV that had been selected for the coming Saturday. So there I was, facing the likes of Yannick Jauzion, Florian Fritz, Vincent Clerc, Cédric Heymans; in other words, some of the best players in Europe. To face those guys in full-on contact in a prolonged session of attack and defence was all the examination I needed, and I came through it well.

After that, I just didn't feel a match represented any kind of fresh mental hurdle, because that session had been as intense as any game. I gradually eased myself back into first-team action, getting through games again and feeling like I was well on the road to being my

It's amazing how a few words can hurt so much.

old self. I was confident in my physical shape, because I had trained like a maniac that summer, putting on loads of muscle mass, eating really well and drinking hardly at all. But what turned out to be my final season at Toulouse did not exactly go smoothly, and the unfortunate events of one horrible January afternoon, not to mention their repercussions, stick out in my mind more than anything else.

We were in the death throes of the failed 2006–07 Heineken Cup campaign and were entertaining Ulster at the Stade Ernest-Wallon in the knowledge that neither side had any realistic chance of reaching the quarter-finals because

Llanelli Scarlets had stormed away with the pool. It was indeed a rare situation for a team like us, so used to challenging for the trophy itself and so accustomed to reaching the knockout stages at a bare minimum. There was some motivation, because Ulster had given us a real hiding at Ravenhill on a horrible windy October day a few months earlier. But all the signs pointed to it being a fairly tame affair with nothing much at stake.

Well, for me and Trevor Brennan, that's not quite how it turned out. We both started on the bench. The stadium was fairly full, but the crowd were no more revved up than usual, and the afternoon seemed to be ticking over quite harmlessly. Then Guy Novès told

230

Trev to go and warm up, and off he jogged. Moments later, there appeared to be some commotion in the crowd.

From where I was in the dugout, I couldn't see that well, but because I automatically assumed that someone had fainted or something, I didn't even attempt to get a better view and just leant back in my seat. But within seconds, Trevor appeared next to me again. He was soaking wet, and his eyes were bulging and his body shaking. He was clearly in one hell of a state. He turned to me and said, 'I've just been in the crowd.'

'What d'you mean?' I said, aghast.

'They called my mother a whore, and I wasn't going to take that,' Trevor continued.

He went on to explain that while he had been warming up he had been subjected to a volley of sustained personal abuse from Ulster supporters. Predictably, when he turned around to confront them, they all shut up, apart from one guy who carried on. Now, when a whole section of a crowd is insulting you with a chant, it is easy to brush it aside, but when it's coming from one individual, it is much harder to let it go.

I again refer you to the infamous Eric Cantona kung-fu kick at Selhurst Park when the Frenchman lost his head because of the vitriol coming from just one moron who saw fit to charge down the steps of the main stand and abuse him as he made his way back to the dressing-room after a red card. Anyway, Guy sent Trevor on to play soon after, even though I tried to signal to him that he was in no fit state.

That was the point at which I got involved. As I got up to stretch my legs and begin warming up, I was met with a barrage of 'sheep shagger' taunts and with other assorted insults. To be quite honest, I couldn't believe this was coming from a rugby crowd. I'd played in some hostile atmospheres around the world in my time, but I can safely say I had never experienced the level of venom that was coming from these people.

I turned around to a few of them and asked them why they were behaving like this, but it was to no avail. I do not want to stereotype Ulster supporters. I'm sure there are a good many of them who are decent people who are just passionate about their sport. But I have spoken to a few people I know from the area since, and they have said that an unsavoury element has crept into their crowd in recent seasons. And it seemed that element had decided on a day out in Toulouse.

The abuse continued to cascade down from the stand accompanied by flying plastic cups, and after a while I flipped and gave them all the one-finger salute, something I have always conceded I should never have done, no matter what was coming my way. As I did so, two of the Toulouse back-room staff grabbed me and dragged me away. Just at that point, a photograph was taken that makes it look as though I was ready to

jump into the stand and commit murder. This went around the world and created a totally misleading impression, and I'm sure it contributed to my later ban.

I went onto the pitch late in the game and thought nothing more of it, putting the incident down to the effects of booze. But that was far from the end of the matter. After the match, we were in the changing-room when one of the back-room boys suddenly came up to me and told me to go and get my car. I didn't understand at first, but then he explained that I would have to park it right outside the door of the players' entrance and quickly drive away with Trevor, because a group of Ulster fans had congregated outside the ground waiting for him.

I'm not trying to play the hard man here, but there was no way I was going to scuttle away anywhere, because I had done nothing wrong. I was going to walk out of that ground with my head held high if it was the last thing I did, right through the middle of the Ulster throng if needs be – and that's precisely what I did.

As I went through the car park to get to my motor, I was approached by a couple of them, and they said they had no argument with me. 'Fine, guys,' I replied. 'I've no argument with you either.' I got my car up to the exit, and as Trevor and I left there was more abuse and throwing of plastic cups, but we got away unscathed.

The pair of us went for a pizza afterwards, and as we chatted about the extraordinary events of the afternoon, Trevor's phone started to go mad. It was becoming clear that the situation was spiralling out of control. There were even claims filtering through to us that the confrontation between Trevor and the Ulster fans was being viewed as sectarian. By that stage, I think Trevor knew he was going to be called to book. He told me that he had hit one fellow, and once he said that I knew it didn't look good for him, even though he had my 100 per cent support. What I hadn't bargained for was the way things were about to blow up in my own face.

Within a matter of days, I was facing charges of threatening behaviour from the Heineken Cup tournament organisers, European Rugby Cup, and it wasn't long before I was making my way over to Dublin for a hearing that I knew could see me banned for the entire Six Nations. And this is where it really started to become pathetic.

Even though I still have another few years of playing the game left in me, I don't know if I would waste my time going to such a farcical thing ever again. Gareth Williams, my solicitor, was brilliant, but the mindset of the panel was clear from the start – the case had become so big in the media that it seemed to me they were going to throw the book at me as well as Trevor no matter what. I was confident when I first arrived, because I knew that I had done nothing wrong, other than give a one-

Arriving for the disciplinary hearing in Dublin after the fracas with Ulster fans.

fingered salute, which, let's face it, is hardly a hanging offence. Didn't David Beckham do the same in an England shirt once after taking personal abuse about his family from so-called fans and escape punishment?

When the hearing got under way, three or four Ulster fans came in to give their version of events, and in my opinion their accounts were completely non-compatible. I was unable to believe what I was hearing. On many occasions, I was reduced to tears because I felt so helpless. I thought about all the things I had done in the name of rugby, especially the work I had done with kids through my academy, but my sport was making me feel like a common criminal.

My solicitor put forward a compelling case, and I held my hands up about the one-fingered salute, saying that I was sorry but that I could not undo it now. But the picture came back to haunt me. The panel referred to it, pointing to the fact that my hand was on the wall in front of the first row of the stand, suggesting that I was about to go in and start a fight. But I was never going to do that.

If I had wanted to, I could have, because Serge Laïrle, the Toulouse forwards coach who held me back, is about 70 years old, and he could never have stopped me in a month of Sundays if that had been my intention. I cannot stress enough that I never intended to jump into the crowd, probably because I was so scared at the time.

The staggering thing was that in the summary from the panel at the end nothing made sense. It was a case of them saying, 'You have told us you did this, but we are telling you what you actually did.' At that point, I wondered why we had bothered wasting an afternoon. They had listened to me, they had listened to three or four Ulster people with contradictory stories and they'd concluded by more or less calling me a liar. There was no empathy with my position whatsoever. We had sat there all afternoon, and I had been judged by people who didn't even know me.

When the guilty verdict was delivered, I had a feeling of abject hopelessness. I would rather have had the case heard in a proper court of law, where at least I would have been assured that every minor detail would have been raked over with no preconceived ideas. The ban they gave me, which ruled me out of the first three matches of the 2007 Six Nations, left me in a total daze. I had really thought that I was about to make a triumphant comeback for Wales in that tournament. I felt fit and raring to go, and incredibly excited that I had the chance to play for my country again on such a stage, even though I had featured in the earlier autumn internationals that season. We had pleaded with the panel that it could be my last-ever Six Nations, which it almost certainly was, but they weren't interested. To them, the opportunity to play in the final two games against Italy and England was

enough of a consolation, as if I should have been grateful for that.

So, that was the end of the matter. There was no point arguing any more, no point appealing. And that was more or less it for me at Toulouse. The final few months of the season just petered out, and I have to say as the summer neared I couldn't wait to get back to Wales. The club had asked me to sign for another year before Christmas, and I had agreed, but then, all of a sudden, Cardiff Blues showed an interest. That was it. I immediately wanted to go home.

Three years was long enough in France, and the bonus was that the Blues were prepared to try and get me an early release from my contract with Toulouse so that I could finish the season with them. I was bang up for that and hoped some agreement could be reached. The truth was, I had become homesick, and my family was also fed up with me being away. Life was becoming a strain. I really hoped for an early exit, but to my dismay Toulouse were having none of it, insisting that they needed me and that I would have to see out my contract to the bitter end.

That gutted me. I wasn't desperately unhappy with my lot, but I really wanted to return home and my hopes had been raised. I still had my two-year contract with Cardiff to come back to, but I had been on the phone to my mates in the Blues team, and the prospect of a quick return had excited me. Don't get me wrong, Toulouse had been great with

me, in particular standing by me when I was ill. But I wanted to be honest with them – I was ready to go and there was no point denying it. I tried to argue that Toulouse would not lose out financially and that my departure was best for everyone. But it was no good.

Carrying on with them became such a drain. What made it worse was that Trevor had been banned, so I was now deprived of my best mate with whom I had built up such a bond. Trev was still coming down to the club from time to time, but it was never the same with him not playing. We played away games that would involve six-hour bus journeys, and because my French was not the best the loneliness started to wear on me. There is only a certain amount of music and DVDs you can get through, and my mind would wander, wishing I was back in Cardiff, just driving back and forth a few miles to training and seeing all the lads.

The pity is that my time with Toulouse ended on something of a sour note when they kicked up a fuss about me touring Australia with Wales and missing the last few games of the season. I will never criticise the club, but the fact is that I was required by Wales to make the trip, and I had all the regulations on my side. What's more, I really wanted to go Down Under in the run-up to the World Cup, and the chance to captain the party was another huge incentive. In fact, if I had stayed in Toulouse, I would have been in more trouble, and so probably would the club have been.

Once more a Cardiff man, but this time a Blue, too.

I learned so much in my three years with Toulouse, and I will always hold them in the highest regard for the rugby lessons they taught me and for the lifestyle. I would have loved to have ended on a brighter note, but *c'est la vie*. The important thing for me now is how much I want to finish my career at the Blues. I never wanted to finish my rugby-playing days anywhere else. I really want to be successful with them, but the main thing for me is being home and happy again. It is a very different set-up at the Arms Park now from the one I left, but I still feel a real affiliation with the place.

I had a season of Welsh regional rugby with the Warriors before going to Toulouse, but the whole thing was in its infancy then, so it will be interesting to find out what it is like. I know nothing about the rivalry between the current Welsh regions or about the standard of the Magners League, about which I hear conflicting reports. I have watched it on television, of course, but that's so different to actually playing.

One thing I will say is that I will miss the really big clashes in France, which were played out in front of enormous crowds. Even when we played a team like Agen, who were relegated after the 2006–07 season, there would be a crowd well into five figures. But that doesn't mean I regret the decision to return to Wales. And it certainly wasn't for the money, because I earn far less in Wales than I did in France. I could have earned far more had I stayed put, but the key was that I wouldn't have been happy.

16

WALES IN THE JENKINS ERA

When Gareth Jenkins took over as Wales coach in April 2006, so many people asked me what I thought of the appointment. Well, I was honestly no different from most of the country. I felt that with the position vacant yet again, Gareth deserved his chance to show what he could do. There had been a right old stink when Mike Ruddock pipped him to the post a couple of years earlier, with Gareth being held up by some sections of the media as the people's choice who had been unforgivably passed over. But here he was with a second chance, and his fine track record with the Scarlets decreed that it was his time. If he hadn't got the nod then, he really never would have.

I have never made any secret of the fact that the boys were upset to see Scott Johnson go back to Australia. I could fill a book with the positive things Scott brought to bear on us as players and people, and we all hoped he would stay. Johnno was criticised by the press for not engineering wins in the second half of the 2006 Six Nations after Mike's exit left him holding the baby, so to speak. But what chance did he ever stand in circumstances like those? To a man, we understood Scott's need to go back to Australia, which was due to personal family reasons as much as anything, but I was gutted to see him go.

Gareth came in at a time when I was not available to play for Wales because of my neck injury, and I wasn't considered for the tour to Argentina that summer. But when the 2006–07 season started to crank up, I felt his impact for the first time. Shortly before the autumn series was due to begin, and after months of debate in the newspapers, Gareth decided that I would not be his captain and appointed Stephen Jones instead. How did I react? In all truthfulness, I was fine with it, and the reason for that was because the honour was going to Stephen, who is one of my best mates in the world. I could trust him with

You can't change it, so don't dwell on it.

Regardless of who is captain, Stephen Jones
and I will always stand shoulder to shoulder.

When I lost the captaincy, I was unsure how to act around the squad.

anything. Don't get me wrong, I was disappointed, because I really felt that I was growing into the captain's role and getting better at it every game. But I had to put those feelings aside.

In fairness to Gareth, he handled it well, making the effort to come all the way out to Belfast, where I was preparing for a Heineken Cup game against Ulster, to tell me face-to-face. I told him that he really needn't have worried about doing it that way, but he was adamant.

My first reaction was to telephone Stephen to congratulate him and assure him that I would be on hand to help him in any way I could. I told him that I had learned a lot doing the job myself and would not hide any of it from him

to make myself look good. 'You deserve to have a good shot at it,' I said. 'But to help you do that, there are things I can share with you.'

As pleased as I was for Stephen, I have learned one thing in the past 18 months or so – I am better around the squad when I am captain. When I am not, I tend to go into my shell a little and be more prepared to take the easy track, though nowhere near the extent of what I used to be like. Sometimes when I don't have the armband, I get caught up in just rolling along in neutral gear, but when I am skipper it is more of a challenge, and it brings the best out of me. It is not that I don't try when I'm not captain, far from it, just that I

thrive on the extra responsibility, the responsibility of looking after your own performance as well as making sure so many other things are right. Perhaps it is because I spent so many years hiding in the background earlier in my career that I now relish leadership so much. I don't know.

One of the problems I found when we met up for the first time as a squad with Stephen as captain was striking the balance between me having an input as a senior player and former captain, and allowing Stephen to grow into the role himself without overpowering him. I just couldn't find that balance, and it ended up affecting my rugby. To me, the preparation in the week building up to a Test match is as important as the game itself, and it knocked me out of my stride to find myself suddenly not doing the things I was used to. I stress, though, that Stephen always had my 100 per cent backing and always will.

I felt for him in the first few months of his captaincy. He would admit his own form was not quite there, and the team was struggling to deliver the results the public demands. Added to that was the emergence of James Hook as an outside-half of real quality. Now, Hooky will concede he still has plenty to learn, but the fearless way he played in the number 10 jersey when he first came into the side had most of Wales hailing him as some kind of magician. That's what we do in Wales, particularly with outside-halves. We either build

them up into gods or knock them down as no-hopers, and Stephen was getting the rough end of it all, while Hooky was unable to do anything wrong in the eyes of the media.

Stephen never lost the famous smile that is almost permanently etched on his face, but I worried about the effect it was having on him and how he was feeling behind closed doors. I know how I felt during stormy times when I was skipper. I used to think that when I got home I would be able to shut my front door and lock the rest of the world out, but things get into your head and prevent you from escaping. I would have sleepless nights about various issues and periods of enormous worry. I don't think the public realise how much it affects you – it really does hurt. I have no doubt at all that Stephen found the first few months of his captaincy extremely hard going.

The one thing I used to tell Stephen was that as long as he had the support of his teammates, nothing else mattered. I know you are only talking about twenty-odd guys in a population of three million, but they are the only ones who really count when push comes to shove. When the going gets tough, when the shit hits the fan, they are the ones who can change it for you. If they believe in you, then you have to believe in yourself.

And they did. I know that if any of the lads had been stopped in their local corner shop and harangued by a punter claiming that James Hook should replace Stephen Jones in the team, they would

have stuck up for Stephen. When that is the case, it is the only ray of light you need. Slowly but surely that light will then start illuminating all the dark. In the end, I felt Stephen got through it OK.

I was made captain for the final 2007 Six Nations game against England, a game we won 28–17 to prevent a tournament whitewash, because Stephen was out injured. Yes, it was an honour, and, yes, it was a great day for me and the team, but throughout I could not stop wishing that Stephen was with us. At the post-match dinner, I was introduced as 'Gareth Thomas, captain of Wales' when I was called up to make the customary speech, and there was also the usual toast to 'Gareth Thomas and his Wales team'. But before I sat down, I stressed to everybody that I was merely the stand-in captain, and, just to emphasise the point, I toasted Stephen as 'our captain'. As far as I was concerned, I was not the Wales captain. It was not my team, and the last thing I wanted was for people to get caught up in the euphoria of having beaten England and forget about Stephen.

Of course, none of this is to say that I did not savour that day. It marked the end of what had turned into a deeply frustrating Six Nations, because of the ban that had been served on me after the nonsense with the Ulster fans. I looked upon the three games I was forced to sit out – defeats at home to Ireland and away to Scotland and France – as a test of

character. I have always been fortunate enough to be involved in Wales squads in the past, more often than not as one of the starting XV or at least on the bench. But there have always been ten or twelve lads who turn up for training every day who are not involved. During match week, they have to come into camp and train in a professional manner, all the while knowing that the reward of playing the game and maybe grabbing a bit of glory at the end of the week is not coming their way. Instead, they attend the stadium on a Saturday in their suits, doing their bit of idle chit-chat around the hospitality boxes and probably feeling like spare parts before reporting back for training on Monday. Believe me, it is an existence that is not easy, but that's what I had to do this time around.

I set myself the challenge – I always have to have a challenge – of taking over as captain of this little group. I tried to get us all having a laugh and enjoying the situation as much as we possibly could, and when we trained together I tried to take a lead and make it fun. I didn't want these fellows to feel like dirt-trackers who were just there to hold tackle bags and carry water bottles. I wanted them to feel worthwhile. I ended up enjoying it, and I'd like to think I played a part in getting us all to form a really good bond. We would train together, eat together, everything, and it showed me a different side of rugby. I was grateful for that, even though I would far rather have been in my usual position.

I tried to chip in with the odd bit of advice for the main team, but it is never the same when you are not available to play. However, the situation was never going to last, and by the time the match against Italy in Rome came into view I was back in the squad, albeit as a replacement. It felt great to be back, but, as ever, controversy was waiting for me. I am now able to laugh about the fact that I was only on the pitch for five minutes at the Stadio Flaminio yet still managed to get entangled in the one rumpus for which the match will always be remembered. At the time, though, it didn't seem quite so funny.

When I ran onto the field as a late replacement, things had been going steadily downhill for us. And as the final minutes approached, we were trailing 23–20 and facing a defeat that would mean humiliation, even though the Italians had improved immeasurably. We were trying desperately to pinch the result and launched what we knew could be the last attack of the game, an attack that yielded a penalty in a position from which James Hook was almost certain to bag three points.

With Stephen off the field injured, it fell to me to make the decision about whether to kick for goal and take a probable draw or go for touch and the win, although nobody had officially given me the captaincy armband. My initial train of thought was simple: I wanted the referee, Englishman Chris White, to effectively take it out of my

There are times when I can't resist ruining photographs!

hands by saying that there was only time for a kick at goal. I wanted us to win, of course I did, but I also knew that while a draw would be heavily criticised back in Wales, a defeat would be seen as a total disaster. In other words, I hoped time would be against us so that I could not possibly be wrong in deciding to go for goal. But life is not that simple.

Before I had the chance to make a decision, Hooky booted the ball into touch anyway. However, I must stress that a split second before he kicked it, the referee said that we had time to take a lineout and go for a try. The rest is

Sitting out most of the Six Nations was so hard.

history, as they say. Mr White blew up before we could take the lineout, and all hell broke loose. I stormed over to him demanding an explanation, which was not forthcoming. I said that I would now have to go into the changing-room and explain to everyone in the Wales camp why we went for touch when there was no time left, and I added that I needed an answer straight away. But he said he could not explain at that moment and told me to come to his room after we had left the pitch.

When I went to see him, I was told by one of the touch judges that he did not want to speak and certainly not publicly. It wasn't good enough as far as I was concerned, and I hit back by saying that in just a few minutes I would have no choice but to speak about it publicly, because I would have to face the press. What was I supposed to tell everybody?

In the end, we had to be vague about the whole thing, which was not satisfactory to the press, and it wasn't until later that evening that we finally got to the bottom of it all. In the post-match get-together, Mr White pulled me, Gareth Jenkins and Hooky to one side and admitted that he was the one at fault, that he would take the rap and that he was sorry for the mistake. Credit to him for owning up to us, but you can understand why the whole affair left a sour taste.

Thankfully, we did not have too much

Surfing on the tour of Australia in 2007.

time to dwell on it, because England were next up at the Millennium Stadium just a week later. I knew early in the week that I was going to be captain, because Stephen wasn't going to make it back from injury, and with all I had been through in the past year I went into the game thinking that it could well be my last-ever for my country. Part of me wondered if it was fate – the gods' way of giving me the perfect stage to finish on as captain of Wales at home to England – and a win would be the icing on the cake.

I can honestly say that after the game when victory was secured, I clapped the crowd and left the field thinking that I would never go on it again. For days after, I thought the same way, as if this was the tailor-made ending to a book about the career of Gareth Thomas: he came back from a life-threatening injury to captain Wales to victory against England. What's more, in the week leading up to the game I knew that we would win, because the preparation had been enjoyable and the camaraderie among the lads had been so strong. I felt I had given a lot of input into the way we approached the game, and I had some great feedback from the players. It had been an example of players and coaches

Ahead of setting a new Wales caps record in Australia 2007,
beating Gareth Llewellyn's mark of 92.

working really well together as a team. Everything had gone almost too well. It was scary, and it only reinforced in my mind the idea that this would be a great time to call it quits. And I also realised that when it did come to me quitting, it could be in the midst of a really sour occasion if I carried on.

However, as is quite often the case with me, I gradually began to have a change of heart in the following weeks. It started with the most basic fear of missing playing for Wales too much if I was to go. Then, gradually, I began to think about the finality of retirement and how there would be no coming back from the decision.

I've seen a lot of players returning to the game after announcing their international retirement, but I have always vowed that I would never do that. For me, retirement means just that. There's no going back on it – you either have the balls to say you're calling it quits and carry it through, or you keep your mouth shut and carry on. And there was still too much I wanted to do with Wales. There was the carrot of becoming the only Welshman to play in four World Cups, the carrot of captaining the tour party to Australia in the summer, the carrot of breaking the all-time Wales caps record. In short, there were too many carrots to refuse. But I stress again

that I do not want to hang around past my sell-by date.

I recall a conversation I once had with Scott Johnson. He said that the Australian cricketer Steve Waugh had a great take on his retirement. Waugh said that he would far rather have people questioning why he had called it a day than agreeing with him that the decision was the right one.

I know that I am not the same player I was some years ago – that I cannot do the same things. Don't ask me to be specific – I just sense it. And I do not want to drag my career out to the point that people say, 'I wish he'd retire.' At 33, I don't consider myself that old by modern rugby standards. Plenty of others have gone on past that age. But it's what I have done that counts. I feel I've packed an awful lot into my best years, and it takes its toll. But I'll say this: I wouldn't have done it any other way.

17

RUGBY WORLD CUP 2007

As the rain hit the window and I glared out at the grey October morning, I thought, 'I shouldn't be here. I should be in Marseilles.'

It was just a few days after our World Cup exit, and I was at the gym in the Vale of Glamorgan Hotel. It felt almost surreal, as if I shouldn't be there. I was home too early. There was supposed to be so much more for us as a team to go through at the biggest tournament of them all. I snapped out of my daydream and reality came thudding back. 'Get used to it, you daft sod,' I told myself. 'It's happened. Just move on.' But it was difficult. So bloody difficult.

After our defeat to Fiji in the final pool game of the competition on 29 September, I stood up in the changing-room at Stade de la Beaujoire. It was a scene of utter devastation. Boys were hanging their heads, and you could have heard a pin drop, such was the silence. Tears welled up in the eyes of many of the lads, and my overriding thought

was, 'How could this have happened?'

'Whatever has happened, the world will keep spinning,' I told the rest of the team. 'So get your heads up, and let's go home to our families and our loved ones. Life goes on.' Of course, life has gone on, but it will take more than a few rallying words to heal the wounds of our failure.

Failure: it's such a tough word to say let alone to experience, but there's no getting away from it. It sums up the way we performed at France 2007. Before the competition began, my view was that we had to at least make the quarter-finals. However, I stress that reaching that stage was a minimum goal, because it was so obviously achievable. In 2003, we were patted on the back for reaching the last eight, but I wanted it to be different this time. The route to the semis and beyond was there for us. The challenge was to make the most of home advantage by beating Australia in our pool clash at the Millennium Stadium, which was the

Ready for World Cup action.

second match of Pool B. If we could do that, then the odds were that we would meet with England in the quarter-finals, a game we felt we could win, despite the 62–5 trouncing they had given us in the warm-up friendly at Twickenham in early August. Then, after the quarter-final, who knew what might happen? The point is that we travelled with so much optimism, hope and expectation, and I believed that it was right for us to expect a lot of ourselves.

We had received a real bashing at the hands of England in the summer, and

it was one hell of a day. The press went to town on the result and performance, which was admittedly awful, but I can honestly say that it didn't have that much of an impact on us as a squad. It hurt like hell to go down by such a margin against the old enemy, but I felt that the players kept it in far better perspective than the media. We knew we had fielded what was far from our strongest side, and we knew it was just a friendly and would mean little come the important business that lay ahead of us. And for me personally, it didn't change my view about what would happen at the World Cup or how capable I thought we were of making an impression on the tournament.

Things got better for us against Argentina a fortnight after the England match when we held on for a 27–20 win, but then we were well beaten by France in Cardiff – 34–7 to be precise. Even that hiding at the hands of some of my old Toulouse teammates meant little to me in the context of the task that lay ahead, though, and I felt we were well on track by the time we went over to our base near La Baule.

We began preparing well as soon as we crossed the Channel, so much so that even now the way we went out of the tournament is something of a mystery to me. I just don't know why we weren't able to do better. Gareth Jenkins bore the brunt of it all, losing his job almost immediately after we had been eliminated. But let's be clear about this: we were all to blame – players as well as

Preparing at our training base at St Nazaire rugby club.

management. We take the plaudits as a group when we do well, so we cop the flak as a group when we mess up – that's my attitude to it.

Unfortunately, in professional sport, the buck always stops with the coach. That's the way it is, and it is never going to change. When Gareth accepted the job as Wales coach, he will have known the price of failure and that the world of sport can be cut-throat, but it was difficult not to feel for him when he was shown the door. I couldn't help but conclude that it was easy for us players to go back to our clubs or regions and carry on, but for him it was all so final.

Gareth will admit himself that he, like the rest of the management staff, had things to learn about coaching at international level, but I'm sure he thought he was growing into the role and wanted time to take the team through to the 2011 World Cup. I'm also positive that part of him will feel that he wasn't given enough time in the post and that he needed longer to work with the team. Others will disagree, though, and point to the fact that it is results that count.

The World Cup hadn't even begun when the controversy that seems to have plagued me in recent years reared its head again. Having captained the squad on the summer tour to Australia, which Stephen Jones had sat out, there had been something of a prolonged debate about who would do the job in France. I was keen, because I knew it would bring the best out of me as a player, but Stephen was the one who had originally been named skipper, so I wasn't sure which way it was going to go.

As it turned out, the big decision was made easier for Gareth in the end. Stephen had damaged his groin while we were at the training camp in La Baule a month before the start of the tournament and missed the warm-up matches. Thankfully, he was kept in the squad when the medics declared that he would definitely be fit for the opening game against Canada, but the fact that the announcement about who would be captain had to be made at a time when Stephen couldn't play might have had an impact on Gareth's decision to hand the honour back to me.

I was naturally chuffed to bits to get the armband back, but when it came to the big moment I was hit by what was at the time a crushing decision by Gareth Jenkins. I've never taken for granted my selection to any team, but I would be lying if I said I didn't expect, as skipper, to be leading the boys out for our opening match of the World Cup. I mean that's what captains do, isn't it? That's certainly what all the other captains at the World Cup were doing: O'Driscoll for Ireland, Vickery for England, and so on.

Smiles turned to grimaces for Gareth Jenkins.

Therefore, you can imagine my horror when Gareth called me in shortly before he was due to announce the team for the opener and told me that I would be on the bench. I was devastated, absolutely gutted, and I couldn't understand it. I wondered if he even thought that I was part of his best XV.

The trouble was that I was being informed so close to the announcement of the team that I didn't really have time to react. I just had to accept the decision, which I did, even though I have since heard some silly rumours that I went potty at Gareth. I didn't want a long rambling explanation about why I

wasn't starting – I've never requested that from any coach – but I did demand to know why I had been omitted. Gareth's answer was simply that he wanted to give other players game time, and I had to swallow it.

There is no way I would ever want anyone to think that I considered myself to be bigger than the team, but I struggled with the whole business, I really did. I had played the role of captain for weeks, with all the extra responsibility that goes with that, and now when the big moment arrived my troops were going into battle without me, even though all I wanted to do was lead them into the

fight. What's more, I couldn't hide from any of it, because I was on the bench. Dwayne Peel had been named captain for the game, and I just had to watch it all unfold before my eyes, taking a back seat in terms of the leadership role. I think the world of Peely and wanted only the best for him, but I'm only human, and I couldn't get away from the feeling that someone else was doing my job.

In the event, it was a mixed sort of afternoon for us against the Canadians. We ran out 42–17 winners in the end, but we trailed for 50 minutes and were put out of our rhythm good and proper by a fiercely determined opposition. Before the game, Martyn Williams said to me and Stephen Jones, who was also on the bench, 'You pair are jammy bastards. Canada are so up for this game they will probably hammer at us for 60 minutes, then when we've tired them out you two will come on and grab the glory, and the rest of us will be the villains!'

Whether Martyn has a secret crystal ball, I don't know, but that is exactly what happened. The introduction of me and Stephen coincided with a purple patch in which we ran in a clutch of tries to kill the game off, something we should have done far earlier. We laughed about it afterwards, but there was no real sense of satisfaction in the camp, because we knew we had been poor for too long in the match. And if Canada had allowed us back into the game, we knew there was no way Australia would do likewise a week later.

Sparking the fightback against Canada.

The build-up to the clash with the Wallabies on 15 September began months and months in advance. I had tried so hard to deflect attention away from it by emphasising that our World Cup bid was not simply about Wales versus Australia, but I was wasting my time. It was all anyone wanted to focus on, which was understandable, I suppose, as it was clearly the pivotal game of the pool. But when 15 September finally arrived, the day turned into one of abject despair for me, not just because of the result – we lost 32–20 – but because

my involvement ended after 20 minutes when I clashed with Stirling Mortlock and damaged a rib cartilage.

I've mentioned already how difficult it is to identify precisely why the World Cup went so poorly for us, and this match was typical of that. As a group, we were buzzing going into the game. The atmosphere was great, we felt confident and I personally believed 100 per cent that we were going to win. But – and I don't know why this was the case – things seemed to change as soon as we got out onto the pitch. When we

were standing in our positions waiting for kick-off, I just sensed a fear envelope us all. Suddenly, the mood had changed. It was as though we were all alone, and that feeling was reflected in the way we played in the first half, during which we effectively lost the game.

By the time the interval came, we were 25–3 behind, having conceded three tries, and although we rallied in the second half we were never really in it. However, my involvement in the match was long over by that point. I had been lucky not to be yellow carded in the opening exchanges after I crashed into Berrick Barnes, Australia's young outside-half, well after he had released the ball. It was pure frustration on my part after I had kicked loosely to the Wallabies and they had gone though five or six phases to score from my mistake. On another day, with another referee officiating, I would have got my marching orders.

After Mortlock collided with me, I was off not just for ten minutes but for the rest of the game. I have no qualms about the challenge, even though there were claims that Mortlock had done me in retaliation for my clattering of Barnes. I don't buy that for a moment. It was innocuous, and it was just my bad luck that it resulted in me having to go off, even though that consequence was devastating for me to accept.

I sloped off to the medical room and watched the rest of the game there, believing that my World Cup and my

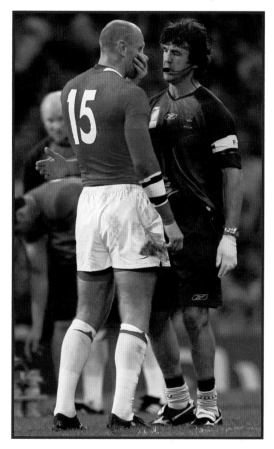

Physio Mark Davies delivers the bad news about my injury against Australia.

Wales career was over. Sonny Parker was also there, having hurt is groin, and the atmosphere was just horrible. I got up ready to go back out to the stadium, but then I just couldn't face it. I didn't want to be seen sitting in some seat with my arm in a sling. Afterwards, I went to hospital – having given what proved to be some hasty quotes to the press about finishing my Wales career on 99 caps – and had a series of X-rays. But the doctors told me the swelling was so bad that they couldn't make out what the problem was. It was 48 hours before

I discovered that things were a lot better than I'd first feared and that I would get the chance to win my 100th cap and taste World Cup action again.

I missed the Japan game the following Thursday, which was the only pool encounter we won without any real scares, even though they scored a magnificent first-half try. After that it was back to France to prepare for what had become a winner-takes-all showdown with Fiji. I was totally confident that if we played to our strengths, we would beat them comfortably.

All week, I tried to instil into the boys the need to be confident about the game. Yes, Fiji were dangerous, and, yes, they had their strengths, but I didn't want us to focus on what they might do to us. Instead, I wanted us to concentrate on what we could do to them. 'Fiji are a good team,' I said, 'but if we perform, we can blow them out of the water.'

For a start, I felt that for once our set-piece was going to be by far the dominant force and that as long as we could play the game to our tempo and style and not let things become too open they would not be in the same league as us. Once again, I tried to keep things low-key in the days running up to the match, and by the time the game was upon us I was super-confident that we would get the outcome we wanted.

We hadn't really watched Fiji that much, which only meant the shock we had on the day was all the more acute. I

Leading the team out for cap 100.

don't know if Fiji will ever perform that well when it really counts again. All I know is that we caught them on one hell of day. I can only compare the first 20 minutes of the match to when we played France in Paris on the way to the Grand Slam win in 2005. That day, the French battered us for the first 40 minutes, and the match against Fiji was a case of déjà vu. We were being annihilated, and from the full-back's spot it just seemed as though the white jerseys were raining down on top of me – they came from everywhere. I remember one instance

26 minutes, and all I could think was, 'This is not supposed to be happening.' Even at that early stage, I wondered how on earth we were going to get back into the match. Then, all of a sudden, we lifted our game after half-time, just as we had against Canada. We were helped by the sin-binning of their flanker Akapusi Qera just before half-time – another of their guys who was everywhere that afternoon – and after Shane Williams, Mark Jones and I had all scored tries I began to hope that we were going to get over the finishing line after all.

It didn't quite work like that, though. Fiji came roaring back, and with their fly-half Nicky Little slotting all his kicks at goal they led once more in the closing stages. Again we hit back, and when Martyn Williams intercepted a pass and streaked away for a try with only about five minutes left on the clock I assumed that we had done enough to win.

'Let's just keep the ball,' I thought to myself. But we couldn't. And that, in my opinion, is the difference between us and sides like New Zealand. As soon as we were faced with the pressure of being in front, we couldn't close the game out, whereas teams like the All Blacks always know how to turn the screw. The Fijians summoned up one last effort and piled over late on, with the television official awarding a try after a melee had formed on our line. There was no coming back this time.

When the final whistle went, there was disbelief among our boys. To lose like

in particular when they broke from the middle of a ruck, and I muttered under my breath, 'Where the hell did he come from? How has that happened?'

I lost count of the number of times that their wing Vilimoni Delasau, who scored a majestic chip-and-chase try before going on to torment us for 80 minutes, caused havoc. 'Boys, you've got to make your tackles!' I kept yelling. But all they could reply was, 'We're trying. We just can't pin him down.'

This time, instead of being 25–3 down at half-time, we were 25–3 down after

Touching down against Fiji – to no avail in the end.

that and then have the Fijians dancing and screaming with delight in victory was an appalling feeling, although I didn't begrudge them their euphoria. We just didn't know where to put ourselves. There were blank faces among our boys, which seemed to say, 'What do we do now?'

We couldn't just slope off the pitch, because there was some token medal ceremony to go through, and to have done that would have been poor sportsmanship anyway. I pulled the lads together. 'We're going home tomorrow to people who love us,' I said. 'Today is a bad day for Welsh rugby and an even worse day for us. But life goes on, so when we go around and clap the crowd

we have to hold our heads up high, no matter what abuse we take.'

And if we had taken a barrage of flak, we wouldn't have been able to complain. Thankfully, though, we didn't; in fact, the response was better than I expected. However, to walk around the pitch in those circumstances was still extremely tough. There was obviously no question of it being a lap of honour, but at the same time we felt we had to acknowledge our fans for the backing they had given us throughout the tournament. I do remember one guy who was wearing a Scarlets jersey. He was just standing there shaking his head with a look of utter disgust on his face. That hurt, but I knew it was part of the deal at

that moment. It was not our proudest moment, to say the least.

In the changing-room afterwards, I cried. I was just floored by the whole episode. Gareth said a couple of words – not much, just that we were going home because things hadn't gone right for us, and he thanked us for everything we had put into it.

A little while later, one of my sayings cropped into my head: 'You can't change it, so don't dwell on it.' It was then that I walked over and put on the stereo, which belted out a few happy tunes that I had put on a CD expecting us to be in a celebratory mood. I knew I couldn't mope for the rest of my days.

Then it was up to the press conference, where I said my piece. I spoke from the heart about our failure, and I'd like to think that the gathered journalists appreciated my honesty. I didn't try to make excuses. When we were done, I decided, totally off the cuff, to go around the room and shake as many hands as possible. You see, the press almost become part of the camp itself. Yes, they give us loads of stick, and, yes, they cause us a lot of frustration at times, but I think some of the boys conveniently forget just how much promotion they get out of newspapers and broadcasters, and I know deep down that the media who travel with us from Wales all support us and want us to do well. So, if this was going to be my swansong, I wanted to show these people a bit of appreciation, and if I could have shaken the hand of

every single person in that room, I think I would have. It just felt right.

That night, back at the team hotel, some of the boys really went for it with the drink, and good luck to them. Yes, we had failed, but that didn't mean we weren't allowed to let off a bit of steam. However, I just couldn't get into it at all – I couldn't let myself go. I was so down that I didn't even feel like drinking. Because I'd won my 100th cap, I was expected to throw a load of shorts down my neck, and the boys were lining them up for me, but I just couldn't and went off to bed. I had already got wind of what might be happening the next day as far as Gareth Jenkins was concerned, because there was talk that Roger Lewis was on his way to see us all. I kind of knew that Sunday was likely to be a fairly intense day. It was.

Putting two and two together, it was clear that Roger was coming to see us for a purpose and not just to make small talk. In the event, it was strange. We saw Roger arrive, and we also saw the press circling. Then Roger came to see me. 'Look, we've just asked Gareth to step down,' he said. 'We are going to announce it to the squad, but as captain I wanted you to be the first to know.' He also asked me to stand up and say a few words when he made the announcement to the rest of team. We were then all herded into the team room. The atmosphere was surreal, because we were all still trying to come to terms with the previous day's defeat and now

The 100th cap meant little in the aftermath of the Fiji defeat.

we were being asked to absorb another bombshell. Things were moving so fast that we barely knew where we were.

Roger spoke first. He thanked Gareth for his efforts but informed the players that for the build-up to the next World Cup there would be a new coach. There was numbed silence. I had never before been in a situation in which things had been done like that. Gareth thanked us, but he was emotional and didn't say a lot, then I stood up and said that although Gareth had taken the bullet we were all in this together and, in a way, all to blame. And that was it – before we knew it, we were on the bus. It must have been difficult for Gareth in those circumstances, but

he had our respect and he certainly had our sympathy. The bus journey was more or less silent, except for the odd bit of muffled talking at the back.

When we eventually reached the Vale of Glamorgan Hotel, there were journalists everywhere. I was asked by a radio guy to comment but declined, and then we were filmed getting off the bus and made to feel a bit like naughty schoolchildren. I couldn't for the life of me think who would enjoy watching footage of blokes unloading bags off a bus, but I'm not a media man.

It was such a strange end to it all. We had begun preparing for the World Cup so long ago that I could barely remember

when we had started, and now it was over in circumstances that I could never have foreseen. I spoke to Martyn Williams a short while later. I told him that the 12 years in which I had played for Wales had been more or less summed up by the events surrounding my 100th and last game – highs, lows, not knowing where you are or what the hell is going on. It seemed as though my whole Wales career had been played out in 24 hours or so.

I've been asked countless times how I feel about being the first Welshman to win 100 caps. Of course, I feel honoured. It is one hell of an achievement and I do feel proud and chuffed to bits. But I also have a sense of perspective on the whole thing. I'm not sure I really deserved a lot of those caps. I'm talking about earlier in my career when my mindset for Wales was different. For so many of those caps, I was not functioning to my potential, and I class those times as wasted years.

But I don't dwell on that. I'm not one for regrets. I'm Alfie. I did things my way, and there are no second chances in life, no opportunities to turn back the clock. I also think that my 100 caps is not just my achievement, it is the achievement of all the guys I have played with during 12 years of pulling on the red jersey. The team ethic has become so central to my thinking that I struggle to think of any success as belonging to anyone other than the group as a whole.

I won't retire – I'm not the type – but I do not expect to play for Wales again. I base that on the fact that the team now has to build for the World Cup in 2011, and I am clearly not going to be around for that tournament. The new coach has to invest in younger players who will be there. The bottom line these days is that rugby moves in four-year cycles.

Where do we go as a rugby nation from here? I'm not sure how to even begin to answer that question. However, I do believe that everyone involved in the national set-up has to stand back and take stock. The building for 2011 has to start more or less straight away, and it may be that results have to be put on the backburner. But that is so difficult in Wales, where a passionate rugby public wants immediate success. There is no magic formula, though, and the debate will go on for some time yet. I will look on with fascination, I will long for Wales to be successful again and I will cherish my memories. Cherish them.

18

....

FAMILY

One morning, during the stormy days following Mike Ruddock's departure and my mini-stroke, I was out on one of the many long walks that I used to take at that time to keep up some level of fitness when my phone rang. It was my wife Jemma, who at the time was ten weeks' pregnant. She had already suffered two miscarriages, the last of which had been in the summer of 2003 when I stayed home from the Wales tour to Australia and New Zealand to comfort her. That meant that when she fell pregnant this time we were fully aware of the dangers and had been given information by doctors as to why she might have lost the baby the other two times, although even the best medics in the world can never be 100 per cent sure about the reasons for miscarriage.

Having a child is something we both wanted immensely, and it goes without saying that we were praying, just like any couple would be, that everything would work out OK this time – that Jemma would have a normal, healthy pregnancy and that in nine months' time we would be parents to a happy, healthy little boy or girl. But when I pressed the answer button on my phone, the words that greeted me made me go cold. 'I'm not feeling well. I'm going to the hospital,' she said. 'Don't panic,' she tried to reassure me. 'I think everything is all right.'

I froze. I was still about half an hour's walk away on one of the many beautiful routes through the fields and woods near us, but I immediately headed for home. My mind was racing. 'This can't be true,' I thought to myself. 'I can't have gone through everything that I have been through in the last few weeks and have this happen to me on top of it all. What have I done wrong?'

A million other thoughts crashed through my head. As much as some people may envy me, I was asking myself what had I done to deserve a life like this? As if talking to some higher authority, I

Me and Jemma on our wedding day. Carys, my niece, is the bridesmaid.
(Courtesy of the author.)

offered to give up everything that people might envy about my life, such as the rugby and good salary, if it could guarantee the health and happiness of my family, who mean more to me than anything in the world. All the other stuff, as far as I was concerned, could go to hell.

Throughout the Ruddock affair and my subsequent health scare, Jemma's pregnancy had been the one thing that had kept me going. The two of us had wanted children more than anything, and the fact Jemma was pregnant was the one fantastic and positive thing that I had going for me at that time. But as I walked home, I thought, 'What's going to keep me going if we lose this baby? What will I do?'

Because of the previous two miscarriages, I had found myself waking up every morning since Jemma had told me that she was pregnant, thinking, 'Oh my God. Is our baby still there?' I was in a ridiculous state of mind as I walked home after Jemma's phone call. I was even thinking to myself that it would be easier if I just closed my eyes and never woke up again. For a fleeting moment, I really did feel like not going on. With all the bullshit that had been flying since Mike walked, it felt like I was drowning, and as soon as I managed to get my head above water, someone or something else would come along to tread on top of my head again.

At the hospital, Jemma had a scan, and we waited for news. Then we were called into a room by a nurse to be told that while the baby was still there, it had no heartbeat. 'Not again. Please, not again,' I thought to myself.

In a way, Jemma being pregnant was a nightmare in itself, because we were constantly expecting another miscarriage and permanently on edge. However, this time also coincided with when my sanity was on the edge anyway. The rumpus surrounding Mike's departure as coach was everywhere – there was no getting away from it and an example of that was a little incident I found myself faced with shortly after our bad news. It was just after the Six Nations match against Italy in Cardiff in which we had slipped to a disappointing 18–18 draw, a game I had watched from the bench because of my state of health. Jemma and I had gone to the hospital so that she could have a check-up, and while she was being seen I nipped down to the canteen to get a coffee.

The woman behind the counter was nice as pie to me. 'Hiya, love,' she said. 'How are you now?' She had obviously heard all about my problems.

'Thanks for asking,' I said. 'Yes, I'm feeling a lot better now.'

All of a sudden, this other woman chirped up from the background. 'Did you see his T-shirt when he was on TV the other day? It said England on it,' she screeched. She was referring to my now infamous appearance in front of the *Scrum V* cameras when I happened to

be wearing a Motorhead T-shirt that has the word England on the bottom of it.

'No, no, love,' I said. 'It's just a tour T-shirt of a band I follow. It didn't mean anything.'

'Yes, it did,' she snapped back. 'It means you support England!' I looked at her as if to ask what on earth she was on about, and then she got up as if readying herself to have a real go.

Fair play to the woman behind the counter, who tried to stick up for me. 'No, he's from Bridgend,' she said. 'I know him. He's a lovely boy, and he's Welsh through and through.'

'Yes, but he doesn't have to pay £50 a ticket to go and watch the rugby – and it's a total bag of shit!' she said.

I could scarcely believe the situation I was in. I was in hospital with my wife upstairs being tended to after a miscarriage and this woman was banging on at me. I found myself wanting to ask her, 'Aren't there more important things in your life than the price of a rugby ticket?' At that stage, I knew where rugby ranked on my list of priorities. I merely pointed out that everyone had a choice whether to part with the money to watch us, and then the woman behind the counter butted in with, 'Yeah, and more bloody fool you for paying it, love!' And with that, my detractor sloped off.

I took stock for a moment. My wife and I had just been through a miscarriage only days after I had suffered a potentially life-threatening mini-stroke. I'm sorry, but £50 didn't even warrant a second thought at that moment in time. If that woman could have ensured that my wife would be able to have a baby and that I could continue to play rugby safely, she would have been welcome to empty my bank account, never mind quibble about £50 when it was her choice in the first place to part with it. It takes incidents like that, at times like that, to make you realise that in the normal course of life some people simply have no perspective whatsoever on what is really important.

As I have said, miscarriage had happened to us twice before. The first occasion was, on its own, the hardest of all to deal with, for the simple fact that it was all new to us. Until it happens to you once, you never think it will ever happen. But it did happen in October 2002, during my second stint at Bridgend.

Just before the first scheduled scan, Jemma had not been feeling too good, and when we got to the hospital they told us that the baby had died somewhere between six and eight weeks. I cried and cried. I was devastated, because we hadn't expected it. We just assumed that everything would run its course as normal. That is what made the second and third times easier, because by then we at least had an expectation that miscarriage was a possibility.

But not that first time. I was ruined for a good while afterwards. It really took some getting over, because we were simply not ready for it in any way. Nothing can prepare you for going into a doctor's office when your wife is supposed to be pregnant only to be told, 'Sorry, but there's nothing there.' I remember that for a split second I thought I'd misheard. You find yourself looking blankly at the medics as if to ask, 'What do you mean there's nothing there?'

The second time occurred just before I was due to tour Australia and New Zealand with Wales in the summer of 2003. It happened four or five days before we were scheduled to go, and there was no way I could travel after the news. Luckily, Steve Hansen, who was in charge of Wales at that time, could not have been more understanding. Straight away, he assured me there would be no problem for me to stay at home, but it wasn't as if he then boarded the plane and forgot about me. No, he regularly rang from New Zealand and Australia to see how things were and to make sure that I knew I could join up with them whenever I wanted – even in a support capacity – if that was what I wanted to do. Best of all, he never put any pressure on me at all. He even said that both Jemma and I could go if we wanted, just to get away from it all.

Steve's attitude to the whole thing was magnificent. And it typified the one good thing to come out of all the tough times in my life – that I have truly discovered who my friends are. I have the best friends and family anyone could ask for. If I were to go through the rest of my life having these people

as the only ones I knew, then I would be happy, because I know that they are there for me no matter what. I owe so much to my mam and dad for the way they brought me up. They did so much for me. I remember all the things my dad used to do for me, like working my post round for me in the early hours of a Saturday morning when I was trying to conserve energy for a game that afternoon. Like most blokes, I think my dad is the best in the world.

Yet there has been one real rock in my life apart from mam and dad – my wife Jemma. Our circumstances have changed in the past year or so. We live apart now. But nothing will ever alter the way I feel about her. Nothing.

Funnily enough, I dated a girl called Amanda, who ended up being one of Jemma's bridesmaids, before Jemma and I got together. I first met Jemma at an 18th birthday party for a mutual friend at a local pub. We ended up slow dancing to 'Wind of Change' by the Scorpions! I was wearing a green Pringle V-neck jumper, which I don't think was very comfortable for Jemma, whom I was pulling up close. It was on–off for a long time after that – our relationship, not my sweater – with me going off to play rugby all the time and usually forgetting to ring her. But we were married in the summer of 2002.

What I love about Jemma is that she doesn't really have a clue about rugby, even though she has been watching

Me, Mam, Dad and brothers Steve and Dickie in my teenage years.
(Courtesy of the author.)

me play for the last ten years. She left me speechless a couple of years ago during one conversation I had with her. I was trying to talk to her through the window, and she wasn't making much sense to me. I said, 'I'd get more sense out of someone on the touchline than you.' She simply replied, 'Which line is the touchline?'

We've been through some tough times, but she will always mean everything to me. When I have been dropped from a team or had a bad game or felt low about something, Jemma has always been there for me. She is someone I can always count on for a reassuring word. Jemma always knows what to say and when to say it.

I also have two brothers. The eldest of us is Steven, who is nine years older than me and spent most of his early years getting the better of me in countless scraps. We get on really well now, though. He's married with kids and our relationship is totally different nowadays. Then there's Richard, the middle one and the brains of the family. I'm the youngest. I've always been close to Richard, who is now a chemical engineer. He has never been a swot but is naturally intelligent.

Sometimes, I get texts from my brothers, saying things like, 'We are so proud of you. Whatever you do doesn't matter. We are so proud to have you as our brother.' I read them and realise that

it doesn't matter what anyone else in the world thinks of me.

But there are also people such as my aunty Denise, who was like a sister to me when we were growing up and has been massively supportive of me throughout my career. Then, of course, there is my mam and dad – Vonny, short for Yvonne, and Baz, for Barry. I couldn't begin to say what they have done for me – they have been amazing. They have guided me from day one. There have been so many times when I could have gone off the rails. To tell you the truth, I have gone off the rails a couple of times, but they have always been there to put me back on.

When I won the BBC Wales Sports Personality of the Year award for 2005, I saw it as more for them than for me. And, in any case, I accepted the accolade on behalf of my teammates. It felt great that the public had voted for me, but the things I had been through that year – the Grand Slam, the Heineken Cup victory and captaining the British Lions – had been done with others. I didn't see them as my achievements, more as things I had been able to accomplish through the efforts of whole teams.

And on the same score, it was great that a lot of the old brigade from Pencoed were there that night to see me win – people who had helped me get to the top of the game. It was a real honour to win, but I knew the award probably meant a lot more to my parents, and I gave the trophy to my mother to

take home with her the night I won. I told her that I felt I had won it largely because of my personality, and they deserved the award, seeing as they had done more than anyone to mould me. If the award had truly been down to an individual achievement, then I believe one of Wales's top amateur swimmers or cyclists should have got it – people who get up at all hours of the morning to train in a quest for excellence for which they receive no real financial reward. Although I do like to think that I have a good personality, and I repeat that is down to my parents.

Which is why something that appeared on an Internet message board at the height of the Ruddock saga really got to me. There was a posting from somebody using the name Gareth Thomas's dad. They were sticking up for me after the *Scrum V* incident. However, below that message, somebody else had posted a response saying something along the lines of, 'Well, if you're his dad, you should have brought him up properly.' That really upset and angered me. Sadly, it was typical of some of the spineless snipers that have nothing better to do than contribute to these message boards. They spout their poison, but haven't got the guts to reveal who they are.

When I read about how my upbringing had apparently been so bad, I really felt like emailing or even telephoning whoever was responsible and giving them a piece of my mind. More than

anything, I wanted to challenge them to say it to my face. But, of course, I had no way of doing that. Whoever had posted the message must surely have known that it was not my real dad who had written the original statement. So, to reply to it in the first place was in itself insane.

I could not help but think of all the things my father has done for me, and it enraged me that some person thought they could post ignorant statements like that for the consumption of the public. Every father looks after his son, I realise that, but not every father has a son who has been under the spotlight quite like I have at times in my career. Dad will stand back a lot of the time. He can be cool and very laid back. But as soon as someone has a go at me or either of my brothers, he will defend us vigorously, even though he is the type of person who will always listen to two sides of an argument.

It is only when I get texts from my brothers and other members of my family, the likes of which I have mentioned, that I calm down a little and realise that things like stupid Internet postings don't matter in the grand scheme of things. I do not class myself as above

anyone else: never have done; never will do. But I know that some people make a judgement on me before they have even met me.

I always said in the aftermath of my mini-stroke that if my family were concerned about me playing rugby again and were happier for me to give the game up, I would do just that. I meant every word. I play rugby because it is a passion, and it gives me an incredible buzz. It has also made me some amazing friends in more than a decade of playing the game. It's been amazing. But it pales in comparison with what my family means to me.

Rugby will come, and rugby will go. You'll have your fun. If you're lucky enough, like me, you'll win a few things. You'll have a few decent pay days if you make it to the top level. But before you start playing and you're nobody and on the breadline, and when you finish playing, that is when your family are there. Rugby is only there for a fleeting time, like a fair-weather friend that sticks around only in the good times. Then one day it leaves you. And it never returns. Who is there to pick up the pieces? Your family, that's who.

19

THE FUTURE

The main trap many professional rugby players fall into, unless they are very well educated, is that they will only start planning for their future the day after they retire from playing. Unfortunately, I have always been like that too. Whenever it has come down to putting some building blocks in place for when I have to hang up my boots, my attitude has been that I'll do it next year. Then, next year comes and it becomes the year after that.

Apart from having been a postman and worked briefly in a local factory fetching and carrying, my life has always been rugby. I left school with one GCSE – a C in English, and I can't even remember whether it was English literature or English language! School and I just didn't get on; classrooms and I just didn't get on. I'm the same now. Whenever anything is done in the environment of a classroom, I find that I really struggle.

My plan was always to do something outside rugby for the simple reason that because the sport has always been such a massive part of my life, it would be nice to concentrate on doing something else. But I have since come to the conclusion that I have had so much positive experience from rugby, that I must – I want to – give something back to the game. For that reason, I became involved with a company called Sport Matters to establish the Gareth Thomas Rugby Academy, which started in the summer of 2006 with a series of three-day academy courses across Wales.

I am doing all my coaching badges, and I have found that I get an amazing kick out of guiding youngsters through the academy and elsewhere. I absolutely love it. I find the kids respond to me, and because of their passion and the way they call things as they see them, I find myself learning things from them all the time. So, coaching youngsters with the Welsh Rugby Union or one of the regions is something I would very much

To lose a game is not important; to lose someone special is.

like to pursue.

When I was a kid and a decent rugby player but a bit of a tearaway, nobody really came to me or my parents and truly guided me in the game. And I know there must still be thousands of great young players who turn away from rugby because life takes over. I bet there are many people who look back on their childhoods and can recall ten or so players who they reckon would have been brilliant had they been nurtured through the ranks instead of being lost to the game because something in their lives took over.

I was lucky in that I did have my parents to guide me to a certain degree, and that was enough to keep me involved. It is easy to find youngsters who, given the chance, would play the game morning, noon and night, seven days a week. I would like to be able to have a positive effect, particularly on the youngsters who have real ability but who cannot be bothered to harness it themselves. I was one of those youngsters, until I realised that I had talent and that rugby could be a great way for me to make a living.

I also have my sights on opening a coffee shop when I finish playing. I would love to have something to call my own, a business that I can work on and hopefully see flourish. I always said that my dream was to have my house paid for by the time I finish playing rugby, so I would forever have something that

I get such a buzz out of my academy.

More academy kicks!

Hindsight is a wonderful thing.

was mine and could never be taken away from me. If I had that, I always said I would be willing to go back and work on the post.

I know one thing: I won't be playing rugby beyond the age of 35. Saying that, I always said I would finish playing for Wales when I had 50 caps and that I would retire from the game altogether by the time I was 30. I now have more Wales caps than anyone in the history of the game, and I'm still going strong aged 33. So, if there's one thing I have learned, it's to never say never.

But for me to play beyond 35 is extremely unlikely, especially in the wake of my health scare. That episode has made me think not so much about the rest of my rugby career but the rest of my life.

I now know the damage just one punch or one knock can cause you, and when you have been through an experience that you know on another day might have changed the whole course of your life, it makes you think differently. Who knows how much longer I will continue to play?

Playing for club and country will always mean the world to me, and captaining Wales has been the pinnacle. I savour it and will continue to pour as much of what I have into it as possible. But maybe it will never mean as much to me because of that experience. And that is simply because something like a mini-stroke forces you to think about things in a different way. It gives you a whole new perspective.

20

WHAT'S ALFIE ALL ABOUT?

SIR CLIVE WOODWARD

My clearest memory of Alfie is when I went to the Vale of Glamorgan Hotel to visit the Wales team management shortly after getting the Lions job. I turned up there alone, feeling very much like the enemy, and walked into the restaurant where the Wales team were having breakfast. There were no team management staff there at all. It went quiet, but Alfie was up out of his seat straight away and bounding over to greet me. He gave me a really positive handshake and then said, 'Great to see you, butt. Come and have some breakfast with the boys.' I remember thinking, 'Wow.' He made a huge first impression on me.

Later, of course, we worked together with the British Lions. It was a disappointing trip in so many respects, but all I can say is that his contribution was just fantastic. Not long after we had returned from the tour, I found a note had been placed under the front door of my house. It was from Alfie, and I can say without question that it is the best note I have ever received from anyone in rugby. While I don't want to reveal the contents, I have it framed and on the wall of my bathroom. That's how much it means to me.

The impression I have of Alfie is that he comes from a fairly tough background, but his heart is always in the right place. He is straightforward, honest and what you see is what you get with him. He never gives you any bullshit. I still send him the odd text, and I've felt for him when he has got himself into strife.

Why did I make him captain of the British Lions? The one thing Alfie had was the respect of all the players: Welsh, Scottish, English, Irish. And without that as a captain, you have nothing. Furthermore, on the Lions tour he was, in my view, guaranteed of his place in the team. But respect was the most important thing.

In my time as England coach, our side contained many great leaders, but there was only one guy who was above anyone in having the total and unwavering respect of everyone – Martin Johnson. Alfie actually reminds me of Martin Johnson in lots of ways. In terms of the captaincy, he doesn't waste words. He says what he thinks needs to be said and leaves it at that. He has had a remarkable career, and there could well be a few more chapters to come.

STEVE HANSEN

From the first time I met Alfie, I saw a guy with tremendous leadership potential who had huge athletic ability. Unfortunately, he had no idea how, or at that point any real desire, to harness that ability to improve his performance or that of others on the rugby field. He was happy to do just enough to make the team. He was only too happy to be one of the lads rather than a leader. Being one of the boys meant bingeing on the booze big time whenever an opportunity presented itself, Sunday being the day he loved best, because he could kick back with his mates and be carefree.

My problem at that time was I needed to change the culture of the Wales team from one of being just happy to be in the team, to one of wanting to be the best player/team we could possibly be. That meant Alfie, as one of the natural leaders within the team, had to change.

He couldn't do this initially, so after a couple of talks I told him he had to go. I told him even though he had played 63-odd Test matches he would be no good to Wales or the team if he wasn't prepared to be what he was capable of being – a leader.

The thing was, though, Alfie really did care. He is one of the proudest Welshmen I have met. He cares deeply about his family, Wales and the Wales national side, along with the guys who play in the team. He just didn't know how to show it, or maybe he felt he might be seen as a softie or something for trying to be the best. I don't know, but what I do know is while he spent time away from the Test team he realised that he really wanted to be part of it.

On receiving word from Allan Lewis, Alfie's coach at Bridgend, that Alfie had changed, I sent Scott Johnson to see him and report back. Scott came back positive, so I asked Alfie in for a chat to assess for myself where he was at. He was then brought back into the fold with the understanding that he would only be judged on what he did from that day forward. It was without doubt one of the best decisions I have ever made concerning rugby.

Alfie had become true to himself, which allowed him to change the way he lived his life. As a result, he became a better person and an even better player. For that, he deserves a lot of credit, because only he could have turned it all around – no one else. It allowed him to become

one of the key figures in returning Welsh rugby to a more respected level in world rugby.

Not only is he one of the best athletes I have ever coached (big, strong, fast and very, very skilled), but he is able to play international rugby in any jersey from 12 to 15, which he makes look easy when in reality it is not. He is also one of the best natural leaders I've been associated with. He has empathy for his fellow players, along with an outstanding nature which brings the best out of others.

I guess the key with Alfie is that he has no favourites. He loves his family, country and his mates. With Alfie, you get what you see – a fun-loving, caring bloke, who will tell you what he thinks straight up with no bullshit. For me, the world would be a better place if there were more people that way inclined.

It's with a great sense of pride that I say I feel very lucky and very fortunate to have had a small involvement in his rugby career. But it's with pleasure and honour that I call Alfie a mate. He is a top bloke for whom I have immense respect. He is a man whom his family, mates and, most of all, his country should be very, very proud of.

GRAHAM HENRY

Alfie as a young rugby player was physically gifted and had great skills. But early in his career he lacked the discipline and confidence to develop those natural talents and become a world-class rugby international. He played a number of Tests during my time in Wales and generally played well. But in the big games against the best teams in the world, he lacked the confidence to make it happen and show his obvious ability. He was also probably a bit of a Jack the Lad who didn't want to show his peers that he was totally dedicated to the cause because that was not 'cool'. I was sure that behind the scenes he was doing the work. However, the balance wasn't quite right.

When Steve Hansen in particular, Scott Johnson and Andrew Hore took over the Wales team, they found the right button to press for Alfie, something that I obviously failed to do in the years before. Since then, he has developed into a world-class player, highly respected by his peers for his qualities as a person, his talent as a rugby player and his ability to lead. He should look back with real pride on how he changed and developed into this person, and he will be very thankful to those who helped in this process.

His performances for the Wales Grand Slam-winning team of 2005, and for a disappointing Lions team that same year, were inspirational. To see Alfie virtually take over the Lions team and inspire them was special. Alfie is now a world-class player whether at full-back, centre or wing, which is extremely rare.

 Alfie!

ANDREW HORE

Like all great champions, Alfie has a drive and determination, which can be his greatest strength and also his greatest weakness. You really have to be on your game to change his mind on a topic if he feels what he is doing is right. It's a great trait, and as a consequence it has made him a great leader. That is not to say that if you put up a sound and logical argument, he wouldn't change his mind – he would, and he would support your idea 100 per cent. This strength is exactly what we needed as a team on many occasions.

Alfie is prepared to say and do what is best for the team, even if that means having a quiet word with the members of the management team. And it's that ability to confront issues and be prepared to enter into conflict which helps make the team so strong.

Alfie is prepared to accept criticism, be challenged and change if it is warranted.

As a great leader, Alfie also has the ability to watch out for those people who may be struggling a bit and then send in the right person to talk to them and deal with the situation. These traits make him a special person to have worked with.

I was lucky enough to be involved with him many times in my role on the pitch, and, as a consequence, I have seen Alfie in action as captain. He is great in this role – calm with his team and challenging to authority when need be. He can process a lot of information in a short space of time, and this ensures he makes things clear for others.

Off the pitch, people do not see all the work he does for others away from the rugby environment, especially young people who have challenges to confront in life. I feel very lucky to have worked with one of rugby's special people. My only advice to Alfie is that once he retires, he should make sure that he finds a decent dentist!

Epilogue

AND FINALLY . . .

I hope you have enjoyed reading about my life.

I said at the start of the book that it was not my intention to deliberately offend anyone for the sake of selling a few extra copies, and I stand by that 100 per cent. I don't doubt there may have been certain things that didn't go down well with one or two people, but I hope they will accept that I have spoken as I have found.

On reflection, my life's been a bit of a roller coaster, never more so than in these last few years. I hope you will agree that it's a life that has been lived to the full, and I hope my story kept you entertained.

I've done some stupid things, yet I can honestly say that there is nothing I look back upon with any real regret – the good and the bad have made me what I am. I'm Gareth Thomas, Alfie, the guy from Bridgend who in going from postman to captain of Wales and the British Lions lived out a dream. But above all, I'm just an ordinary bloke who in telling his story has hopefully given a little bit of inspiration to anyone who has taken the time to read it.

Thank you all.

Appendix I

CLUB STATISTICS

BRIDGEND

October 1993 to December 1997
Bridgend debut: v. Birchgrove (friendly),
    Brewery Field, 5 October 1993
88 matches; 38 tries

Bridgend Team on Debut:

Don Davies; Glenn Webbe (captain),
Lloyd Davies, Carl Yardley, Gareth
Thomas; David Griffiths, Jason Lewis;
Dinlle Francis, Paul Morgan, Tony
Bumford, Nathan Jones, Neil Spratt,
Julian Derrick, Paul Evans, Owain Lloyd.
Replacements: Phil Wintle, Sean Gale
(used); Ian Greenslade, Chris Bradshaw,
Graham Evans, Nick Thatcher (unused).

CARDIFF

December 1997 to May 2001
Cardiff debut: v. Newport (Welsh
    Premier Division), Rodney Parade,
    6 December 1997
76 games; 47 tries

Cardiff Team on Debut:

Bobby Ross; Justin Thomas, Mike Hall
(captain), Leigh Davies, Gareth Thomas;
Lee Jarvis, Steve Wake; Spencer John,
Paul Young, David Young, Keith Stewart,
Derwyn Jones, Steve Williams, Emyr
Lewis, Jamie Ringer. Replacements:
Jonathan Humphreys for Paul Young;
Gwyn Jones for Stewart.

BRIDGEND (SECOND SPELL)

August 2001 to May 2003
Celtic League: 12 matches; 5 tries
Heineken Cup and European Challenge
    Cup: 9 matches; 4 tries

CELTIC WARRIORS

September 2003 to May 2004
Celtic League: 6 matches; 4 tries
Heineken Cup: 6 matches; 1 try

Celtic Warriors Team on Debut:

Kevin Morgan; Daffyd James, Gareth
Thomas, Jon Bryant, Aisea Havili; Neil

278

Jenkins, Sililo Martens, Gethin Jenkins, Matthew Rees, Chris Horsman, Deiniol Jones, Rob Sidoli, Maama Molitika, Cory Harris, Richard Parks. Replacement: Paul John (used), Mefin Davies, Chris Loader, Brent Cockbain, Nick Kelly, Ceri Sweeney, Gareth Wyatt (unused).

TOULOUSE

August 2004 to June 2007
Debut: v. Pau (French Championship), Pau, 18 August 2004
60 (48+12) matches; 20 tries

2004–2005

French Championship Top 16: 21 (18+3) matches; 8 tries
Heineken Cup: 7 (3+4); 1 try

2005–2006

French Championship Top 14:
13 (11+2) matches; 7 tries
Heineken Cup: 6 matches; 3 tries

2006–2007

French Championship Top 14 matches:
9 (8+1); 1 try
Heineken Cup: 4 (2+2)
(Figures in brackets refer to games started + games as a replacement.)

Toulouse Team on Debut:

Gareth Thomas; Nicolas Jeanjean, Florian Fritz, Yannick Jauzion, Xavier Garbajosa; Jean-Frédéric Dubois, Jean-Baptiste Elisalde; Jean-Baptiste Poux, Yannick Bru (captain), Omar Hasan, Grégory Lambouley, Trevor Brennan, Jean Bouilhou, Finau Maka, Christian Labit.

Statistics supplied by Westgate Sports Agency

Appendix II

NATIONAL TEAM STATISTICS

GARETH THOMAS TEST APPEARANCES (UP TO 29 SEPTEMBER 2007)

Key: FB = Full-back; WG = Wing; C = Centre; R = Replacement; RWC = Rugby World Cup; W = Win; L = Loss; D = Draw; * = Captain; MS = Millennium Stadium

Cap	Pos	Year	Against	Venue	Result
Bridgend					
1	WG	1995	Japan (RWC)	Bloemfontein	W 57–10
2	C	1995	N. Zealand (RWC)	Johannesburg	L 34–9
3	WG	1995	Ireland (RWC)	Johannesburg	L 24–23
4	C	1995	South Africa	Johannesburg	L 40–11
5	C	1995	Fiji	Cardiff	W 19–15
6	WG	1996	France	Cardiff	W 16–15
7	WG	1996	Australia	Brisbane	L 56–25
8	C	1996	Australia	Sydney	L 42–3
9	WG	1996	Barbarians	Cardiff	W 31–10
10	WG	1996	France	Cardiff	L 40–33
11	C	1996	Italy	Rome	W 31–22
12	C	1996	Australia	Cardiff	L 28–19
13	WG	1997	USA	Cardiff	W 34–14
14	WG	1997	Scotland	Murrayfield	W 34–19
15	C	1997	Ireland	Cardiff	L 26–25
16	WG	1997	France	Paris	L 27–22
17	WG	1997	England	Cardiff	L 34–13
18	C	1997	USA	Wilmington	W 30–20
19	C	1997	USA	San Francisco	W 28–23
20	C	1997	Canada	Toronto	W 28–25
21	WG	1997	Romania	Wrexham	W 70–21
22	WG	1997	Tonga	Swansea	W 46–12
23	WG	1997	N. Zealand	Wembley	L 42–7

Cardiff						
24	WG	1998	Italy	Llanelli	W 23–20	
25	WG	1998	England	Twickenham	L 60–26	
26	WG	1998	Scotland	Wembley	W 19–13	
27	WG	1998	Ireland	Dublin	W 30–21	
28	WG	1998	France	Wembley	L 51–0	
29	WG	1998	South Africa	Wembley	L 28–20	
30	WG	1998	Argentina	Llanelli	W 43–30	
31	R(WG)	1999	France	Paris	W 34–33	
32	WG	1999	Italy	Treviso	W 60–21	
33	WG	1999	England	Wembley	W 32–31	
34	WG	1999	Argentina	Buenos Aires	W 23–16	
35	WG	1999	South Africa	Cardiff (MS)	W 29–19	
36	WG	1999	France	Cardiff (MS)	W 34–23	
37	WG	1999	Argentina (RWC)	Cardiff (MS)	W 23–18	
38	R(WG)	1999	Japan (RWC)	Cardiff (MS)	W 64–15	
39	WG	1999	Samoa (RWC)	Cardiff (MS)	L 38–31	
40	WG	1999	Australia (RWC)	Cardiff (MS)	L 24–9	
41	WG	2000	France	Cardiff (MS)	L 36–3	
42	WG	2000	Italy	Cardiff (MS)	W 47–16	
43	WG	2000	England	Twickenham	L 46–12	
44	WG	2000	Scotland	Cardiff (MS)	W 26–18	
45	WG	2000	Ireland	Dublin	W 23–19	
46	R(C)	2000	USA	Cardiff (MS)	W 42–11	
47	WG	2000	South Africa	Cardiff (MS)	L 23–13	
48	WG	2001	England	Cardiff (MS)	L 44–15	
49	WG	2001	France	Paris	W 43–35	
50	WG	2001	Italy	Rome	W 33–23	
Bridgend						
51	C	2001	Japan	Osaka	W 64–10	
52	C	2001	Japan	Tokyo	W 53–30	
53	WG	2001	Romania	Wrexham	W 81–9	
54	C	2001	Argentina	Cardiff (MS)	L 30–16	
55	WG	2001	Tonga	Cardiff (MS)	W 51–7	
56	WG	2001	Australia	Cardiff (MS)	L 21–13	
57	C	2002	England	Twickenham	L 50–10	
58	WG	2002	Romania	Wrexham	W 40–3	
59	WG	2002	Fiji	Cardiff (MS)	W 58–14	
60	WG	2002	Canada	Cardiff (MS)	W 32–21	
61	WG	2002	N. Zealand	Cardiff (MS)	L 43–17	
62	WG	2003	Italy	Rome	L 30–22	
63	WG	2003	England	Cardiff (MS)	L 26–9	
64	WG	2003	Scotland	Murrayfield	L 30–22	
65	WG	2003	Ireland	Cardiff (MS)	L 25–24	
66	WG	2003	France	Paris	L 33–5	
Celtic Warriors						
67*	WG	2003	Ireland	Dublin	L 35–12	
68	WG	2003	England	Cardiff (MS)	L 43–9	
69	WG	2003	Canada (RWC)	Melbourne	W 41–10	

70	WG	2003	Italy (RWC)	Canberra	W 27–15
71	R(FB)	2003	N. Zealand (RWC)	Sydney	L 53–37
72	FB	2003	England (RWC)	Brisbane	L 28–17
73	FB	2004	Scotland	Cardiff (MS)	W 23–10
74	FB	2004	Ireland	Dublin	L 36–15
75	FB	2004	France	Cardiff (MS)	L 29–22
76	FB	2004	England	Twickenham	L 31–21
77	FB	2004	Italy	Cardiff (MS)	W 44–10
Toulouse					
78*	FB	2004	South Africa	Cardiff (MS)	L 38–36
79*	FB	2004	Romania	Cardiff (MS)	W 66–7
80*	FB	2004	New Zealand	Cardiff (MS)	L 26–25
81*	FB	2005	England	Cardiff (MS)	W 11–9
82*	FB	2005	Italy	Rome	W 38–8
83*	FB	2005	France	Paris	W 24–18
84*	FB	2005	New Zealand	Cardiff (MS)	L 41–3
85*	C	2005	South Africa	Cardiff (MS)	L 33–16
86*	FB	2005	Australia	Cardiff (MS)	W 24–22
87*	FB	2006	England	Twickenham	L 47–13
88*	FB	2006	Scotland	Cardiff (MS)	W 28–18
89	WG	2006	Australia	Cardiff (MS)	D 29–29
90*	FB	2006	Canada	Cardiff (MS)	W 61–26
91	R(C)	2007	Italy	Rome	L 23–20
92*	C	2007	England	Cardiff (MS)	W 27–18
93*	WG	2007	Australia	Sydney	L 29–23
94*	FB	2007	Australia	Brisbane	L 31–0
Cardiff Blues					
95*	C	2007	England	Twickenham	L 62–5
96*	C	2007	Argentina	Cardiff (MS)	W 27–20
97*	C	2007	France	Cardiff (MS)	L 34–7
98	R(FB)	2007	Canada (RWC)	Nantes	W 42–17
99*	FB	2007	Australia (RWC)	Cardiff (MS)	L 32–20
100*	FB	2007	Fiji (RWC)	Nantes	L 38–34

CAPS – 100 (W 51; D 1; L 48)
CAPTAIN – 21 (W 9; L 12)
FULL-BACK – 19
WING – 55
CENTRE – 20
REPLACEMENT – 6 (FB 2, WG 2, C 2)

Wales Team on Debut

Tony Clement (Swansea); Ieuan Evans (Llanelli), Mike Hall (Cardiff, captain), Neil Jenkins (Pontypridd), Gareth Thomas (Bridgend); Adrian Davies (Cardiff), Andy Moore (Cardiff); Mike Griffiths (Cardiff), Garin Jenkins (Swansea), John Davies (Neath), Derwyn Jones (Cardiff), Gareth Llewellyn (Neath), Stuart Davies (Swansea), Emyr Lewis (Llanelli), Hemi Taylor (Cardiff). Replacements: David Evans (Treorchy) for A. Davies; Stuart Roy for D. Jones.

THE APPEARANCES – COUNTRY BY COUNTRY (UP TO 29 SEPTEMBER 2007)

14 – England (W 3, L 11)
12 – France (W 5, L 7)
10 – Italy (W 8, L 2), Australia (W 1, D 1, L 8)
7 – Ireland (W 2, L 5)
6 – New Zealand (L 6), Scotland (W 5, L 1), South Africa (W 1, L 5)
5 – Argentina (W 4, L 1), Canada (W 5)
4 – Japan (W 4), Romania (W 4), USA (W 4)
3 – Fiji (W 2, L 1), Tonga (W 2)
1 – Barbarians (W 1), Samoa (L 1)

GARETH THOMAS'S 40 TRIES (UP TO 29 SEPTEMBER 2007)

Try	Pos	Cap	Year	Against	Venue	Result
1–3	WG	1	1995	Japan (RWC)	Bloemfontein	W
4	WG	10	1996	France	Cardiff	L
5–6	C	11	1996	Italy	Rome	W
7	C	12	1996	Australia	Cardiff	L
8	WG	16	1997	France	Paris	L
9	C	20	1997	Canada	Toronto	W
10–11	WG	22	1997	Tonga	Swansea	W
12	WG	24	1998	Italy	Llanelli	W
13	WG	25	1998	England	Twickenham	L
14	WG	29	1998	South Africa	Wembley	L
15–18	WG	32	1999	Italy	Treviso	W
19	WG	35	1999	South Africa	Cardiff	W
20	R(WG)	38	1999	Japan (RWC)	Cardiff	W
21	WG	39	1999	Samoa (RWC)	Cardiff	L
22	C	51	2001	Japan	Osaka	W
23–25	C	52	2001	Japan	Tokyo	W
26	WG	55	2001	Tonga	Cardiff	W
27	WG	58	2002	Romania	Wrexham	W
28	WG	59	2002	Fiji	Cardiff	W
29	WG	65	2003	Ireland	Cardiff	L
30	WG	66	2003	France	Paris	L
31	WG	67	2003	Ireland	Dublin	L
32	WG	69	2003	Canada (RWC)	Melbourne	W
33	FB	76	2004	England	Twickenham	L
34	FB	77	2004	Italy	Cardiff	W
35–36	FB	88	2006	Scotland	Cardiff	W
37	FB	90	2006	Canada	Cardiff	W
38	WG	93	2007	Australia	Sydney	L
39	C	96	2007	Argentina	Cardiff	W
40	FB	100	2007	Fiji	Nantes	L

THE TRIES – COUNTRY BY COUNTRY (UP TO 29 SEPTEMBER 2007)

8 – Japan, Italy

3 – France, Tonga, Canada

2 – South Africa, Ireland, England, Australia, Scotland, Fiji

1 – Samoa, Romania, Argentina

APPEARANCES/TRIES FOR BRITISH & IRISH LIONS

Game	Pos	Year	Against	Venue	Result	Tries
1	WG	2005	Wellington	Wellington	W 23–6	1
2	WG	2005	N. Zealand	Christchurch	L 21–3	
3	C	2005	N. Zealand	Wellington	L 48–18	1
4	C	2005	N. Zealand	Auckland	L 38–19	

Lions Team on Debut

Josh Lewsey (Shane Horgan 68); Gareth Thomas, Brian O'Driscoll (captain), Gavin Henson (Stephen Jones 63), Jason Robinson; Jonny Wilkinson, Dwayne Peel (Chris Cusiter 72); Gethin Jenkins, Shane Byrne, Julian White (Matt Stevens 72), Danny Grewcock, Ben Kay, Simon Easterby, Neil Back, Martin Corry.

APPEARANCES/TRIES FOR WALES XV

Game	Pos	Year	Against	Venue	Result	Tries
1	C	1996	Western Australia	Perth	W 62–20	5
2	WG	1996	ACT	Canberra	L 69–30	
3	C	1996	NSW	Sydney	L 27–20	
4	C	1996	Australia B	Brisbane	L 51–41	1
5	R(C)	1996	NSW Country	Moree	W 49–3	
6	C	1997	Souths	Charlotte	W 94–3	1
7	WG	1999	Buenos Aires	Buenos Aires	L 31–29	
8	WG	1999	Argentina A	Rosario	L 47–34	
9	WG	2000	French Baa-Baas	Cardiff (MS)	W 40–33	
10	FB	2004	Barbarians	Bristol	W 42–0	1

APPEARANCES/TRIES FOR WALES A

Game	Pos	Year	Against	Venue	Result	Tries
1	C	1995	Fiji	Bridgend	L 25–10	
2	WG	1997	N. Zealand	Pontypridd	L 51–8	
3	C	2002	Ireland	Cork	L 55–22	
4	C	2002	Italy	Swansea	W 50–23	1
5	C	2002	Scotland	Wrexham	W 30–23	1

Wales A Team on Debut

Justin Thomas (Llanelli); Alan Harris (Swansea), Mark Taylor (Swansea), Gareth Thomas (Bridgend), Wayne Proctor (Llanelli); Adrian Davies (Cardiff), Paul John (Pontypridd, captain); Andrew Lewis (Cardiff), Robin McBryde (Llanelli), Spencer John (Llanelli), Greg Prosser (Pontypridd), Andy Moore (Swansea), Andrew Gibbs (Newbridge), Steve Williams (Neath), Owain Lloyd (Llanelli).
Replacements: Mike Voyle (Newport) for Prosser; Lyndon Mustoe (Cardiff) for Lewis.

APPEARANCES/TRIES FOR WALES UNDER-21

Game	Pos	Year	Against	Venue	Result	Tries
1	WG	1994	Romania	Bridgend	W 20–8	1
2	WG	1995	Scotland			
3	WG	1995	Ireland	G. Wands	W 16–9	1

Wales Under-21 Team on Debut

Justin Thomas (Cardiff Inst); Gareth Thomas (Bridgend), Jason Hewlett (Cardiff), Gareth Jones (Bridgend), Craig Moir (Northampton); Lyndon Griffiths (Swansea), Pat Horgan (Aberavon); Christian Loader (Swansea, capt), Marcus Thomas (Swansea), Spencer John (Llanelli), Steve Martin (Cardiff Inst), Steve Johnson (Llanelli), Chay Billen (Pontypool), Richard Morris (Neath), Paul Beard (Cardiff).
Replacement: Jason Strange (Llanelli) for Griffiths.

APPEARANCES/TRIES FOR WALES YOUTH

Game	Pos	Year	Against	Venue	Result	Tries
1	R(C)	1993	France	Swansea	L 27–23	
2	C	1993	England	Bath	L 17–16	

Wales Youth Team on Debut

Steffan Jones (Llangennech); Nathan John (Cardiff), Stuart Prendeville (Llangennech), Shane Webley (Blackwood), Leigh Morgan (Maesteg); Lyndon Griffiths (Pencoed), Jason Hewlett (Cardiff); Steffan Ohlsson (Pontardulais), Barrie Williams (Llanelli, captain), Aled Griffiths (Llandybie), Steve Mellalieu (Dunvant), Steve Martin (Neath Colts), Chris Morgan (Swansea), Andrew Moore (Wrexham), Glen John (Treorchy).
Replacements: Austin Howells (Maesteg) for Prendeville; Gareth Thomas (Pencoed) for Webley

WALES SEVENS

1995 Tokyo
1996 Hong Kong
1997 RWC Sevens, Hong Kong
1998 Commonwealth Games, Kuala Lumpur
2002 Commonwealth Games, Manchester

Wales Sevens Squad on Debut in Tokyo

Justin Thomas (Cardiff Inst.), Alan Harris (Swansea), Gareth Thomas (Bridgend), Matthew Wintle (Llanelli), Arwel Thomas (Neath), Jason Hewlett (Cardiff), Marcus Thomas (Swansea), Gary Jones (Llanelli), Colin Charvis (London Welsh), Chris Wyatt (Neath).

MOST TRIES FOR WALES IN A CALENDAR YEAR

Tries	Player	Year
11	Tom Shanklin	2004
9	Ieuan Evans	1994
8	Shane Williams	2004
7	Rhys Williams	2004
7	Gareth Thomas	1999
7	Nigel Walker	1994
7	Maurice Richards	1969

MOST GAMES AS CAPTAIN OF WALES

Matches	Player	W	D	L
28	Ieuan Evans	13	0	15
22	Rob Howley	15	0	7
22	Colin Charvis	11	0	11
21	Gareth Thomas	9	0	11
19	Jonathan Humphreys	6	0	13
18	Arthur Gould	8	1	9
14	Clive Rowlands	6	2	6
14	Billy Trew	12	0	2

MOST MILLENNIUM STADIUM APPEARANCES

Matches	Player	W	D	L
38 (36+2)	Gareth Thomas	20	1	17
38 (34+4)	Colin Charvis	19	1	18
35 (32+3)	Stephen Jones	16	2	17
35 (30+5)	Martyn Williams	17	2	16
27 (24+3)	Shane Williams	14	2	11
26 (18+8)	Dwayne Peel	15	2	9
24 (22+2)	Ian Gough	11	2	11

MOST TRIES FOR WALES AT THE MILLENNIUM STADIUM

Tries	Player
13	Shane Williams
12	Rhys Williams
10	Gareth Thomas
10	Tom Shanklin

PLAYERS WHO HAVE SCORED FOUR TRIES FOR WALES IN ONE MATCH

Player	Opposition	Venue	Year
Willie Llewellyn	England	Swansea	1899
Reggie Gibbs	France	Cardiff	1969
Maurice Richards	England	Cardiff	1969
Ieuan Evans	Canada	Invercargill	1987
Nigel Walker	Portugal	Lisbon	1995
Gareth Thomas	Italy	Treviso	1999
Shane Williams	Japan	Osaka	2001
Tom Shanklin	Romania	Cardiff	2004
Colin Charvis	Japan	Cardiff	2004

Statistics supplied by Westgate Sports Agency